GREEN
ECONOMICS

GREEN
ECONOMICS
CONFRONTING THE ECOLOGICAL CRISIS

ROBIN HAHNEL

M.E.Sharpe
Armonk, New York
London, England

Library of Congress Cataloging-in-Publication Data

Hahnel, Robin.
   Green economics : confronting the ecological crisis / Robin Hahnel.
      p. cm.
   Includes bibliographical references and index.
   ISBN 978-0-7656-2795-7 (cloth : alk. paper)—ISBN 978-0-7656-2796-4 (pbk. : alk. paper)
   1. Environmental economics. 2. Sustainable living. I. Title.

HC79.E5H3165 2011
333.7—dc22   2010027020

Printed in the United States of America

This book is dedicated to Kristen Sheeran, who gave up tenure at the University of Maryland to become Executive Director of Economics for Equity and the Environment because she knew the ecological crisis we face must be confronted more quickly than wheels turn in ivory towers.

Contents

Acknowledgments

This book is written in desperation. The human species has launched the planet on a trajectory that threatens to make all previous environmental disasters pale by comparison. Despite the fact that more and more people do "get it," our leaders, and the current political and economic systems we labor under, have proved unable to make any progress whatsoever toward heading off climate change disaster.

The much-anticipated climate meetings in Copenhagen in December 2009 ended in disaster, threatening to undo diplomatic progress that had consumed decades of precious time. And as Bill McKibben, cofounder of the campaign to stabilize atmospheric concentrations of greenhouse gases at 350 parts per million, recently lamented, after "the planet has just come through the warmest decade, the warmest 12 months, the warmest six months, and the warmest April, May, and June on record . . . in late July, the U.S. Senate decided to do exactly nothing about climate change. They didn't do less than they could have—they did *nothing*, preserving a perfect two-decade bipartisan record of no action" (TomDispatch.com, August 4, 2010).

This book is not written because the author thinks he has all the answers we need. Quite the contrary, I believe it may be some time before anyone provides a grand theoretical synthesis suitable to analyzing all facets of the relationship between human economic activity and the natural environment. While we can build from insights provided by various heterodox approaches as well as by mainstream economics, unfortunately all schools of economic thought fall short of what is needed in one way or another. And while the efforts of those who advocate on behalf of the environment have often been inspirational and heroic, unless political strategies improve there is little reason to expect the environmental movement to achieve better results in the future.

After acknowledging pioneering work by environmental, ecological, institutional, Marxist, and other economists, it may appear unseemly to proceed to criticize them. But improvements will not come without criticism, which should not be confused with pointing the finger of blame at those we owe a debt of gratitude for all they have done. Those who study and work to protect the environment are not the reason the environment is in serious danger, even if better analyses and more effective political strategies will be required to better protect the environment.

I want to thank all the students in my environmental economics classes over the past decades at American University, Lewis and Clark College, and Portland State University who worked with me to separate the wheat from the chaff in received wisdom. I thank my editors at M.E. Sharpe—Lynn Taylor, who rescued this project when it was all but lost, and Henrietta Toth and Laurie Lieb, who labored mightily to make the book more readable. But mostly I thank Kristen Sheeran for teaching a long-time radical economist that he needed to take environmental issues more seriously.

As much as I owe to these and others, the views expressed here are entirely my own responsibility.

Introduction

Green Economics: Confronting the Ecological Crisis is an attempt to provide environmentalists and progressives with the kind of economics that suits their needs today. It is written by a professional economist who has taught environmental economics, mainstream economic theory, radical political economy, institutional economics, and post-Keynesian economics at the graduate and undergraduate levels for more than thirty-five years in one of the few economics departments in the United States with a PhD program that features heterodox as well as mainstream schools of thought. The author of *Green Economics* has also worked as an activist in a variety of progressive and environmental campaigns and organizations for more than forty-five years. He understands why activists mistrust economists, yet desperately need helpful economic analysis.

Unfortunately, there is no grand synthesis for analyzing economics and the environment. There are useful insights from mainstream economics when its theories are properly interpreted, and ecological economics and several other heterodox schools of economic thought provide important ideas as well. However, every theoretical framework for analyzing the relations between our economic activities and the natural environment remains incomplete and flawed. As a result, there is no single place to turn for someone seeking to understand what is necessary to protect the environment in ways that are effective and fair. *Green Economics* does not pretend to provide the grand synthesis that, unfortunately, still lies beyond our reach. However, those who struggle to protect the environment can ill afford to wait for a grand synthesis. *Green Economics* gathers together useful insights available from many sources and dispels debilitating myths independent of origin. The three brief sections that follow in this introduction offer a glimpse of where mainstream economics can be helpful, where mainstream economics can be misleading, and where heterodox ideas can provide important insights but also create unnecessary confusion.

What If 250 Years Ago . . .

. . . Americans had put a price on carbon? Of course, nobody understood 250 years ago that carbon emissions from burning fossil fuels were going to destabilize the earth's carbon cycle and that increasing concentrations of greenhouse gases in the atmosphere would threaten to unleash cataclysmic changes in the earth's climate systems by the end of the twenty-first century. But now, with the benefit of hindsight, we do know that we should have imposed a tax on carbon emissions as far back as colonial days when the market system was just getting up a head of steam in the New World. One place mainstream economics can be useful is helping us understand how much damage getting an important price wrong can cause in a market economy.

Comparing the timelines of important discoveries in the evolution of coal and of solar energy suggests that had damage from carbon emissions been factored into the price system our economy might well have evolved quite differently. In colonial America, blacksmiths used small amounts of "stone coal" to supplement the charcoal normally burned in their forges. While underground coal deposits were first discovered near Richmond, Virginia, in 1701, large deposits in Pennsylvania, Ohio, Kentucky, and western Virginia were only discovered in the 1750s, and it was not until the mid-1800s that significant amounts of coal were mined in the United States. And it was not until 1882—when coal was plentiful, cheap, and available at the end of any railroad line—that a coal-fired, electric generating station invented by Thomas Edison was first used to supply electricity to households in New York City. Meanwhile, Horace de Saussure had built a solar collector by 1767; by 1816 Robert Stirling had built a solar thermal electric heat engine that Lord Kelvin used in his university classrooms; August Mouchet had converted solar radiation into mechanical power and together with Abel Pifre had constructed solar-powered engines for various uses by 1860; Charles Fritts had built the first genuine solar cell by 1883; and Baltimore inventor Clarence Kemp patented the first commercial solar water heater in 1891.

These two timelines do not suggest that we were condemned to embrace the most environmentally damaging part of our current fossil fuel–based energy system to produce electricity for lack of any technological alternative. It is more likely that significant mispricing, combined with path dependency, explains why "king coal" won out over solar power in the United States, leading us in 2007 to produce 48.5 percent of our electricity by burning coal but only .015 percent from solar thermal and photovoltaic sources.

When You Ask the Wrong Question . . .

. . . you get the wrong answer. This is why mainstream environmental economic modelers can erroneously conclude that taking strong measures now to avert climate change is not "cost-effective," while climate scientists warn us correctly that failure to reduce greenhouse gas emissions immediately and dramatically would be tomfoolery. When people feel safe and secure, it makes sense to weigh the costs and benefits of doing a little more or less of something. And if some outcomes are unlikely to occur, it makes good sense to ignore these improbable outcomes provided their consequences do not dwarf those of more probable outcomes. In effect, this is what mainstream economic climate modelers do when they estimate the benefits of avoiding the effects of only mild to moderate climate change, which is most likely, discount those benefits since they will occur many decades in the future, and then conclude that the discounted benefits do not warrant the cost of significant emissions reductions in the present. They have answered the wrong question. They have ignored the main fact, which is that absent any serious response we run an unacceptable risk of inducing cataclysmic climate change, and until we are safe we can ill afford to be weighing pros and cons of tolerating a little more or less mild climate change.

Climate scientists have answered the right question, which is: "How much do we have to reduce emissions now to reduce the risk of cataclysmic climate change to an acceptable level so we can feel reasonably safe?" When answering the right question, climate scientists focus on the central issue—cataclysmic climate change that we can ill afford—even though it is far less likely than the kind of mild to moderate climate change mainstream economic climate modelers focus on instead. When mainstream economic modelers ignore cataclysmic climate change because it is less likely and because they cannot even begin to estimate the damages if it does occur, they make themselves irrelevant to the primary issue at hand. Climate scientists, on the other hand, correctly treat the problem as an insurance problem: Can we afford the premiums we have to pay to make ourselves reasonably safe? The answer to this question in the case of cataclysmic climate change turns out to be a resounding "yes." As insurance policies go, it is easily affordable and, in fact, quite a good buy!

When mainstream economists conclude that the expected benefits of avoiding moderate climate change do not warrant the costs of significant emission reductions, all they have discovered is that the expected value of an insurance policy we do not need is negative. The policy we need is the one they did not even consider since their models do not take cataclysmic climate change into account. Moreover, the expected value of most insurance policies for buyers is always negative since it must be positive for sellers if the insurance industry is to be profitable! However, this does not mean we are foolish whenever we buy insurance. Insurance is about avoiding unlikely consequences you cannot afford, and to do this sensible people happily buy insurance policies with an expected negative value all the time. This is why we should pay an affordable premium and reduce carbon emissions dramatically now to avoid cataclysmic climate change—an outcome whose consequences are not just incalculable but unthinkable. Weighing costs and benefits of a little more or less moderate climate change is completely beside the point.

Growth of What?

Economists have long worshipped at the altar of economic growth. If economists had a motto, it would likely be "A rising tide raises all boats." Not long ago a dissident group of ecological economists issued a blunt challenge to this conventional wisdom: "Infinite growth on a finite planet is impossible." It was a showstopper, although the cast in the mainstream economics show paid it little attention, and their show goes on.

How can it make sense to strive for something that is impossible to achieve? Why should we hope to grow faster if faster growth only exhausts our finite resources and fouls the environment with our wastes that much sooner? If infinite growth is not sustainable, then should we not be searching for a steady state economy that is sustainable and does not impoverish future generations?

Ecological economists have done a great service by issuing their bold challenge. However, as we discover in Chapter 5, it is important to ask "growth of what" when considering this issue. Much time has been wasted because people have been talking past each other and talking about the growth of very different things. What ecological economists call *throughput* and insist cannot continue to grow is not the same as the gross domestic product that mainstream economists talk about growing. In the shouting match that has ensued, important issues that we will need to explore have been pushed into the background.

Organization of This Book

Part I explains why we need a new environmental economic paradigm in order to develop a much broader intellectual framework than the simplistic problematic of allocating scarce natural resources to competing insatiable wants and disposing of the wastes of economic activity in the least costly way. Chapter 1 considers the implications of a full-world as opposed to an empty-world mind-set. Chapter 2 explains why cost-benefit analysis (CBA) is far from value-free and not always the appropriate method for making environmental policy choices. Chapter 3 explores complicated issues that arise when we try to define "sustainable development" and measure "progress."

Moving discussion beyond platitudes about population growth and industrialization, Part II focuses attention instead on perverse incentives intrinsic to our economic institutions that put the natural environment at much greater risk than people realized until forty years ago, when the modern environmental movement was born. Chapter 4 explains the implications of externalities, public goods, free access to common property resources, and discrepancies between profit rates and the social rate of time discount. When these mainstream theories are properly interpreted, they reveal a great deal about why the environment is endangered. Chapter 5 confirms the concerns emphasized by heterodox schools of economic thought that private enterprise and market economies contain an unhealthy "growth imperative" that is environmentally destructive are well founded, even if some who make this argument fail to present their case in a convincing way.

Many people, including some economists, suffer from fundamental confusions about how different environmental policies work. Part III equips environmentalists and progressives to confront professional economists who often do not share their values or priorities in debates over environmental policy. Chapter 6 begins by explaining why free-market environmentalism is not the answer to environmental problems its proponents would have us believe, but is instead an ideological and political obstacle to solving environmental problems. Chapter 7 goes on to explain the logic, as well as the strengths and weaknesses, of different environmental policies from a progressive perspective.

Part IV applies our new understanding to climate change, the greatest environmental problem humanity has ever faced. Unfortunately, averting climate change, and doing so fairly, requires overcoming serious obstacles that have stymied progress to date. Chapter 8 reviews the history of climate negotiations leading up to the disastrous meetings in Copenhagen in December 2009. Chapter 9 evaluates criticisms of the Kyoto Protocol and identifies important lessons to be learned. Chapter 10 applies those lessons to designing an effective, efficient, and fair post-Kyoto treaty.

The conclusion briefly discusses political strategy and ideas about more far-reaching, systemic changes that might prove necessary to alter our relations with the natural environment before damage becomes irreversible.

Part I

Toward a New Paradigm

Part I explores important components of a new environmental economic paradigm needed to broaden the intellectual framework beyond the simplistic problematic of allocating scarce natural resources to competing insatiable wants and disposing of the wastes of economic activity in the least costly way.

Chapter 1

Something Happened on the Way to the Twenty-First Century

Mainstream economic theory is based on a paradigm that dates back to the eighteenth century, and critics argue that is part of the problem. The world was a very different place when a Scottish moral philosopher wandered the grounds of the University of Glasgow in absent-minded reverie, thinking thoughts that would launch a new economic discipline that was called "political economy" before becoming simply "economics." When Adam Smith published *An Inquiry into the Nature and Causes of the Wealth of Nations* in 1776, there were less than 800 million people roaming the earth, only the indigenous tribes and a handful of French Canadian trappers had any idea what lay between the Mississippi River and the Pacific coast of North America, and Captain James Cook, spurred on by a British Admiralty reward of 20,000 pounds, was searching in vain off the coast of Alaska for a Northwest Passage back to the Atlantic Ocean. With the exception of small parts of China, India, and Europe, the world was a mostly empty place when the discipline of economics was launched.

No wonder Adam Smith believed the value of goods and services was determined entirely by the amount of labor it took to produce them and never integrated the opportunity costs of using natural resources into his explanation of prices. No wonder it never dawned on Adam Smith that there might be effects on people other than buyers and sellers of producing and consuming the goods they bartered over in market exchanges. In a largely empty world, neither resource exhaustion nor effects on external parties were likely to be top concerns for creative minds trying to unravel the important economic conundrums of their day.

Full-World Economics: Limits to Growth

By the time this book is printed, roughly 7 billion people will be crowding into the same space occupied by only 800 million in Adam Smith's day. The world is different today. It is now more full than empty, and one would think the underlying presumptions that make up the gestalt that informs our economic paradigm would reflect this difference. But as ecological economists point out, modern-day economics, to its detriment, remains largely an empty-world economics as our colleagues in the mainstream continue to operate under the influence of a paradigm pioneered well over 200 years ago (Costanza et al. 1997).

Mainstream economic theory managed to integrate the opportunity cost of using scarce resources into its theory of prices long ago. But ecological economists are right to point out that mainstream economics continues to largely ignore potentially problematic relations between human economic activity and the natural environment *in the aggregate*. Again, the history of economic thought can help us understand how this could have happened.

Only the Great Depression and incessant prodding by John Maynard Keynes forced the profession to acknowledge that traditional economic theory was not up to the task of dealing with important *macro*economic issues. When mainstream economics underwent its great makeover in the mid-twentieth century and economic theory was divided into two distinct branches, microeconomic theory and macroeconomic theory, the field of natural resource economics was assigned to the micro branch, where theories of optimal pricing and extraction rates for nonrenewable and renewable resources were further elaborated. Afterward, any concerns about potential macro problems between the economy and the natural environment in a world that was filling quickly were implicitly assigned to macroeconomists. But macroeconomists' attention was long focused elsewhere.

Early macroeconomists, preoccupied with fallacies that Keynes exposed in traditional economic thinking that had nothing to do with environmental issues, quickly became very busy tackling the job of building new macroeconomic models that no longer rested on a false premise known as Say's Law. This was a compelling priority because otherwise economists would continue to be unable to provide sensible advice about appropriate fiscal and monetary policies to address macroeconomic problems such as unemployment and inflation. Unfortunately, none of this important work lent itself to creation of a macro environmental economics to compliment micro natural resource economics.

When macroeconomists finally turned their attention to long-run issues, they built on early work by Roy Harrod (1939) and Evsey Domar (1946) on the relation between saving rates, capital output ratios, and the rate of growth of output. They used an aggregate production function that defined output as a function of labor and produced capital with no reference to natural resources whatsoever, instead focusing on how to incorporate technical change into their analysis to help explain what was an embarrassingly large residual that the growth of labor supplies and capital stocks did not seem to account for (Solow 1956, 1957). As a result, even among macroeconomists whose primary concern was long-run economic growth, there was little interest in how natural resources might impose limits on the growth of output. Concerned with other problems and increasingly isolated from natural resource economists who worked on the micro side of the profession's theoretical partition, mainstream macroeconomists continued to function with an empty-world paradigm.

Publication of a study titled *Limits to Growth* (Meadows et al.) commissioned by the influential Club of Rome think tank in 1972 marked a turning point in popular thinking, but not in thinking inside the mainstream of the economics profession. Robert Solow, for example, questioned the quality of some of the data the authors of the report used in a critical article published in *Newsweek*. And Allen Kneese and Ronald Ridker from Resources for the Future questioned what they called the report's overly conservative assumptions about technological change. Chapters 3 and 5 review what has been an ongoing debate ever since between so-called technological pessimists and optimists about environmental limits to growth. But the point for now is that mainstream macroeconomic growth theory continued to ignore any constraints imposed by nonrenewable natural resources, as well as resources that were renewable but only at rates that were often lower than the rates at which the world's economies were exploiting them.

Ecological economists also point out that an empty-world vision blinds mainstream economists to danger from wastes that the production of desirable goods and services generates as by-products. The harmful effects of particular pollutants on humans are now widely recognized by mainstream environmental economists, and this subject has been dutifully added to the study of natural resources in mainstream environmental economics curricula and textbooks. But ecological economists point to an additional problem caused by wastes based on their full-worldview. Just as a full-world paradigm sensitizes researchers to ways in which the natural environment is overtaxed as a *source* of resources as inputs into economic activities, it also draws attention to limits on the capacity of the biosphere to serve as a *sink* to absorb and store wastes that are outputs of economic activities in relatively harmless ways. In effect, the Club of Rome report suggested that humans were on a trajectory to die of starvation as they exhausted needed environmental resources. Thirty years later, many environmentalists began to worry that people might asphyxiate themselves first as they exhaust even faster the capacity of the biosphere to act as their sink.

Ecological economists introduced a very useful concept they call through-put to reorient thinking about how the natural environment limits growth as both a source of natural resources and as a sink for wastes. *Throughput* is defined as physical matter of one kind or another that enters the economic system and physical matter that exits the economic system as waste of some kind. As ecological economists point out, as long as the human species remains earthbound and since physical stocks of different categories of natural resources are finite, and the capacity of the biosphere and upper atmosphere to absorb physical wastes of different kinds is also finite, economic through-put cannot grow infinitely. Ecological economists turn this fact—which is undeniable in and of itself—into a relevant point by arguing that (1) much thinking about economic goals and strategies implicitly ignores this fact, and (2) the future of our present economic system seems to be predicated on the false assumption that throughput can grow infinitely.

Full-World Economics: Externalities Are the Rule, Not the Exception

There is a second important consequence of changing from an empty-world to a full-world mind-set that ecological economists do not emphasize sufficiently. Not only are people more likely to bump into the limits of the physical world when there are more of them, but also people are more likely to bump into each other when there are 7 billion of them than when there were only 800 million. Changing from an empty- to a full-world economic paradigm reverses an assumption that is crucial to every major conclusion and economic theorem about markets and market systems.

An *externality* is defined as an effect on any party other than the buyer or seller when a good or service is produced, exchanged, and consumed. In other words, whenever anyone who is "external" to the market decision-making process is affected by the decision a buyer and seller agree to, this is termed an external or third-party effect. An externality can occur either when a good or service is produced or when it is consumed, and an external effect can be either negative or positive.

According to Adam Smith's theory of the "invisible hand" (Smith [1776] 1999), when self-interested behavior on the part of buyers and sellers in competitive markets drives the market toward its equilibrium price and quantity, this quantity will also be the socially efficient amount of the good or service to produce and consume. But as we will discover in Chapter 4, Adam Smith's invisible hand works in a market *only if* there are no externalities. The first fundamental theorem of welfare economics states that any general equilibrium of a private enterprise, competitive market economy will be socially efficient. But this theorem is true *only if* there are no externalities. The second fundamental theorem of welfare economics states that any socially efficient outcome—of whatever degree of equality or inequality one might desire—can be achieved as the general equilibrium of a private enterprise market economy with the appropriate initial assignment of ownership rights over productive resources. But this theorem is true *only if* there are no externalities. In sum, the conclusion that markets can be relied on to allocate scarce productive resources and distribute consumption goods efficiently is warranted *only if* externalities are the exception and not the rule, which is where the difference between an empty- and full-world mind-set comes in.

In an empty world it is far more reasonable to presume—as a general operating principle, or default option—that externalities are the exception, not the rule. A careful reading of his work suggests that it never occurred to Adam Smith that there might sometimes be costs to society above and beyond the costs producers pay for. Operating with an eighteenth-century, empty-world mind-set, Smith assumed that the costs to private producers covered all the costs anyone in society bore when goods were produced.[1] The notion that this assumption might not always be warranted, that there might sometimes be negative effects associated with production on third parties, parties external to the market decision-making process, and therefore that the cost to society as a whole of making a good might sometimes differ from the cost borne by the private producer did not occur to anyone in the economics profession until the twentieth century, when the world was much fuller and A.C. Pigou first defined the concept of an externality (Pigou [1912] 2009). But even after Pigou succeeded Alfred Marshall at Cambridge University in 1908 and served as the primary lecturer on welfare economics for thirty-five years, externalities, and corrective measures economists still call *Pigovian taxes and subsidies* in his honor, remained a minor, technical footnote in the profession's thinking about the market system. Externalities were not taken seriously until popular concern over pollution—which economic theory defines as a negative externality—led to the rise of the modern environmental movement in the 1970s, when the world was *much* fuller. Yet mainstream microeconomic theory continues to operate under the implicit assumption that external effects are insignificant in all but a few markets, despite compelling reasons to believe otherwise that we explore in Chapter 4.

7

Ecosystem Complexity

The bottom line is that the biological world turns out to be more of a mystery than many people once assumed. This comes as something of a surprise because the rate of growth of knowledge in the biological sciences has been astounding over the past few decades. Just as there was an age when scientific discoveries were most notable in physics, there have probably been more pathbreaking discoveries in biology recently than in any other scientific field. But while discoveries have deepened our understanding of how *individual* organisms and parts of organisms work, and arguably made the effects of interventions on individual organisms and microorganisms more predictable, new knowledge concerning how biological *systems* function suggests that predicting the effects of interventions on system trajectory is more difficult than previously believed.

We are now smart enough to know that eliminating one species in an ecosystem may well unleash a chain of effects reaching many other species that appeared to be far removed. But this new knowledge often makes us less, not more, certain of what to predict. Even when biologists successfully unravel one long causal chain with many surprising links, it only heightens awareness of how many other long causal chains must also be out there about which we remain clueless. We are now smart enough to know that ecosystems can have tipping points where the effects of applying pressure of one kind or another suddenly change dramatically. But knowing tipping points exist without knowing how to pinpoint where they are only makes us feel less certain about our ability to predict outcomes. We are now smart enough to know that even if an ecological system were deterministic with no random elements, if it is a chaotic, complex dynamic system, outcomes can be surprisingly sensitive to small variations in initial conditions, making long-run predictions impossible.[2] And of course random elements are numerous and greatly magnify our ability to predict outcomes. Again, knowing more only makes us less certain about predicting the effects of human interactions on ecosystems. In sum, in the field of biological *systems* much new knowledge has been humbling for any who were paying attention.

As we will see in Chapter 2, *long causal chains*, *tipping points*, and *butterfly effects* are all phrases that should strike fear into the heart of anyone trying to apply cost-benefit analysis to the environment because cost-benefit analysis relies on predictable and continuous responses to changes in an economic activity. Instead, to put it crudely, what much new knowledge about ecosystem complexity suggests is precaution when poking Mother Nature. More specifically, ecological scientists have identified a number of critical planetary thresholds where ecosystem complexity makes a strong case for exercising precaution. Ecologists warn that avoiding crossing thresholds with regard to climate change, ocean acidification, ozone depletion, the biogeo-chemical flow boundary for nitrogen and phosphorus, global freshwater use, biodiversity loss, and toxic chemical pollution is essential to maintaining the relatively benign climate and environmental conditions that have existed during the last 12,000 years.

Notes

1. Although Adam Smith was oblivious to the problem externalities cause for his beloved invisible hand, he was fully aware that noncompetitive market structures keep the invisible hand from working its magic, which is why he singled out monopoly as the great danger to the efficient functioning of market economies. While the world may still have been largely empty in Smith's day, it was certainly not free from monopolies.

2. There is now a large literature applying insights from what is popularly known as chaos theory to the interaction between complex ecological and economic systems. For example, see Rosser (1999, 2005).

Chapter 2

Cost-Benefit Analysis
Beware

Mainstream economists often give the impression that *cost-benefit analysis* (CBA) does not involve value judgments, when, in fact, CBA rests on a number of questionable value judgments, and pretending otherwise only serves to disguise important choices incorporated into the analysis. Mainstream economists also present CBA as the only rational and objective method for making social choices about the environment, when in fact there are many situations where CBA is not the appropriate methodology at all. In particular, CBA is inappropriate when compensation is unlikely to rectify inequities, when people have rights, when power differentials bias estimates of costs and benefits, when time frames are long and the choice of a rate of time discount is overwhelmingly determinant, when continuity is unlikely, when benefits are hard to quantify, and when the consequences of improbable outcomes are very large relative to those of more probable outcomes.

The Lure of CBA

"If the benefits of doing something outweigh the costs, it should be done. But if the costs outweigh the benefits, then it would be a mistake to do it." What could be more sensible? What could be more obvious? This has the markings of a "truth" that requires no explanation. One might even offer this as a simple definition of *rational* behavior.

It is hard to imagine a more straightforward approach to social choice, and

11

Figure 2.1   **Standard CBA Diagram**

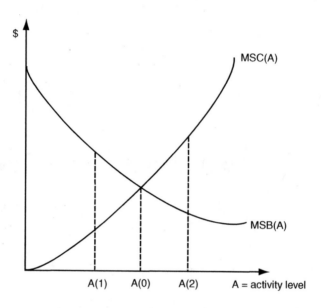

indeed, this is precisely the attraction of CBA and one reason that challenging it is so difficult. The common sense expressed above is formally stated by economists as the *efficiency criterion*: If the overall benefits to all people of doing something outweigh the overall costs to all people of doing it, it is socially "efficient" to do it; however, if the overall costs outweigh the overall benefits, it is "inefficient" to do it.[1]

Economists like to think in terms of the effects of making small changes, called *marginal* changes, in one direction or another, and economists also have a penchant for expressing their theories graphically. The standard way to demonstrate the logic of CBA uses the concepts of marginal social cost (MSC) and marginal social benefit (MSB) and the graph represented in Figure 2.1.

A represents any "action" we could take. As we move rightward along the horizontal axis, we undertake more and more of whatever this action is. A could be the percentage of glass bottles recycled in the City of Portland, the percentage reduction in the average arsenic content in drinking water in West Virginia, the reduction in the number of tons of sulfur dioxide emitted from power plants in the United States, or the reduction in the number of tons of greenhouse gases emitted worldwide in 2012 compared to 1990. The MSC curve shows the cost *to society* of engaging in the *last unit* of action A at different levels of action. If we choose the cheapest way of doing things

12

first, the cost of doing *yet more* will increase as we do more and more, and the MSC curve will rise as A increases. The MSB curve shows the benefit *to society* of engaging in the *last unit* of action A at different levels of action. If the more of something we have done already, the smaller the benefit will be from doing *yet more*, the MSB curve will fall as A increases. What is exceedingly useful about this diagram is that it allows us to determine the socially efficient or "optimal" level of action to engage in, A(0). It is the amount where the MSC of the last unit of action A is equal to the MSB from the last unit of action A. This is demonstrated easily by eliminating all other possibilities.

For any level of action A less than A(0), such as A(1), what would be the effect of increasing activity A one more unit? To see what the additional cost to society would be, we go up from A(1) to the MSC curve. To see what the additional benefit to society would be, we go up from A(1) to the MSB curve. But when we are at level A(1), the MSB curve is higher than the MSC curve, indicating that engaging in more of activity A increases social benefits more than it increases social costs. In other words, there are positive *net* social benefits from expanding activity A at activity level A(1), and therefore A(1) cannot be optimal, or socially efficient. For any level of production greater than A(0), such as A(2), what would be the effect of decreasing activity A by one unit? To see what the savings in social cost would be, we go up from A(2) to the MSC curve. To see what the lost social benefit would be, we go up from A(2) to the MSB curve. But when we are at A(2), the MSC curve is higher than the MSB curve, indicating that reducing activity A by one unit reduces social benefits by less than it reduces social costs. So there are positive *net* social benefits from reducing activity A at A(2), and therefore A(2) cannot be socially efficient.

So for all A < A(0) we should expand activity A to increase net benefits, and for all A > A(0) we should reduce activity A to increase net benefits. Therefore, the only level of activity A that is efficient from society's point of view is the level where the MSB of the last unit of activity A engaged in is equal to the MSC of the last unit of activity A, which in Figure 2.1 is A(0). At any other level of activity A, we could increase net social benefits by expanding or reducing activity A.

This is a powerful tool indeed! The efficiency criteria as illustrated in Figure 2.1 appears to tell us how much we should recycle in Portland, how much we should reduce arsenic in drinking water in West Virginia, how much we should reduce sulfur dioxide emissions from power plants in the United States, and how much we should reduce global greenhouse gas emissions. Can it really be this simple? The remainder of this chapter explores why it is usually *not* this simple.

CBA and Value Judgments

Despite the appearance of objectivity, a host of value judgments lies behind CBA. This, in and of itself, is not objectionable because value judgments necessarily lie behind any approach to social choice. What is misleading is the pretense that this is somehow not the case when we use CBA and the consequent failure to provide justification for important value judgments that underlie analyses.

Whereas the efficiency criterion and CBA may be the "rational" way for an individual to approach decision-making, society, of course, is comprised of many different people and many different interest groups. Since different people and groups will be affected differently by any social choice, it is immediately apparent that matters are a bit more complicated than CBA suggests. There will be losers as well as winners if the environment is better protected, just as there are always winners as well as losers when it is degraded. In other words, there are always distributive issues as well as efficiency issues involved in environmental policy choices, and pretending otherwise, which is the practical effect of CBA as usually practiced, would appear to be an obvious oversight.

However, it would be a mistake to assume this is simply an egregious oversight on the part of the economics profession. In fact, economists have historically engaged in self-doubt and much soul-searching surrounding precisely this complication. Unfortunately, the soul-searching has been conducted almost entirely when the economics "court" is in "closed session." When results of CBA studies are released, they are seldom accompanied by a disclosure that recounts the history of economic thought about the disadvantages of cardinal versus ordinal theories of utility, much less the perils of interpersonal utility comparisons.

To use CBA, one must be willing to do two things mainstream economists have historically shown a great reluctance to engage in. One must embrace a cardinal theory of individual utility rather than an ordinal theory of utility, and one must engage in interpersonal utility comparisons. Those who apply CBA must first measure changes in costs and benefits to different people quantitatively. It is not enough to say Peter will be made better off while Susan will be made worse off. To carry out CBA, we need to know Peter will be nine units better off than he was before, while Susan will be five units worse off than she was before. This amounts to committing to what economists call a *cardinal* rather than an *ordinal* model of utility for individuals, which mainstream economists have historically been very uneasy about and often go to great lengths to avoid. Next, the scale used for measuring utility, or benefit, for Peter and Susan must be the same because CBA requires us to compare the magnitude of the benefit gained by Peter to the magnitude of the benefit lost by Susan.

However, before the benefits that have been quantified for Peter and Susan using the same scale are added together, we must also decide how much to count a unit of benefit for Peter compared to the loss of a unit of benefit to Susan. While many would never give a second thought to what they were implicitly assuming before adding nine and subtracting five, economists have historically been more self-conscious and cautious. What if Susan is more deserving than Peter? Economists historically acknowledge that at this point in the application of CBA a decision must be made about how to weigh benefits to Peter and Susan before we add them. We may wish to weigh losses to Susan "the deserving" twice as heavily as gains to Peter "the unworthy"—in which case we would add nine and subtract two times five, which gives a very different result.

In sum, historically and as a profession, economists have pondered the most immediate complications of applying CBA: Can benefits to *different* people be quantified, compared, and conflated, and if they can, should they be? But when economists practice CBA today, they more often than not put all these self-doubts out of mind and invariably hide them from public view. Without admitting as much, economists who practice CBA also lose claim to much of the theoretical progress neoclassical welfare theory pretends to over the past hundred years. Neoclassical theorists pride themselves as having "progressed" from the "primitive" classical utilitarian notion of knowable, additive, interpersonally comparable cardinal utilities, first to ordinal utilities, then to indifference curves, then to the theory of revealed preferences, and finally to the "axioms" of rational choice—where each of these stations of the cross is portrayed as a significant theoretical advance. Whether or not all the self-congratulation is deserved, one thing is clear: CBA takes its practitioners all the way back to the "primitive" nineteenth-century world of classical utilitarianism.

Putting theoretical niceties aside, the bottom line is this: We cannot apply CBA without making value judgments. Even if it is possible to accurately estimate benefits and costs quantitatively—which is by no means a trivial task, as discussed below—we must make a value judgment that benefits and costs for different individuals and groups of people are quantifiable and comparable. We must make a value judgment about how much to weigh the welfare of different individuals and groups. Finally, as discussed below, we must make a value judgment that no individual or group rights are at stake, so that maximizing our measure of social welfare is all that matters.

It would also be naive not to recognize that, on a very practical level, when people argue over CBA it is often not really maximizing social welfare they care about. Different constituencies have different interests in whether or not to protect the environment and how to protect it. But to argue for or against environmental policies on the basis of what will most favor one's group is not usually persuasive, except among members of a group trying to identify their own self-interest. So, instead, interested parties usually try to argue that what happens to be best for them is coincidentally in the social interest. One way to slant a CBA to favor the outcome one personally prefers is through choice of value judgments. When value judgments are implicit rather than explicit, and especially when practitioners pretend there are no value judgments involved in CBA, deception is all the more likely.

Compensation

It is a truism that if aggregate benefits exceed aggregate costs, then it is *possible* for those who benefit from a policy to fully compensate those whom the policy disadvantages for their losses and still enjoy positive benefits for themselves. If this were done, it would prevent the policy from harming anyone, but it would mean that the entire efficiency gain from the policy had been appropriated by those the policy advantages. Of course, it is also possible to distribute the entire efficiency gain from any policy to those who are disadvantaged by the policy itself. If those who "won" compensated all who "lost" to the point where the winners were no longer any better off than they had been originally, again the policy would have harmed no one, but in this case the entire efficiency gain from the policy would have been awarded to those the policy itself harmed in some way. When a policy passes muster according to CBA, this simply means there is an efficiency gain. Once we realize this, it is obvious that *in theory* the efficiency gain from any policy can be distributed in an infinite number of ways.[2]

But it is important to realize that in general policies that bear the CBA stamp of approval do more than generate and distribute an efficiency gain. They also redistribute pre-policy welfare. Suppose there is no compensation following implementation of a policy. Not only will the winners capture the entire efficiency gain from the policy, they will also capture whatever those disadvantaged by the policy lose! In other words, if a policy generates an efficiency gain but also creates losers as well as winners, absent compensation the winners will capture 100 percent of the efficiency gain from the policy *plus* 100 percent of everyone else's losses.

The first problem with talk about compensation is that it is all too often just that—only talk. Knowing that *in theory* any policy that passes their CBA test *need not* harm anyone may ease economists' consciences, but theoretical compensation that is not actually paid does nothing to ease the pain of those

16

the policy harmed. As a matter of fact, knowing that the harm was not necessary might make the damage inflicted even more painful!

But there is a second problem when economists talk about compensation that progressives are often oblivious to. When economists do talk about actual rather than theoretical compensation, they are only talking about compensation for the redistributive effects of a policy. Discussion is invariably about whether or not some of the benefits of winners will be transferred to losers. The standard operating assumption is that fully compensating the losers for their losses would be the most that anyone could hope for, and since reasonable people understand the world is never perfect, losers should be happy to settle for something less than full compensation. But notice that this mind-set implicitly assumes that those who benefit from a policy deserve to capture the entire efficiency gain from the policy! This mind-set not only implicitly assumes that the pre-policy distribution of welfare was fair in the first place, it also assumes that those whom a policy benefits deserve to capture the entire efficiency gain while others deserve not to benefit at all.

Progressives should always approach compensation in a very different way. We should start by asking whether or not the pre-policy distribution of welfare was fair in the first place. If not, we need to identify who has more welfare than they deserve and who has less than they deserve. Only then does it make sense for progressives to join in where others begin, namely identifying whom a policy benefits and whom it harms, and considering if compensation is in order. If the winners happily coincide with those whom progressives regard as more deserving, and if the losers are those we consider less deserving, then the redistributive effect of the policy is progressive and reduces economic injustice. In this case, progressives have no reason to support compensation since this will only reduce the amount by which the policy serves the cause of economic justice.[3] On the other hand, if a policy advantages those progressives find less deserving and disadvantages those we find more deserving, progressives should fight hard for compensation. But we should not merely insist on compensation only for the regressive redistributive effect of the policy. We should point out that in addition to whatever compensation is necessary to make the more deserving victims of a policy "whole"—that is, restore them to their pre-policy level of welfare—unless they also receive additional compensation sufficient to award them at least half of the efficiency gain, the policy will have had the effect of aggravating preexisting economic injustice. When we consider different domestic environmental policies in Chapter 7 and international climate policy in Chapters 8, 9, and 10, these lessons are very important to keep in mind.

When People Have Rights

In the example above, what if Susan and Peter are equally deserving, but the loss of five units of benefit to Susan violates Susan's *rights* in some way? In this case, weighing Susan's well-being more heavily than Peter's is no solution and, in fact, misses the point altogether. If Susan has a right that would be violated by a policy that provides Peter with greater welfare, then unless Susan agrees to waive her right it does not matter how much better off Peter will be.

The philosopher John Rawls has made this point most recently (Rawls 1971), and most persuasively, but philosophers who subscribe to "contractarian" theories of social justice have made this criticism of utilitarianism for centuries, and CBA is nothing more than applied utilitarianism. In short, the notion of "rights" is intrinsically incompatible with utilitarianism and CBA.

One important category of "right" is *safety standards*. According to this reasoning, no matter who you are or where you live, you should be able to have access to water that is safe to drink. Of course, nothing is ever completely safe, and safety standards must be quantified also. For example, in 1992 the Environmental Protection Agency (EPA) defined a "safe" level of lead in drinking water as anything less than 15 micrograms of lead per liter of water, and a safe level of copper as anything less than 1.3 milligrams of copper per liter of water. Obviously 10 micrograms of lead and 1.0 milligrams of copper would be safer, so ultimately safety standards come down to estimating the likelihood of adverse affects on human health of different standards and deciding how much health risk we are willing to tolerate. In other words, in the case of standards, the value judgment takes the form of how safe is safe enough.

A recent hot debate over arsenic standards for drinking water illustrates the difference between CBA and a rights-based, safety standard approach. Arsenic standards for drinking water were set in 1946 at 50 parts per billion. In 1999 a report by the National Academy of Sciences based on new toxicological evidence concluded that 50 ppb was not safe enough and recommended tightening the standard. After studying the issue, the EPA initially proposed to lower the arsenic standard to 10 ppb. However, in March 2001 the Bush administration announced it was not accepting the new standard on grounds that CBA analysis revealed that the estimated benefits of lowering the standard to 10 ppb did not outweigh the estimated costs. In response to public outcry, the House of Representatives voted to direct the EPA to implement the 10 ppb standard anyway—implicitly rejecting CBA and endorsing a safety standard based on the best available health science as the appropriate methodology in this situation.

How Power and Wealth Matter

We consider two examples to illustrate how ignoring differences of power and wealth adversely affects environmental economics as traditionally practiced.

Asking the wrong question: The activity that employs more environmental economists than any other is conducting *contingent valuation* (CV) *surveys.* The problem these surveys address is that we often have no quantitative estimate of how much people benefit from protecting the environment to weigh against the costs of more protection, which are often presented in dollars, right down to the last penny. Below we discuss the strengths and weaknesses of CV surveys compared to other methods used to provide quantitative estimates of environmental benefits. But a simple example of how applied environmental economics ignores wealth and power is illustrated by an obvious error in the question CV surveys invariably ask respondents.

Suppose we are trying to determine where it is most efficient to locate a waste dump and we want to get a quantitative estimate of how strongly residents of different communities feel they would be adversely affected if the dump were located near them; that is, we want to measure differences in communities' "preferences" for a safer environment compared to their preferences for other things, like food and clothing. In Washington, DC, when survey-takers ask residents of Chevy Chase, a wealthy enclave in the northwest quadrant of the city, how much they would be willing to pay not to have a toxic dump in their neighborhood, they will predictably answer much larger dollar amounts than residents of Anacostia, a poor ward in the southeast quadrant of the city. But does this mean it is efficient to locate the dump in Anacostia rather than Chevy Chase?

Even if residents in Anacostia placed a higher priority on their health compared to other goods than the residents of Chevy Chase, and therefore it was actually more efficient to locate the dump in Chevy Chase, and even if residents of both neighborhoods responded truthfully, the dollar amounts Anacostia residents would answer would be far lower than the dollar amounts Chevy Chase residents would answer simply because people's incomes in Anacostia are much lower than people's incomes in Chevy Chase. The problem is that when respondents answer the question typically asked in CV surveys, their answer reflects not only the strength of their preference, or aversion in this case, but also how much income they have with which to express their preferences for everything. In other words, CV surveys invariably ask the wrong question and thereby bias estimates of environmental benefits.

What is striking is how easy it would be to correct this mistake, and yet it is almost never done. Either by asking respondents what percentage of their income they would be willing to pay, or by asking respondents their incomes as well as their willingness to pay in dollars, one could correct for this obvious bias and practice CV to measure strength of environmental preferences in a way that gives one person one vote rather than one dollar one vote. However, failure to conduct CV surveys fairly is not the likely explanation for the fact that hazardous waste sites are disproportionately located near where racial minorities and poor people live in the United States (Commission on Racial Justice 1987). That is best explained by the power-weighted decision rule.

The power-weighted decision rule: Suppose activity A in Figure 2.1 is some form of environmental degradation. If those who benefit from the degradation are more powerful on average than those who are harmed, James Boyce (2002) explains the outcome is likely to lie to the right of A(0), whereas if those who benefit are less powerful on average than those who are damaged, the outcome is likely to lie to the left of A(0). There are, of course, many reasons that people and groups have more or less power, including differences in wealth, race, gender, and political connections. These are factors that political economists like Boyce take seriously and integrate into their studies, while such factors are generally ignored in mainstream treatments. But just as mainstream economic theory infers utility from what individuals reveal when they buy in markets, Boyce suggests we can infer power from the revealed preferences of society regarding social decisions. The farther to the right of A(0) we actually end up, the more powerful those who benefit from degradation must be compared to those who are harmed.

For example, why are Brazilian forests converted to cattle ranches even though an objective estimation would reveal that the costs outweigh the benefits of doing so? In other words, why is the outcome far to the right of A(0) when it comes to destruction and degradation of tropical forests in Brazil? Boyce explains it is because the beneficiaries include the landed aristocracy in Brazil and those living primarily in advanced economies and enjoying high enough income to eat beef frequently, while those who bear the costs are primarily indigenous forest dwellers, small farmers living downstream, and future generations who will suffer from climate change (Boyce 2002, chapter 4).

When the Rate of Time Discount Is Determinant

The benefits of environmental degradation typically occur sooner than the costs, while the benefits of environmental protection invariably come later than the costs. This means that environmental cost-benefit studies will be sensitive to the rate of time discount chosen by the analyst. If a benefit or cost is treated in the same way no matter when it occurs, then there is no "discounting" and the rate of time discount is zero. However, if net benefits farther in the future are deemed less important than net benefits in the present, a positive rate of time discount is used, and the higher the rate of discount the more strongly future consequences will be discounted compared to more immediate consequences. Chapter 4 reviews the debate over what the appropriate rate of time discount should be for environmental policies and explains the effects of discount rates on extraction rates of natural resource deposits. Here the point is only to illustrate how sensitive CBA is to choice of a discount rate.

Suppose we use CBA to decide whether or not to protect our grandchildren from a climate-related loss of $100 they will suffer sixty years from now. According to CBA, how much should we be willing to pay today to prevent their loss sixty years from now?[4] If we use a zero discount rate, we should be willing to pay up to $100 today for this $100 benefit for our grandchildren sixty years from now. However, if we use a discount rate of even 1 percent, CBA indicates that we should not pay more than $55. If we use a 3 percent discount rate, CBA will tell us not to pay anything over $17. If we use a 5 percent discount, CBA will instruct us not to pay much more than $5. Clearly, the amount that CBA shows is "rational" to spend now to avoid environmental damages later is highly sensitive to choice of a discount rate.

Of course, when time frames are even longer, sensitivity is even greater. If the climate-related loss of $100 will occur 200 years from now instead of sixty years from now, CBA suggests that avoiding it is worth paying only $13.70 now if we use a 1 percent discount rate, only $0.30 now if we use a 3 percent discount rate, and not even a penny now if we use a 5 percent discount rate. Clearly any consequences 200 years down the road will be rendered effectively invisible by CBA at discount rates that are typically used. Do we really want to ignore the environmental consequences of our choices that occur 200 years or more in the future? How would we feel if those who ruled in 1810 had decided that none of us alive today mattered at all?[5]

As Figure 2.2 shows, if activity A is protecting the environment in some way or another, and if we assume that the benefits of greater protection occur in the future while the costs occur in the present, the effect of increasing the rate of time discount, d, is to rotate the MSB line downward. This moves the point where the MSB line crosses the MSC line to the left, and A(0), the optimal level of protection, will therefore be lower than before. Again we see that the higher the rate of time discount used, the lower the level of environmental protection CBA will recommend as optimal.

When Continuity Is Unlikely

Tipping points mean that marginal damage curves are not continuous and no longer look like the MSC curve in Figure 2.1. Suppose the activity measured

Figure 2.2   **CBA With a Positive Rate of Time Discount**

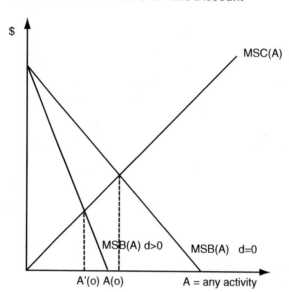

on the horizontal axis is annual, global, net carbon dioxide emissions (i.e., tons of carbon dioxide released into the atmosphere during a year, minus tons of carbon dioxide sequestered, or taken out of the atmosphere during the year). The marginal benefit curve, MSB, may still look something like the one drawn in Figure 2.1 since there continue to be positive but continuously declining benefits from burning more and more fossil fuels while technologies and infrastructure to produce and distribute renewable energy sources are still being developed. But the MSC curve will no longer be rising continuously. It may rise continuously in the beginning as burning more fossil fuels generates slightly more "mild" climate change, but once we reach a climate tipping point there will be a break in the MSC curve, the curve will skip significantly upward, and then perhaps continue to rise slowly again, as depicted in Figure 2.3.

Scientists devote a great deal of attention to what might possibly trigger a climate tipping point. Melting of Greenland or Antarctic glaciers; disappearance of the polar ice caps, which reflect a great deal of sunlight; thawing of the permafrost in northern tundra, releasing large quantities of methane frozen there; die-offs of whole forests as tree species cannot travel fast enough away from the equator as temperatures warm; reversal of ocean currents like the Gulf Stream, which warms Europe; and other possibilities that could unleash positive feedback affects that would further accelerate climate change to cataclysmic levels are taken more seriously by scientists every year.

Figure 2.3 **CBA With a Tipping Point**

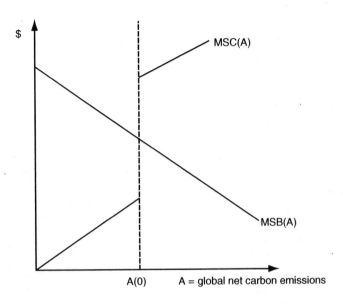

In theory, CBA is still applicable even if there is a tipping point. Accord-ing to Figure 2.3, we should continue to increase net carbon emissions up to A(0), just as before. According to Figure 2.3, every ton of net emissions up to A(0) will increase social benefits by more than it increases social costs. Only further reductions beyond A(0) would cause more damage than benefits. But this is the key point: We had better be very sure exactly where the tipping point is or we risk making a very, very big mistake. Initially, as we increase net emissions, the benefits of doing so will be significantly higher than the costs—sending a strong signal that we should keep increasing emissions. But the problem is that this strong signal will continue right up to the tipping point. When we compare benefits to costs one ton before the tipping point, A(0), the signal will still be strong that marginal benefits are much higher than marginal costs, telling us to keep on increasing greenhouse gas (GHG) emissions. If we had some other way to pinpoint precisely where the tipping point is, we could ignore this misleading economic signal and there need be no problem. Or if, having passed the tipping point, we could simply backtrack once we realized our error, the mistake would not be disastrous. But scientists have told us very clearly that they do not think they can predict exactly where the tipping point will come, and of course once we have passed a climate tipping point there is no going back to correct for our mistake. This means that comparing costs and benefits of increasing carbon emissions to decide if

23

further emissions are "efficient" may be a disastrous methodology to use for making this social decision.

When Benefits Are Hard to Quantify

In 1960, if you asked the manager of a power plant using coal how much it would cost to reduce emissions of sulfur dioxide from his plant, he would have had a hard time giving you a number, although he would have assured you that it would be very expensive. The reason he would not have had a number ready is that in 1960 nobody had suggested charging power plants for sulfur dioxide emissions, and therefore he had never asked his engineers to figure out what changes would be necessary to reduce emissions, so his accountants could translate whatever changes they recommended into dollars and cents. But in the 1990s, when it was apparent that a sulfur dioxide cap and trade policy was going to be passed and that power plants were going to pay a price for sulfur dioxide emissions, managers of utilities ordered their engineers and accountants to come up with numbers that they presented in congressional testimony right down to the penny. Of course, there was some legitimate uncertainty, and of course they deliberately inflated the estimates to convince Congress to loosen the cap on aggregate sulfur dioxide emissions from power plants and give power plants more permits to emit sulfur dioxide free of charge. But as soon as there was reason to need them, precise quantitative estimates of how much it would cost to reduce sulfur dioxide emissions were available, and after the Clean Air Act was amended in 1990 to cap emissions of sulfur dioxide from power plants, and plants did switch to coal with a lower sulfur content and installed scrubbers in smokestacks, those numbers were no longer only estimates.

But to apply CBA we also need to know something quantitative about the benefits of reducing emissions, and there lies the rub. While quantitative estimates of the costs of emission reductions are readily available, translating a long list of different ways that reducing emissions will provide benefits into a single number is very difficult. It is so difficult that many people quickly despair, concluding that only a fool would tackle the task of trying to quantify the benefits of environmental protection. The next section of this chapter reviews the problems that arise and then evaluates the methods that economists, driven by necessity if they want to use CBA at all, use to quantify what many noneconomists regard as unquantifiable.

The first problem is that environmental protection is a public good since it benefits many people. So we must identify the affected population and make a choice about how to weigh and sum different degrees of benefit to different people. The most obvious value the environment can have is for people who use it in some way. Those who breathe cleaner air, drink purer water, live on a coast with a beautiful ocean view, or vacation in a national park gain what economists call "use value" from the environment. However, people may value the environment for other reasons as well, further complicating matters. People may value some part of the environment even though they never use it personally in any of the above ways. People who know they will never visit the Arctic National Wildlife Refuge (ANWR) in Alaska may value *knowing* that ANWR exists as a protected habitat for many Arctic wildlife species, off-limits to oil exploration and extraction. Or people may value the existence of the Bengal tiger in its native habitat even though they will never travel to India or Bangladesh. ANWR and the Bengal tiger will never have use value for most people because only a very few will ever see them, but they both may have what environmental economists call "existence value" for tens of millions of people.

Finally, because there is often a great deal of uncertainty about what the effects of permitting the environment to deteriorate may be, and because the decision may be irreversible, preserving the environment can have what economists call "option value" for people. Just as commodity speculators pay money for "options" that give them nothing more than the right to buy a commodity at a particular price later in time if they choose to, people may want to protect the environment because they want to preserve the option of making a decision about the environment at a later date, perhaps when they think the consequences will be more predictable and clear. For example, even if a particular species, such as the snail darter, has no known use value today and, unlike the magnificent Bengal tiger, nobody attributes any value to knowing it exists, people might still wish to protect it for now in order to preserve the option of being able to decide later what to do about it.

The strongest argument for quantifying environmental benefits even when this is difficult is that unless environmental benefits are quantified, it is very difficult to present a case for *how* and to *what extent* they should be weighed against costs that are quantified. Environmental economists use three main methods to tackle what they understand is a difficult practical problem. There are situations in which the results from these methods of quantifying environmental benefits inspire confidence and thereby provide a strong prima facie case for using CBA, provided there are no other reasons to believe that CBA is inappropriate. But often "solutions" to the quantification problem are not robust and inspire little confidence. In these cases, insisting on plowing ahead regardless, making important social choices on the basis of highly questionable CBA analyses, is problematic, to say the least.

CV: The most direct approach to quantifying environmental benefits is to simply *ask* people the dollar value to them of an environmental benefit or the dollar value of the damage to them from environmental degradation. These *CV surveys* come in two forms: *willingness to pay* (WTP) surveys ask respondents the maximum amount they would be willing to pay for a little more environmental protection of one kind or another; *willingness to accept damages* (WTA) surveys ask respondents the minimum amount they would accept to compensate them for tolerating a little more environmental degradation. If people surveyed gave accurate estimates of the benefits (WTP) to them of slightly more protection, or of the costs (WTA) to them of slightly less protection, and if those surveyed were a sufficiently large random sample of all affected parties, then an accurate quantitative estimate of the benefits of environmental protection or costs of environmental degradation could be calculated. Moreover, CV surveys have important advantages over other alternatives. As noted in the last chapter, CV surveys could easily control for differences in income, although they typically do not, whereas the most common alternative method, hedonic regression, cannot. More importantly, CV surveys can capture option and existence value as well as the use value of environmental protection, which, as we will see, other methods cannot.

However, there are serious problems with CV surveys and strong evidence that they are often quite unreliable. Consider the two questions: (1) "How much would you be willing to pay for an incremental improvement in environmental quality of some particular kind?" (2) "How much would you insist on being paid to accept an incremental increase in degradation of the same environmental quality?" Even though respondents *should* give almost identical answers to these two questions, they often do not. While answers might differ slightly since the marginal movements are in opposite directions, reliable answers should differ only slightly. Unfortunately, this is far from the case. It turns out that in cases where both questions are asked, on average WTA estimates are *three to four times* as high as WTP estimates! This obviously casts great doubt on the accuracy of CV estimates in general. Presumably the reasons for inaccuracies are due to "biases" that have been much discussed by environmental economists who carry out CV surveys.

1. Free-rider bias: People deflate WTP answers in an attempt to reduce actual payments they fear will result, and they inflate WTA damage estimates in an attempt to increase actual payments they anticipate. Of course, this is nonsense since respondents should be informed that their answers are completely hypothetical and will not serve as the basis for any actual assessments or payments later. But if those conducting the survey do not convey this fact clearly, or if the respondents are suspicious and do not believe it, or if people who live in market economies simply function in an automatic pilot bargaining mode, free rider bias can be expected. It is obviously a major problem

since it is the most plausible explanation for the wide discrepancy between WTP and WTA estimates.

2. Hypothetical bias: People may not give the questions serious consideration if they understand that they will neither be paid nor assessed any money based on their response. Economists are generally suspicious of people's self-reported valuations whenever they do not have to "put their money where their mouth is," so to speak, and generally trust preferences that are revealed through people's behavior more than preferences that are simply self-reported.

There is an obvious dilemma when trying to correct for both free-rider and hypothetical biases. To reduce free-rider bias risks increasing hypothetical bias, and vice versa. What we are often left with are survey-takers mouthing platitudes about the importance of "good citizenry" to reduce hypothetical bias and conducting both a WTP and WTA survey to get a lower and upper bound, as well as an average estimate, if time and money permit.

3. Embedded bias: Especially in situations where people commonly profess great ignorance and inability to respond, it can help to provide factual information about the predictable consequences of a choice. But what information is provided, even if it is factually accurate, not surprisingly has a large impact on results. Even the order in which questions are asked can influence answers.

4. Ignorance bias: This is not a phrase in the literature, but it may be the root source of problems with CV surveys. People simply do not know as much about environmental "goods" and "bads" as they do about things they buy in the marketplace all the time. There are two kinds of ignorance: (1) How much sicker am I likely to be if particulate pollution rises by 10 percent? Most people do not know; and (2) How will I feel once a trout stream that has always been there is gone because a dam flooded the area? Obviously reducing ignorance bias risks increasing embedded bias, and vice versa, just as reducing free-rider bias risks increasing hypothetical bias, and vice versa.

5. Strategic bias: If I believe that most people value an environmental amenity less than I do, I might be tempted to overstate my own preference when responding to a survey. Alternatively, if I believe most people value the amenity more than I do, I might be tempted to understate my own preference. These would be conscious attempts on my part to manipulate the survey outcome—to deliberately exaggerate my own preferences in order to achieve an outcome closer to what I would truthfully prefer given my beliefs about what others will want and say they want. But strategic bias may be less of a problem than researchers fear. If people to the right and left of the mean engage in this kind of strategic maneuvering to the same extent, their strategic biases should cancel each other out. Moreover, there seems to be no reason to expect strategic bias itself to be skewed.

Travel cost studies: The benefits of environmental recreational amenities such as national parks can be measured by estimating a demand curve for their use, even when no price is charged, by using travel costs. Users are asked how far they traveled, what their travel cost was, and how many visits they have made to use the amenity. Different travel costs are interpreted as different prices, and the number of visits made by people paying different travel costs is interpreted as the demands at different prices. The chief advantage of this method is that people are putting their money where their mouths are. The chief disadvantages are that it applies only to environmental amenities people travel to use, option and existence value are not captured, and unless travelers' income data are collected, the method measures one dollar one vote, not one person one vote.

Hedonic regression: Researchers *impute* the value of an environmental amenity or degradation to the difference or change in value of a different good for which there are market prices, after controlling for all other factors that would produce differences in the market price of the other good. For example, after controlling for city size, average income, and so on, the difference in real estate values between different cities can be attributed to differences in pollution levels. Or the drop in housing prices along a coast can be attributed to the damage from an oil spill after all other factors that would have influenced those housing prices are controlled for. The trick is obviously how well the researcher controls for all other influences, and many times the data necessary to do this are not available. Like travel cost studies, hedonic regression is inherently incapable of capturing option and existence value, and there is no way to turn dollar-weighted votes into people-weighted votes.

Many people are very skeptical about how well these techniques measure the true value of environmental protection. A common reaction from my students after they study these procedures is, "You've got to be kidding me!" And even environmental economists whose livelihood depends on getting paid to carry out these studies often express serious misgivings about how much faith one should put in their results. These reactions are understandable and reasonable. The problem is, however, that in market economies there are no alternatives. Market economies contain no "environmental preference revealing mechanism" that forces people to make frequent choices about the environment in situations where they will be rewarded for behavior that accurately indicates their actual preferences and punishes for deception. In the conclusion of this book we briefly consider such a mechanism, but for now there is no alternative to CV surveys, travel cost studies, and hedonic regressions if we want to estimate the benefits of environmental protection quantitatively.

Moreover, the practical consequences of failure to estimate environmental benefits quantitatively are severe. Environmentalists who criticize efforts to put a dollar value on environmental benefits should be aware of the implications of failure to do so. If important social choices will be based on CBA in market economies where quantitative estimates of the costs of protecting the environment are often readily available but quantitative estimates of the benefits of protecting the environment are not provided, CBA will continue to tilt the playing field strongly against protecting the environment.[6]

Since without an environmental preference revealing mechanism CV surveys are the only available technique that can capture existence and option value as well as use value, and since CV surveys can easily correct for differences in income if the proper questions are asked, environmentalists have a great deal riding on improving the accuracy and credibility of CV estimates. Besides making the adjustments for differences in income, as discussed previously, this means putting more time and money into better surveys. Free-rider bias can be reduced only by making respondents understand that their answers will not influence any actual payments. To minimize the consequent aggravation of hypothetical bias—failure to give serious consideration to weighing the options—respondents should be generously compensated for their time independent of their answers. To reduce ignorance bias, much more information about predictable consequences must be provided, and time necessary to make sure respondents have digested the information must be budgeted as well. To minimize the adverse consequences of aggravating embedded bias—coaching for answers desired—different views and opinions about relevant information should be presented. All these improvements in CV surveys will require much more money and time. On the other hand, given the magnitude of the consequences of many decisions we currently use CBA to make, additional expenses would surely be "cost-effective"!

However, in addition to working to improve the reliability of CV surveys, environmentalists should also challenge those who claim that large discrepancies between WTP and WTA estimates necessarily indicate that CV surveys contain little information of any value. What if the real problem is ignorance bias? What if people simply do not have firm preferences for what economists call "environmental amenities" as they do for different foods, clothes, cars, restaurants, houses, music, and so on? After all, people neither buy nor answer surveys about environmental amenities very often. People are not used to thinking about how much they value environmental amenities and predictably have a large margin of internal error as a result. When the question is posed as "What would you be willing to pay?" the ignorance comes out in the form of a minimal estimate. When the question is posed as "How much would you have to be paid?" the ignorance is expressed as a maximum estimate. In both cases, respondents are merely providing a conservative response in a state of internal ignorance. Not wanting to overreact, given their state of ignorance, they respond to a WTP formulation by naming the least amount they might be willing to pay—not wanting to say more than they would, in fact, be willing to pay if they were less ignorant. Similarly, in responding to a WTA formulation, people name the highest amount they would have to be paid to be fully compensated for the environmental loss—not wanting to say less than might actually turn out to be necessary to compensate them if they were less ignorant.

If this is what is actually going on, then discrepancies between WTP and WTA are not illogical and inconsistent answers to the same question: they are lower and upper bounds that respondents provide in a state of great ignorance. People who give an answer four times bigger to the same question phrased differently do not, admittedly, sound like reliable informants. On the other hand, given that people have a great deal of internal ignorance about their preferences for environmental amenities, answers suggesting a four to one range of possible preferences sound pretty reliable.

This hypothesis could be tested by doing WTP and WTA surveys about goods for which people have much more certain preferences—goods they buy all the time. If I am right, we would get very small differences between their answers in these situations, implying that it is really ignorance bias, not unreliable respondents, that is the explanation for the observed discrepancy between WTPs and WTAs in environmental surveys. Of course, we could quibble with respondents about not construing our phrasing as an implicit request for lower and upper bounds. But it would be better to simply thank them for letting us know (1) the range of their uncertainty due to internal ignorance and (2) the upper and lower bounds of their preferences.

Not All Uncertainty Is Created Equal

Over the past decade, at the same time the warnings of scientists grew louder and more unanimous about the dangers of climate change unless GHG emissions were reduced substantially, the economics profession continued to construct ever more complicated models estimating that the costs of significant emission reductions in the present could not be justified by the future benefits that the models predicted those sacrifices would yield. While misleading results from these economic climate models also derive from some highly questionable assumptions,[7] one reason mainstream economic models yield conclusions disturbingly at odds with the recommendations of climate scientists is that they misconstrue the question they should be addressing and consequently mistreat risk.

How should we take into account events whose likelihood of occurring is extremely small? The answer to this question critically affects how we analyze risk in many situations, most notably climate change. The standard answer is that if the probability of occurrence is small enough we should basically ignore an event. This is not only convenient but also reasonable *if* the consequences associated with highly improbable events are of comparable magnitude to the consequences of much more probable outcomes.

However, what if the consequences of a highly improbable event are exceedingly large—bordering on the incalculable? Combine "incalculable" with "highly improbable" and you have two reasons for analysts to avoid what is now popularly referred to as a *black swan*—an event that is highly improbable but whose consequences if they do occur dwarf the consequences of more probable outcomes. Black swans are the nightmare everyone would like to ignore. However, when seeking to protect the public interest over generations, we ignore black swans at our peril—which is unfortunately what failure to take precautionary measures to avoid climate change amounts to.[8]

Is maximizing the expected value of our actions always the appropriate criterion, which is what CBA implicitly assumes? If a course of action almost always produces small negative payoffs and only yields a large positive payoff once in a blue moon, then we would always reject this course of action in order to maximize expected value if the blue moon occurs seldom enough. However, if people always behaved in this way they would not buy insurance, nor would companies find it profitable to sell insurance policies. The profitability of the insurance industry hinges ultimately on the willingness of buyers to pay more in annual premiums than the expected payout in the event of a blue moon. Put differently, the insurance industry enjoys positive profits only because many of us, fearful of a black swan we can ill afford, buy insurance policies with a negative expected value for the buyer and a positive expected value for the seller. Are we to believe it is foolish to buy insurance against black swans we cannot afford?

Climate scientists have informed us that if we refuse to pay the costs of reducing GHG emissions over the next forty years, there is a high probability of moderate climate change and a much smaller probability of cataclysmic climate change. Even if economic modelers were correct that in the event of moderate climate change the benefits of avoidance fail to outweigh the costs,[9] is it unwise for us to insure ourselves against a climatic black swan whose negative consequences are literally incalculable? Irrespective of whether avoiding moderate climate change is cost-effective, if we use the appropriate risk model even a small probability of cataclysmic climate change would still recommend the precautionary policy of paying the necessary costs of avoiding climate change unless those costs were truly astounding.

In the case of economic climate change modeling, it is inappropriate to assume that our goal is to maximize the expected value of climate change policy—which is what mainstream economic climate models implicitly assume when they apply CBA to determine how much emissions reduction is warranted. Insurance policies by their nature invariably have negative expected values, but that does not mean it is never wise to buy one.

The overwhelming consensus among climate scientists is that the likelihood of cataclysmic climate change if we do little to GHG emissions is far greater than the likelihood of a once-in-a-hundred-years financial crisis, in the words of a chastened Alan Greenspan testifying before Congress in the aftermath of the financial crisis of 2008. And even Greenspan now admits that this small probability warrants precautionary regulations on the financial industry given the magnitude of the damage such a financial black swan unleashes. Since the probability of a climatic black swan and the magnitude of the damage a climatic black swan would wreak upon the planet are both far greater than in the case of a financial black swan, the rational choice is to pony up and pay our precautionary premiums to prevent climate change.

When we feel safe, it makes sense to engage in CBA. When we feel safe, we can weigh the pros and cons of doing a little more of this or that. But when we do not feel safe, what makes sense is to buy insurance. When safety is the primary concern, it is the logic of insurance we should turn to, which is quite different from the logic of CBA. In situations where safety is foremost, arguments to the effect that the expected value of our insurance policy may be negative are completely beside the point.

Notes

1. "All people" refers to any people, anywhere, who are positively or adversely affected by a decision in any way. This includes not only people alive today, but also people who have yet to be born but who will predictably be affected by environmental choices we make today.

2. If the efficiency gain from a policy is distributed in any way that prevents any people from being worse off than they were before the policy was enacted, economists call this a Pareto improvement. However, for a policy that passes the efficiency criteria to also be a Pareto improvement, all losers must actually be compensated.

3. If some compensation for less deserving constituencies is necessary to win sufficient political support to secure the policy—which by hypothesis increases efficiency and equity—it may be wise for progressives to accede to compensating losers even though they are less deserving. But this should be understood as political expediency and not confused with compensation required for equity reasons. Progressives need to understand that every penny paid in compensation in this scenario makes the economy less, not more equitable.

4. This example is taken from chapter 2 of Ackerman (2009).

5. One could argue that when our colonial ancestors chopped down the eastern forests, that was exactly what they did do. A more charitable interpretation of their behavior would be "they knew not what they did." Perhaps this explains why the environmental

movement is so often resented. It has made it harder for our generation to claim ignorance in our self-defense.

6. Environmentalists who reject attempts to quantify environmental benefits should be sure to also strongly oppose CBA for making social choices. Many do understand this and act accordingly. But to criticize and reject quantification of environmental benefits and fail to successfully oppose CBA is a recipe for environmental disaster.

7. See Ackerman (2010), Ackerman, Stanton, and Bueno (2010a), Ackerman et al. (2009a), and DeCanio (2003). These authors demonstrate that behind all the technical bells and whistles, what drives results in mainstream economic climate models are highly questionable assumptions about a few key parameters. In effect, they argue that the MSB curve actually crosses the MSC curve in Figure 2.3 significantly to the left of A(0), meaning that the benefits of averting even moderate climate change outweigh the costs if benefits and costs are properly measured.

8. Financial deregulation amounts to ignoring black swans in the financial sector of the economy. As the world discovered to its shock and dismay in the fall of 2008, while black swans may not appear often, eventually one will show up, and if old insurance policies like the Glass-Steagle Act have been canceled, the consequences can be devastating. See Hahnel (2009a) and Ackerman (2010a).

9. Ironically, as Ackerman et al. (2009b) and Ackerman, Stanton, and Bueno (2010b) demonstrate, this is not the case. When reasonable figures for a few key parameters are chosen, mainstream economic climate models indicate that the benefits of aggressive mitigation to avoid even mild climate change outweigh the costs.

Chapter 3

What on Earth Is Sustainable Development?

It is tempting to seek refuge in the words of former Supreme Court justice Potter Stewart, who, when asked to define pornography famously said, "I shall not today attempt to define it, but I know it when I see it." In the case of *sustainable development*, a more modest claim might be, "I am not sure what it is, but I am quite sure what it is *not*." Or we could attempt to browbeat anyone who persists in pressing for a definition by taunting, "If you are still asking for a definition, you are asking the wrong question." Finally, when exasperation has become unbearable, perhaps we should blurt out the naked truth: "Sustainable development is what we want, stupid!"

The problem is that delving into the meaning of sustainable development opens several Pandora's boxes. If wisdom comes from grappling with the imponderables that emerge, and if failure to tidy up the mess and refasten lids is not too discouraging, then this chapter might prove useful as it explores how we define our goals and how we measure progress toward achieving them.

Sustainable Development: A Definition

The most famous definition of sustainable development is from the report of the United Nations World Commission on Environment and Development (WCED), better known as the Brundtland Commission, after its chair. According to the report, published under the title *Our Common Future* by Oxford University Press in 1987, "Sustainable development is development

35

that meets the needs of the present without compromising the ability of future generations to meet their own needs." This definition has been criticized from every conceivable angle. It has been ridiculed as so vague that it says nothing. As the philosopher Luc Ferry quipped, "Who would like to be a proponent of an untenable development!" When reworded as *sustainable growth* and interpreted broadly to anticipate new technologies and permit full substitution of produced capital for natural capital, many environmentalists regard it as a license to continue to kill the planet, and some propose the goal of a *steady state economy* instead. When defined more strictly as requiring that stocks of different major categories of natural capital must not be permitted to decline, it is criticized by business leaders and economists as imposing unreasonable and unnecessary restrictions. But by beginning with a definition, we have started at the endpoint of efforts to take environmental issues into account when defining economic goals, so it will be helpful to return to the beginning.

What Is GDP?

Attempts to measure the value of economic activity in the aggregate only date back to 1934, when the U.S. Commerce Department began reporting statistics on what it called the net product of the national economy. The national income and product accounts were only systematized during World War II, when the government needed to know how much output was being produced for defense and what this left over for the rest of the economy. After the war, the U.S. government compared its statistical efforts with those of the British and Canadian governments, and the League of Nations convened an international conference on national income accounting as one of its last acts. We have been living ever since in a world where something called gross national product (GNP), or more recently gross domestic product (GDP), has been the principle number associated with national economies.[1]

Some people who despair of problems that inevitably arise when we try to measure something meaningful but complicated—such as how valuable our collective efforts during a year really were, or how much progress we made as a result—point out the advantages of keeping things simple. We could easily measure the dollar value of all recorded market exchanges during a year. But measuring the dollar value of recorded commercial activity would not be terribly meaningful for a number of reasons, which is why this is not where matters were left.

The first problem is called "double counting." When an auto company buys a ton of steel in March and sells the car it used the steel to make in September, we will count the dollar value of the steel production twice if we sum the dollar value of all sales during the year. As long as we remember that we have simply measured the dollar value of all recorded commercial activity and exercise caution about attributing much importance to the result, there is no harm done. But many economists with higher expectations felt little would be accomplished by performing this exercise, and from the beginning procedures were adopted to eliminate double counting and to measure only the dollar value of all recorded market exchanges of *final* goods and services.

The next problem was that not only do relative prices change but also prices often rise on average. In order not to deceive ourselves that production is growing when only prices are rising, procedures were adopted to convert nominal, or *current GDP* (for current prices) into what is called *real GDP*. However, the word *real* should not be misconstrued as "material or physical." Like current GDP, real GDP is a value, not a material category, and is measured in dollars. To control for price inflation, the prices from what is called a *base year* are chosen to evaluate output in a series of years. Because the choice of base year is inherently arbitrary and because relative prices differ from year to year, estimates of real GDP will differ somewhat depending on which base year is chosen. This means the process of converting current to real GDP is inherently imperfect. However, since this difficulty has nothing to do with the problems discussed below, we will assume henceforth that when we refer to GDP we are always talking about real GDP, and we will ignore the fact that methodology dictates that there will inevitably be a margin of error surrounding our estimates of its rate of growth.

The next problem was that not all goods sold during a calendar year were produced in the same calendar year. Since the goal of those creating the national income and product accounts was to measure something about the value of production during a year, procedures to correct for this problem were adopted as well. These procedures quickly made a third problem apparent. Some things that are produced are never exchanged in a market, which in turn creates two new problems. There may be no record that these goods or services were produced because there is no record of a market exchange, and there is no market-generated price to multiply them by in any case. From the beginning, attempts were made to correct for this problem, but only in some cases and not in other cases. For example, an estimate of the market value of food produced by farmers, but never sold because farmers consumed it themselves, was included in GDP. However, no attempt was made to estimate and include the value of housework performed by spouses, even though the same work performed by paid housekeepers was included in GDP. Illegal activity posed a similar problem. In this case, there was a market exchange and price, but it was not recorded, or at least the records were not accessible to government agents. Traditionally no adjustment is made for the production of illegal drugs, although presumably this leads to significant undermeasurement of GDP in countries like Bolivia (coca) and states like California (marijuana.)

Interestingly, a final correction that was made from the beginning reveals that there was always at least an implicit goal of trying to account for a certain kind of sustainability and distinguish progress from treading water. Part of what we produce each year simply replaces machines we wear out during the year. For example, if we produce a hundred drill presses but ten drill presses wear out through use, we are not a hundred drill presses better off at the end of the year than at the beginning: we are only ninety drill presses better off. In this case, no adjustment was made in how we calculate GDP. Instead, a second statistic called net domestic product (NDP) was created by subtracting from GDP an estimate of how much something called the "capital stock" had "depreciated" during the year. While the system of national income and product accounts has undergone several revisions, for the most part this is as far as modification of the dollar value of recorded commercial activity during a year has gone.

What Is Wrong With GDP?

Ecological economists like Herman Daly have waged a thirty-year war to try to force the same treatment for *natural capital* as is used for *produced capital* when transforming GDP into NDP. Their argument is straightforward: If using up the stock of produced capital is not sustainable, then using up the stock of natural capital is also not sustainable. If net changes in the stock of produced capital are what merit inclusion in NDP, whether they are positive or negative, then net changes in the stock of natural capital merit inclusion in NDP as well. Just as we risk deceiving ourselves that we have progressed through our economic endeavors by more than we really have if we do not subtract depreciation of produced capital during a year, we risk deceiving ourselves how much we have progressed if we fail to subtract depreciation of natural capital as well. In other words, ecological economists argue that natural capital should be treated in the same way that produced capital has been traditionally treated. However, few agencies responsible for official estimates of NDP make this adjustment, although some, like the World Bank, have begrudgingly and belatedly conceded that they should attempt to take depreciation of natural capital into account.[2]

As soon as we admit that we are attempting to measure how much progress we made through our economic endeavors during a year, it becomes apparent that we should also account for the fact that when we produce economic goods and services we often produce as *joint products* economic *bads*, like pollution, as well. Of course, there usually is no market where the pollution sells for a negative price that we can use as a signal for how bad these joint products are. Nonetheless, ecological economists and environmentalists urge that we should do the best we can to estimate the damage from pollution and reduce NDP accordingly.

Finally, ecological economists also call for adjusting NDP for *defensive expenditures*. When the *Exxon Valdez* spilled oil off the coast of Alaska in March 1989, this was not a natural but an Exxon-made disaster. It was a joint product of transporting much of the oil consumed globally in large tankers that always pose a risk of a shipping accident. And when BP's Deepwater Horizon underwater oil rig in the Gulf of Mexico blew up in April 2010, spilling roughly twenty times as many barrels of oil as spilled out of the *Exxon Valdez*, this was also not a natural disaster. It was a predictable consequence of permitting all the major oil companies to engage in deep-sea oil operations where the risk of an accident might be small, but is not insignificant, given the number of deep-sea rigs that are licensed and the difficulties of stopping a deep-sea leak when one occurs. Not only was no estimate of the noncommercial damaged caused by the *Valdez* spill subtracted from Alaskan GDP that year because we do not subtract for bads, but the defensive expenditures of paying people to wash otters, seals, and seabirds, and clean up beaches was added to Alaskan GDP, which ironically enjoyed quite a boom in 1989 as the result of the *Valdez* spill! Similarly, statistics will record the defensive expenditures associated with the BP disaster in the gulf as a substantial increase in production for several coastal states and as an increase in U.S. GDP in 2010, thereby misleading us into thinking that the Great Recession slackened in 2010 more than it really did. Ecological economists argue that defensive expenditures against negative consequences of economic activities should be subtracted from NDP.

Obviously, these adjustments require estimating procedures that can become quite elaborate and also contestable—as a plethora of alternative measures devised by different organizations and think tanks to make these and other adjustments attests.[3] Part of the attraction of GDP and NDP as traditionally calculated was that calculations were straightforward, appeared to be noncontroversial, and were difficult for governments to fudge. As soon as everyone agreed to the practical necessity of using market prices, this effectively eliminated the most difficult and potentially contentious problem in the exercise—determining the relative values of different goods and services produced. Making adjustments, no matter how compelling the case to do so, where market prices are not readily available makes the procedure appear much more subjective. I say "appear" because accepting market prices as accurate indicators of the relative values of different goods and services is itself a subjective value judgment and very questionable.

Economic Progress

Even if we could measure NDP perfectly, the rate of increase, or growth, of NDP would hardly be synonymous with economic progress, much less social progress. Unless NDP grows as fast as the population grows, the average person is not progressing. This problem is easily corrected by dividing NDP by population, which gives us average or *per capita NDP*. But while changes in a perfectly measured per capita NDP may tell us something about how much progress we are making with regard to the *efficacy* of our economic endeavors, they tell us nothing about whether or not the distribution of the burdens and benefits of our economic activities is becoming more or less fair. The most common measure of income inequality is the GINI coefficient, where perfect equality yields a value of zero and perfect inequality (one person has all the income or wealth) yields a value of one. Unless we care nothing about income distribution and any inequities that inequalities imply, presumably we should look at changes in the GINI coefficient as well as changes in per capita NDP when assessing a country's economic progress. However, neither per capita NDP nor the GINI coefficient tells us anything about how economic decisions in a country are made. Per capita NDP and the GINI coefficient tell us something only about economic outcomes, not about economic decision-making procedures. So presumably we should also look at whether economic decisions are being made more or less democratically when assessing a country's economic progress. In short, even when we are concerned only with economic progress, there is more than one dimension along which we can progress or regress. The growth rate of a perfectly measured per capita NDP can measure progress only along one of those dimensions, what we might call the efficacy dimension, not whether or not we are making progress in improving economic justice and economic democracy.

But suppose per capita NDP is growing at an impressive rate, the GINI coefficient is falling fast enough to satisfy us we are making excellent progress in reducing economic injustice, and popular participation in economic decision-making is increasing dramatically as well. That is, suppose we are making more than acceptable economic progress on all dimensions. It is still possible that something is very wrong with how the economy is progressing. We might be running down our stock of produced capital to the point where there will soon be no machines for future generations to work with. We might be using up natural resources at a pace that will cause the economy to grind to a halt in only a few years. We might be releasing wastes into the environment at a pace that will collapse one or more major ecosystems.

It is true that if per capita NDP is measured accurately, the depreciation of produced and natural capital and the damage from emissions will have been subtracted and accounted for. But that does not mean that the rate of growth of NDP is environmentally sustainable. It does not mean that we have not seriously compromised the ability of future generations to meet their needs. There is a remaining goal to be dealt with before we can judge to what degree we are making economic progress on all dimensions worthy of consideration. We have still failed to account for sustainability, and in the process we have failed to account for intergenerational equity.

Sustainability as Intergenerational Equity

When we added economic justice to efficacy and economic democracy as an important economic goal to be considered when asking if we are making economic progress, we only took *intragenerational equity* into account. The GINI coefficient only sheds light on whether the benefits of our collective economic activities are being distributed equitably among those of us who are alive today. We did not consider *intergenerational equity* at all. But the main thrust of the Brundtland definition of sustainable development is to insist that the legitimate interests of future generations are not compromised. Sustainability is about intergenerational equity. For economists who operate with an empty-world mind-set, this reduces to how much of what we produce is consumed and how much is saved and invested. For environmentalists and ecological economists, it also has to do with whether or not the biosphere is damaged during the year.

Sir John Hicks (1939) addressed this important issue over seventy years ago when he argued that national income should be defined as what a nation could consume during a year without impoverishing itself. Since Hicks operated with an empty-world mind-set, this meant restricting consumption sufficiently so as to leave a stock of produced capital at the end of the year that was as valuable as the stock had been at the beginning of the year—in effect, not committing the intergenerational sin of eating the seed corn. However, once we recognize the importance of natural capital and the fact that it has become scarce, this must be accounted for as well, along with any other forms of capital Hicks may not have considered. And once we realize that the biosphere also provides valuable services as a sink, we must consider whether or not its ability to process wastes has been impaired.

It is now common to talk of natural capital, produced capital, human capital, and social capital. Whether all these kinds of capital can be kept logically distinct from one another and from technology and whether it is possible to aggregate separate capitals in meaningful and consistent ways is an intriguing Pandora's box, but not one we need open for our purposes. The central idea is that capital is anything that permits people to work more productively than they otherwise might. A hoe allows me to grow more corn than I could grow if I did not have one. An inch of topsoil allows me to grow more corn than if I did not have it. Knowing the optimal depth to plant my corn seeds allows me to grow more corn than if I was uneducated and planted them too deep. And if my neighbor and I are socially primed to plant our gardens together, and if by working together we can plant them faster, with me making the holes and him following me and placing the corn seeds in each hole, than if each of us plants our own garden separately, this will allow us to grow our corn with less work.[4] The central idea of sustainability as intergenerational equity is that we must leave a stock of productive assets for those who follow that is collectively as valuable as the one we had to work with, where the value of what is commonly called the *capital stock* refers to the degree to which it can enhance productivity.[5] This requirement is known as *weak sustainability*, and it is the definition of sustainability that mainstream economists are most comfortable with.

When Capital Is Not Fungible

Environmentalists and ecological economists are very suspicious of interpreting the Brundtland definition of sustainable development as simply complying with the condition of weak sustainability. They point out that weak sustainability allows for substitution of produced capital to make up for deterioration of natural capital without limit. Since their major argument is that this substitution is actually not possible in important regards, one could respond that if something proves to be impossible that will take care of matters itself, without need to abandon the condition of weak sustainability. But critics argue that the condition of weak sustainability is problematic and dangerous because it suggests that something can be done when we already know it cannot. These critics propose additional constrains to protect against this danger. What is defined as *strong sustainability* requires also leaving future generations a stock of natural capital that is at least as valuable as that we enjoy, and what is often called *environmental sustainability* further requires that the physical stocks of major categories of natural resources and sinks must be maintained.

Obviously the critical issue is substitutability. Weak sustainability permits substituting any individual component of the capital stock for any other individual component as long as the value of the overall capital stock is maintained. Strong sustainability permits full substitution within the category of produced capital, and also within the category of natural capital, provided the overall value of the produced capital stock is maintained *and* the overall value of the natural capital stock is maintained. There is now a large literature debating how realistic it is to assume that produced capital can adequately substitute for different components of natural capital, where differences of opinion between technological optimists and pessimists plays a central role. Economists are long accustomed to assuming that everything is infinitely substitutable for everything else at the margin, albeit with diminishing effects, of course. Ecologists generally begin with the opposite assumption that key components of natural systems are irreplaceable. Since in many cases attempts to substitute produced capital for natural capital are irreversible, and since our understanding of ecosystem complexity is often imperfect, many environmentalists argue that the precautionary principle should be applied: Do not assume some part of natural capital can be adequately replaced by produced capital until it has been proven beyond any reasonable doubt to be the case.

It is important to note that both weak and strong definitions of sustainability are defined in terms of the *value* of capital stocks, whether it be the overall capital stock or the overall stock of produced capital and the overall stock of natural capital, whereas environmental sustainability is defined in terms of physical stocks of particular natural resources.[6] We should recognize that measuring and comparing the value of different components of the overall capital stock quickly runs into methodological as well as practical problems. Ecological economists suggest a functional definition of capital as a stock that yields a flow of goods or services. While natural capital sometimes produces a flow of services without aid from any other inputs—as when a natural sink can store and decompose waste—more often natural capital yields a flow of services only in conjunction with other inputs, like labor, produced capital, and human capital. So perhaps a better way to think of capital is as something that enhances human productivity. In that case, when we attempt to quantify the value of any individual component of the capital stock—whether it be natural, produced, or human capital—we would attempt to estimate how much more productive people could be if they had this component available to them, where productivity is defined as increases in the value of what people can produce.

Finally, now that we are aware that exhaustion of sinks for our wastes may be a greater threat to sustainability than exhaustion of natural resources, we must also design ways to incorporate this fact into definitions of weak, strong, and environmental sustainability. Since economists had already addressed sustainability in the form of maintaining the stock of capital, it was relatively straightforward to point out that produced capital was not the only form of capital and to challenge whether traditional assumptions about the substitutability of one kind of capital for another carried over to natural capital. But exhaustion of natural sinks may be even more difficult to quantify and incorporate than exhaustion of natural capital. Can the negative consequences of exhausting a natural sink really be reduced to losses in productive capabilities of future generations?

Social Versus Economic Progress

Just as progress with regard to the efficacy of our economic endeavors should not be confused with overall economic progress—which includes progress along other economic dimensions like intra- and intergenerational equity and more democratic decision-making procedures—economic progress should not be confused with social progress. The common habit of treating the growth of per capita NDP as an indicator of overall social progress for lack of an alternative, quantitative measure of progress has recently spawned efforts to create quantitative measures of social progress that are more meaningful.

Nobel Prize–winning economist Amartya Sen worked for years as a consultant to the United Nations, helping construct a summary index that would capture the extent that basic opportunities were available to people. The Human Development Index (HDI) first appeared in 1990 in the UN's *Human Development Report*, an alternative to the World Bank's *World Development Report*. The HDI is a weighted average of GDP per capita adjusted for purchasing power, income inequality, life expectancy, literacy, and average years of education. It does little to adjust for environmentalist concerns. Related indices, such as the gender development index (GDI), which measures gender disparities, and the gender empowerment index (GEM), have also appeared in the *Human Development Report* since 1995. The genuine progress indicator (GPI), developed by Redefining Progress, attempts to adjust for depreciation of natural capital, environmental damage, and defensive expenditures and also includes income distribution, literacy, and access to higher education. How one measures success can make a great difference. For example, Sri Lanka, Vietnam, and Cuba rank much higher on the UN's HDI index than they do according to per capita GDP, and Canada, whose per capita GDP ranks it below many other developed countries, has the highest HDI index in the world due to low income inequality and high literacy and longevity.

Judging human progress by the rate of growth of per capita GDP is clearly misleading, and all who speak out against this common practice are well justified. It is misleading because economic progress is only one component of human progress. Life expectancy, health, literacy, education, political and civil rights, and a host of other concerns are all relevant to whether or not humans are "progressing." It is misleading because what truly matters is what economic wherewithal permits people to do, not the wherewithal itself. And it is misleading for all the reasons explained above why growth of per capita GDP is an inaccurate measure of economic efficacy, much less overall economic progress. Measuring human progress by the rate of growth of per capita GDP obscures lack of progress in many important noneconomic areas, as well as lack of progress in achieving economic justice and democracy and preventing further environmental degradation. All these problems go unnoticed when human development is equated with mismeasured economic growth.[7]

But there are two possible responses to this misleading practice: (1) we could design a more comprehensive and inclusive indicator of social progress, or (2) we could insist that economic progress should not be equated with human progress or with the rate of growth of per capita GDP and instead measure human *and* economic progress along a number of different dimensions. These two alternative responses share a great deal in common. Both must point out why the standard practice of conflating social progress with the rate of growth of per capita GDP is misleading. Both responses must identify and develop ways to measure all the important components of human progress, including ways to perfect our estimate of per capita NDP that adequately account for environmental degradation. And legitimate debate in both cases concerns (1) whether or not to include a particular dimension, and (2) how best to define and measure progress along any particular dimension. In any attempt to design a comprehensive indicator of social progress, debate over appropriate weights for the different dimensions in the index is inevitable. However, avoiding debate over appropriate weights by forswearing any attempt to construct an overall index of social progress is bought at the expense of multiple and potentially conflicting judgments about how well humans are progressing.[8]

While efforts to construct a worthy quantitative index of social progress to substitute for per capita GDP are still in early stages, all efforts to date are seriously flawed. Sen and his collaborators at the UN included measures of health, education, and income distribution along with economic growth in their HDI, but the HDI ignores environmental issues and economic democracy as well. Those working at Redefining Progress have gone to greater lengths to try to account for environmental degradation as well as income distribution in their GPI, but it ignores education, health, and economic democracy. However, both indices are misleading indicators of overall social progress because of omitted dimensions. Other indices, such as the gender disparity index, the gender empowerment measure, and the right-wing Hoover Institute's economic freedom index, all focus on measuring a single dimension of social progress. In the case of single-dimension indices such as these, the question is whether the definition of the goal and/or the method of measurement are appropriate. For example, anyone who has looked carefully at how the Hoover economic freedom index is constructed should recognize it for what it is—an ideological rather than a scientific tool and a case study in deceptive labeling. But the general problem with single-dimension indices is that even if they define and measure one goal well, it is only one dimension of human progress. The problem with indices that claim to be comprehensive is that even if particular dimensions are defined and measured appropriately, omitted dimensions render them useless, and challenging the weights used is always a logical rebuttal.

Those who seek to broaden the concept of sustainability to include not only economic and environmental sustainability but also what is now called *social sustainability* are motivated by the same concerns that drove people like Sen to broaden attention from a narrow measure of economic progress to a more inclusive measure of overall social progress. In the case of social sustainability, the focus is on communities and social networks, and the potentially destructive effects that particular kinds of economic activities may have on them. Just as environmentalists pointed out that replacement of produced capital does not prevent unsustainable depletion of natural capital, others are now pointing out that conducting ourselves in ways that may be economically and environmentally sustainable still may not sufficiently protect valuable social and cultural institutions and may therefore be socially unsustainable.

The idea of social sustainability quickly raises a question that was of little concern to most people with regard to environmental sustainability: Is preserving the social status quo always desirable? Environmentalists generally assume that the status quo in nature is much to be preferred to alterations we inflict.[9] However, progressives in particular are not generally inclined to give all our existing social institutions the same benefit of the doubt. Traditionally, progressives are about *social progress*, not social stability. This may well make conceptualizing social sustainability more complicated than conceptualizing environmental sustainability, where protecting the status quo provides an easy target to shoot for.

A Workable Definition

A workable definition for sustainable development? If this chapter was good for nothing else, it should have served as a clear warning: "Be careful what you ask for. You might get it!"

Sustainable means repeatable. However, humans in the modern age have not been content with survival, or repeating the same activities, with the same results, year after year. We now generally aspire to more. We hope to progress, and we hope to progress along many dimensions. I think the word *sustainable* can best be used as a warning about dangers we must avoid during our quest to progress if we do not wish to compromise the prospects of those who will follow us in ways that cannot be justified. For our behavior to be sustainable for our species, we must operate under constraints as we struggle to progress.

If the prospects of the next generation depended only on how much seed corn they had to work with on average, the traditional economic concept of maintaining the seed stock would be a sufficient condition for intergenerational equity. When "seed stock" became hoes, plows, and tractors as well as seeds, the notion that as long as the capital stock as a whole equipped our descendants with the means to be as productive as we were, intergenerational equity was observed. But when we came to our senses and realized that the world was filling fast—that is, that per capita stocks of different components of natural capital were already scarce and shrinking fast—sufficient conditions for intergenerational equity became both more complicated and more stringent. In truth, methodological problems associated with aggregation of different components of the capital stock, as well as practical questions of substitutability, became troublesome issues as soon as hoes were added to seed corn. But these problems became acute as soon as we realized that the prospects of the next generation depend on how much natural capital they will have to work with as well as how much produced capital we will have left them. And since the environment also provides a variety of vital sink services that do not neatly fit the metaphor of capital as enhancer of human productivity, the problem of defining how development—that is, human progress—could simultaneously be sustainable—that is, not compromise the ability of future generations to continue to develop—became even more problematic. So . . .

- WHEREAS the natural environment provides valuable services both as the source of resources and as sinks to process wastes,
- WHEREAS the regenerative capacity of different components of the natural environment and ecosystems contained therein are limited,
- WHEREAS ecosystems are complex, contain self-reinforcing feedback dynamics that can accelerate their decline, and often have thresholds that are difficult for us to pinpoint,
- WHEREAS passing important environmental thresholds can be irreversible,
- WHEREAS some social institutions are similar to natural ecosystems in displaying valuable characteristics and responding unpredictably to intervention,
- WE, the present generation, now understand that while striving to meet our economic needs fairly, democratically, and efficiently, we must not impair the ability of future generations to meet their needs and continue to progress.
- In particular, WE, the present generation, understand that intergenerational equity requires leaving future generations conditions at least as favorable

as those we enjoy. These conditions include what have been commonly called produced capital, human capital, natural capital, ecosystem sink services, technical knowledge, and perhaps social capital as well.

- Since the degree to which different kinds of capital and sink services can or cannot be substituted for one another is uncertain and since some changes are irreversible, WE, the present generation, also understand that intergenerational equity requires us to apply the precautionary principle with regard to what is an adequate substitution for some favorable part of overall conditions that we allow to deteriorate. The burden of proof must lie with those among us who argue that a natural resource or sink service, or a valuable social institution that we permit to deteriorate on our watch, is fully and adequately substituted for by some other component of the inheritance we bequeath our heirs.

Notes

1. As we discover in Chapter 5, Simon Kuznets had nothing to do with what is commonly referred to as the environmental Kuznets curve. However, Kuznets did play a major role helping the Commerce Department design and organize the system of national income and product accounts, although he was always at pains to warn that GNP should not be taken as an indication of economic welfare. Note: GNP, which measures the value of production by businesses who are "nationals" of a country regardless of where the production is located, was replaced in the early 1990s by GDP, which measures the value of production that takes place within the territorial boundaries of a country.

2. Herman Daly served as chief environmental economist at the World Bank for years. Only after he resigned, largely in protest over the bank's unwillingness to take depreciation of natural capital into account when evaluating projects for bank financing, did the World Bank relent on this point.

3. Alternative measures include the measure of economic welfare (MEW) (Nordhaus and Tobin 1972), the economic aspects of welfare (EAW) (Zoltas 1981), the index of sustainable economic welfare (ISEW) (Daly and Cobb 1989), and the GPI created by Redefining Progress in 1995 and available (along with an ecological footprint calculator) at www.myfootprint.org/en. The GPI differs from the others because it adjusts not only for environmental factors but also includes income distribution as well as some social categories.

4. Whether this is technology or social capital is just the kind of contentious issue we are sidestepping.

5. Costanza et al. (1997, 123) put it this way: "The main operational implication of Hicksian income is to keep capital intact. Our problem is that the category of capital we have endeavored to maintain intact is only human-created capital. The category 'natural capital' is left out, as is human capital."

6. Presumably environmental sustainability permits substitution between individual components within each major category of natural capital, and presumably this judgment would have to be based on whether the value of the service provided by a category of natural capital was maintained.

7. For a recent summary of contributions from evolutionary, ecological, post-Keynesian, radical, and feminist economists attempting to broaden our understanding of development, see Greenwood and Holt (2010).

8. I am personally inclined toward the second approach for two reasons: (1) I do not believe debate over weights increases understanding of our progress or lack thereof; it merely diverts energy from where it could be more usefully applied—identifying important areas in which we need to progress and refining our ability to measure progress along each dimension; and (2) I fear a single index can serve as an excuse to justify deficiencies in some areas by overall gains according to the index, even though the advance in the overall index might have been possible to achieve without losses along some dimensions.

9. This has not always been the broad consensus. Nature our enemy, nature to be conquered, nature to be mastered and tamed were the consensus among nonindigenous, European cultures until very recently. And many people today look on bioengineering and other similar projects in a positive light as "nature improvements"—not to speak of all of us who plant and mow lawns and tend our flower gardens, even if we do not use chemical fertilizers or pesticides.

Part II

Why the Environment Is at Risk

Part II moves discussion beyond platitudes about population growth and industrialization and focuses attention instead on perverse incentives intrinsic to our economic institutions, which put the natural environment at much greater risk than people realized until forty years ago when the modern environmental movement was born.

Chapter 4

Useful Insights From Mainstream Economics

Regrettably, Part I falls short of providing a complete new paradigm and theoretical framework for analyzing the relations between human economic activity and the natural environment. Hopefully, it will sensitize us to pitfalls in traditional economic thinking and provide useful clues about new thinking we must engage in. In any case, we are now ready to apply our new mind-set to analyzing why the economic system tends to place the environment at risk.

When properly understood, a number of mainstream concepts and theories can help us understand why in private enterprise market economies we overpollute, overexploit, and underprotect the natural environment. Understanding the nature of what economists call "perverse incentives" created by externalities, public goods, free access to common property resources, and resource extraction under private ownership can take us a long way toward understanding the sources of environmental problems. Since mainstream economists invariably defend the private enterprise market system, environmentalists who sense that our major economic institutions are largely responsible for environmental distress assume there is little in mainstream economic theory that sheds light on where problems arise. Surprisingly, this is not the case. The problem is that the mainstream literature on perverse incentives is underadvertised by a profession dedicated to providing ideological support for the dominant economic system of our age, and these perverse incentives are rarely interpreted as reason for concern.

Mainstream economic theory teaches that the problem with externalities is that the buyer and seller have no incentive to take the external cost or benefit for others into account when deciding how much of something to supply or demand. And mainstream theory teaches that the problem with public goods is that nobody can be excluded from benefiting from a public good once anyone buys it, and therefore everyone has an incentive to "ride for free" on the purchases of others rather than revealing a true willingness to pay for public goods by purchasing them in the marketplace. In other words, mainstream economics concedes that the laws of the marketplace will lead to inefficient allocations of productive resources when public goods and externalities come into play because important benefits or costs go unaccounted for in the market decision-making procedure. If anyone cares to listen, standard economic theory predicts that market forces will tend to produce too much of goods whose production and/or consumption entail negative externalities, too little of goods whose production and/or consumption entail positive externalities, and much too little, if any, of public goods. We illustrate the problem of negative externalities by looking at the automobile industry, and the problem of public goods by considering pollution reduction.

Externalities and Professor Pigou

A great deal of mainstream economic theory is devoted to explaining why markets can be relied on to allocate scarce productive resources efficiently. Of course, this vision has been with us since the time of Adam Smith ([1776] 1999), who popularized the idea of a beneficent "invisible hand" at work in capitalist economies over 200 years ago in his *Wealth of Nations*. How does the beneficent invisible hand work, and when do beneficent invisible hands turn into malevolent invisible feet?

Smith reasoned that sellers would keep supplying more of a good as long as the price they received covered the additional costs of producing them. In other words, Smith assumed that market supply curves would be the same as suppliers' marginal cost curves. He also reasoned that buyers would keep demanding more of a good as long as the satisfaction they got from an additional unit was greater than the price they had to pay for it, in which case market demand curves would be the same as buyers' marginal benefit curves. But if market price keeps adjusting until the quantity suppliers want to sell is the same as the quantity buyers want to buy, this means that every unit that benefits buyers more than it costs producers to make will get produced, and no units that would cost more to produce than the benefits buyers would enjoy from them will be produced. Therefore, according to Smith, every unit we should want to be produced will be, while none we should not want produced will be produced—that is, the market will lead us, as if guided by a beneficent invisible hand, to produce exactly the socially optimal, or efficient, amount of the good.

What can go wrong? In his defense, as discussed in Chapter 1, nobody in Smith's day distinguished between private costs to sellers and costs to society as a whole, or between private benefits to buyers and benefits to society as a whole. It fell to A.C. Pigou ([1912] 2009) to raise these disturbing possibilities over 100 years later when it was more apparent that the world was no longer empty. If there are what Professor Pigou first called *external costs* associated with producing something—that is, costs borne not by the seller but by someone else—then the marginal social cost (MSC) of producing something will be greater than the marginal private cost (MPC). And if parties other than the buyer of a good are affected when it is consumed, either positively or negatively—that is, if there are what Professor Pigou first called *external effects* when a buyer consumes a good—then the marginal social benefit (MSB) that comes from consuming the good is different from the marginal private benefit (MPB) to the buyer alone. Problems arise because neither sellers nor buyers have any incentive to take consequences for third parties into account, which means that the market decision-making process, in which only buyers and sellers participate, will fail to take external effects into account. If the external effects are negative consequences for "third" parties, the market will end up leading us to produce and consume more of the good than is socially efficient by effectively disenfranchising parties other than the buyer and seller who are negatively affected. If the effects on external parties are positive, the market will lead us to produce and consume less of the good than is socially efficient by excluding third parties who are positively affected from the decision-making process.

Today professional economists all agree that Adam Smith's vision of the market as a mechanism that successfully harnesses individual desires to the social purpose of using scarce productive resources efficiently hinges on the assumption that external effects are absent, or insignificant. The assumption of no external effects is explicit in theorems about market efficiency in graduate texts, although usually implicit when most mainstream economists conclude that markets are remarkable efficiency machines that require little social effort on our part. However, driven in large part by research into environmental externalities over the past forty years, more economists are challenging this assumption, and a growing number of skeptics outside the mainstream now dare to suggest that externalities are prevalent and often substantial. Or, as Hunt and D'Arge put it, externalities are the rule rather than the exception, and therefore markets often work as if they were guided by a "malevolent invisible foot" that keeps kicking us to produce more of some things and less of others than is socially efficient.[1]

First, critics point to the absence of empirical evidence supporting the claim of external effect exceptionality. It is truly remarkable that this crucial assumption has never been subjected to serious scrutiny. Economists are well known for engaging in exhaustive empirical debates over assumptions that are far less important. But in this case, perhaps the most critical assumption about market economies—the assumption that externalities are small and rare—has not given rise to serious empirical debate and remains unsubstantiated by empirical studies. Instead it remains untested—an assumption of ideological convenience.

Lacking conclusive empirical studies, are there theoretical reasons to believe that externalities *should* be exceptional rather than prevalent? Obviously, increasing the value of goods and services produced, and decreasing the unpleasantness of what we have to do to get them, are two ways producers can increase their profits in a market economy. By increasing the value of goods produced, sellers can reasonably hope to sell more and/or sell at a higher price. By making work less onerous or by reducing labor or nonlabor inputs, producers can hope to lower labor or nonlabor costs. And competitive pressures will drive producers to do both, as Adam Smith argued long ago. But maneuvering to appropriate a greater share of the value of goods and services produced by externalizing costs and internalizing benefits without compensation are also ways to increase profits. And presumably competitive pressures will drive producers to pursue this route to greater profitability just as assiduously. Of course, the problem is that while the first kind of behavior serves the social interest as well as the private interests of producers, the second kind of behavior serves private interests at the expense of the social interest. When buyers or sellers promote their private interests by externalizing costs onto those not party to the market exchange, or internalizing benefits from third parties without compensation, their behavior introduces inefficiencies that lead to a misallocation of productive resources.

Market admirers seldom ask: Where are firms most likely to find the easiest opportunities to expand their profits? How easy is it usually to increase the size or quality of the economic pie we bake, so to speak? How easy is it to reduce the time or discomfort it takes to bake it? Alternatively, how easy is it to enlarge one's slice of the pie by externalizing a cost or by appropriating a benefit without payment? Why should we assume that it is always easier to expand profits by socially productive behavior than by redistributive behavior that leads to inefficient uses of scarce resources and energies and is therefore socially counterproductive? The implicit assumption that it is always easier to increase profits through productive behavior than redistributive maneuvering is what lies behind the view of markets as efficiency machines.

Market enthusiasts fail to notice that the same feature of market exchanges primarily responsible for the small transaction costs so widely admired—excluding all affected parties but two from the transaction—is also a major source of potential gain for the buyer and seller. When the buyer and seller of an automobile strike their convenient deal, the size of the benefit they have to divide between them is greatly enlarged by externalizing the costs of air pollution from auto plants, and the costs of urban smog, noise pollution, traffic congestion, and greenhouse gas emissions caused by car consumption. Those who pay these costs, thereby enlarging carmaker profits and car consumer benefits, are easy "marks" for car sellers and buyers because they are geographically and chronologically dispersed and because the magnitude of the effect on each of them is small yet not equal. Individually, they have little incentive to insist on being party to the transaction. Collectively, they face transaction cost and free-rider obstacles to forming a voluntary coalition to represent a large number of people, each with little, but different amounts at stake.

Moreover, the opportunity for this kind of cost-shifting behavior on the part of buyers and sellers in market economies is not eliminated by making markets more competitive or entry costless, as is commonly assumed. Even if there were countless perfectly informed sellers and buyers in every market, even if the appearance of the slightest differences in average profit rates in different industries induced instantaneous self-correcting entries and exits of firms, even if every market participant were equally powerful and therefore equally powerless—in other words, even if we embrace the full fantasy of market enthusiasts—as long as there are numerous external parties with small but unequal interests in market transactions, those external parties will face greater transaction costs and free-rider obstacles to a full and effective representation of their collective interest than that faced by the buyer and seller in the exchange. It is this unavoidable disadvantage that makes external parties easy prey to cost-shifting behavior on the part of buyers and sellers.

Even if we could organize a market economy so that buyers and sellers never faced a more or less powerful opponent in a market exchange, this would not change the fact that each of us has smaller interests at stake in many transactions where we are neither the buyer nor the seller. Yet there is every reason to believe that the *sum total* interest of *all* external parties can be considerable compared to the interests of the buyer and the seller. It is the transaction cost and free-rider problems that put those with lesser individual interests at a disadvantage compared to buyers and sellers in market exchanges, in turn giving rise to the opportunity for individually profitable but socially counterproductive cost-shifting behavior on the part of buyers and sellers. So not only is there no empirical evidence that external effects are, truly, small and exceptional, there are strong theoretical reasons for expecting just the opposite to be the case. There is every reason to expect that competition for profit will drive buyers and sellers to seek out ways to externalize costs onto large numbers of disempowered third parties who are relatively easy marks, creating significant allocative inefficiencies in the process.

But what does all this have to do with pollution? For economists, pollution is a "negative externality" of production or consumption activity. Since market economies overproduce goods and services whose production or consumption entails negative external effects, as explained above, this means that while it may be efficient to pollute to some extent—when the benefits from the goods or services produced along with the pollution exceed the costs of producing them *including* the damage from the pollution—markets will predictably lead us to pollute beyond this point.

Since there are external costs associated with producing cars, the MSC of producing an automobile is higher than the MPC of producing the automobile, as shown in Figure 4.1. Since there are negative externalities associated with consuming cars, the MSB, of consuming a car is less than the MPB to the car buyer, as shown in Figure 4.1. As we know, the socially efficient number of automobiles to produce and consume is $A(0)$, where MSC = MSB. However, market supply, S, depends on private costs, not social costs, and is therefore equal to MPC, not MSC, and market demand, D, depends on private benefits to buyers, not social benefits, and is therefore equal to MPB, not MSB. So when the laws of supply and demand drive the auto market to its equilibrium, they drive us to produce where S = D, or $A(M)$. As Figure 4.1 demonstrates, since $A(M) > A(0)$, when automobile producers and buyers predictably ignore the negative external effects of sulfur dioxide emissions from plants producing cars, and the negative effects of driving cars on local air quality, congestion, and greenhouse gas accumulations, we predictably produce and consume too many cars. By doing so, we also produce too much local air pollution, congestion, and greenhouse gas emissions.

Although the magnitude of the external effects and consequent inefficiencies is particularly great, the automobile industry is hardly an exception. Besides producing cement, cement factories emit particulates that cause urban air pollution. Besides producing electricity, utility companies emit sulfur dioxide that causes acid rain. Besides producing fruits and vegetables, modern agriculture produces pesticide runoff that contaminates groundwater and rivers. Retail stores generate packaging that ends up in solid waste dumps at best and as litter at worst. The biosphere provides resources, assimilates wastes, provides amenities, and performs life support services. Whenever production or consumption diminishes the usefulness of the environment in any of these regards, it is likely to go unaccounted for in a market system since most of those affected will be third parties whose interests will not be considered by

Figure 4.1 **Externalities and the Automobile Market**

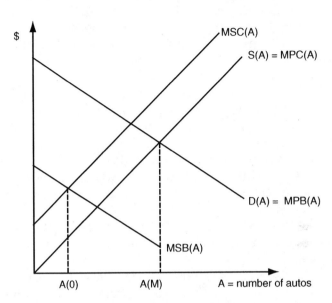

the buyer or seller in a market transaction. Expecting a free market system not to pollute too much is like waiting for a lead balloon to float.

But surely environmentally conscious people take the environmental effects of their actions into account. Is not the answer more environmental education so we all become "green" consumers, thus forcing producers to behave in environmentally responsible ways as well? We *should* consume so as not to pollute, and the environment certainly is better off because many who have become aware of the environmental consequences of their choices take those effects into account. But it is important to realize that a market system provides no incentives for people to engage in green consumerism. Quite the opposite, markets provide powerful incentives for consumers *not* to behave in environmentally responsible ways. To understand this, we need to consider a second major reason why market economies destroy the environment.

Public Goods and the Free-Rider Problem

A public good is a good produced by human economic activity that is consumed, to all intents and purposes, by everyone rather than by an individual consumer. Unlike a private good, such as underwear, which affects its wearer and only its wearer, public goods, like pollution reduction, affect most people. In different terms, nobody can be excluded from "consuming" a public good—or benefiting from its existence. This is not to say that everyone has the same preferences regarding public goods any more than people have the same preferences for private goods. I happen to prefer apples to oranges, and I value pollution reduction more than I value so-called national defense. Other people place greater value on national defense than they do on pollution reduction, just as some prefer oranges to apples. But unlike the case of apples and oranges, where those of us who prefer apples can buy more apples and those who like oranges more can buy more oranges, all U.S. citizens have to "consume" the same amount of federal spending on the military and on pollution reduction. We cannot provide more military spending for U.S. citizens who value that public good more, and more pollution reduction for U.S. citizens who value the environment more.[2] Whereas different Americans can consume different amounts of private goods, we all must live in the same "public good world."

What would happen if we left the decision about how much of our scarce productive resources to devote to producing public goods to the free market? Markets only provide goods for which there is what economists call "effective demand"—that is, buyers willing and able to put their money where their mouth is. But what incentive is there for a buyer to pay for a public good? First of all, no matter how much I value the public good, I only enjoy a tiny fraction of the overall or social benefit that comes from having more of it since I cannot exclude others who do not pay for it from benefiting as well. In different terms: Social rationality demands that an individual purchase a public good up to the point where the cost of the last unit she purchased is as great as the benefits enjoyed by *all* who benefit, *in sum total*, from her purchase of the good. But it is only rational for an individual to buy a public good up to the point where the cost of the last unit she purchased is as great as the benefit *she herself* enjoys from the good. When an individual buys public goods in a free market, she has no incentive to take the benefits others enjoy when she purchases public goods into account when she decides how much to buy. Consequently, she demands far less than is socially efficient, if she purchases any at all. When many behave in this individually rational way market demand grossly underrepresents the marginal *social* benefit of public goods, and consequently very little public goods will be provided.

Another way to see the problem is to recognize that each potential buyer of a public good has an incentive to wait and hope that someone else will buy the public good. A patient buyer can "ride for free" on the purchases of others since nonpayers cannot be excluded from benefiting from public goods. But if everyone is waiting for someone else to plunk down his hard-earned income for a public good, nobody will demonstrate effective demand for public goods in the market place. *Free riding* is individually rational in the case of public goods—but leads to an effective demand for public goods that grossly underestimates their true social benefit, and consequently, if left to the market, far too few public goods will be produced.

But what prevents a group of people who will benefit from a public good from banding together to express their demand for the good collectively? The problem is that there is an incentive for people to lie about how much they benefit. If the associations of public good consumers are voluntary, no matter how much I truly benefit from a public good, I am better off pretending I do not benefit at all. Then I can decline membership in the association and avoid paying anything, knowing full well that I will, in fact, benefit from its existence nonetheless. If the associations are not voluntary—that is, if a government "drafts" people into the public good–consuming coalition—there is still an incentive for people to underrepresent the degree to which they benefit if assessments are based on degree of benefit. This is where the fact that not all people *do* benefit equally from different kinds of public goods becomes an important part of the problem. If we knew that everyone truly valued a large military to the same extent, there would be few objections to making everyone contribute the same amount to pay for it. But there is every reason to believe this is *not* the case. In this context, if we believe that payments should be related to the degree to which someone benefits, there is an incentive for individuals to pretend they benefit less than they do. If the effective demand expressed by the nonvoluntary consuming coalition is based on these individually rational underrepresentations, it will still significantly underrepresent the true social benefits people enjoy from the public good, and consequently effective demand, and therefore supply, will still be less than the socially efficient or optimal amount of the public good.

In sum, because of what economists call the free-rider incentive problem, as well as the transaction costs of organizing and managing a coalition of public good consumers, market demand predictably underrepresents the true social benefits that come from consumption of public goods. If the production of a public good entails no external effects so that the market supply curve accurately represents the MSC of producing the public good, then since market demand will lie considerably under the true MSB curve for the public good, the market equilibrium level of production and consumption will be significantly less than the socially efficient level, as shown in Figure 4.2, where the market equilibrium outcome, A(M), is considerably less than the socially efficient outcome, A(0). In conclusion, if it were left to the free market and voluntary associations, precious little, if any, of our scarce productive resources would be used to produce public goods no matter how valuable they really are. As Robert Heilbroner (1989) put it: "The market has a keen ear for private wants, but a deaf ear for public needs."

But what does all this have to do with environmental protection? Reducing pollution, or acting to protect the environment in any way, is providing a public good. Since everyone benefits from pollution cleanup, and everyone benefits from environmental protection, and nobody can be excluded from the benefits of cleaning up pollution or protecting the environment, reducing pollution and protecting the environment are public goods like good A in Figure 4.2. Consequently, there is an incentive for everyone who benefits from pollution reduction or environmental protection to avoid paying the cost of providing it and instead to ride for free on the purchases of others. But of course, when individuals pursue their individually rational strategy and ride for free, there is little or no demand in the market for pollution reduction or environmental protection even when the social benefit is quite large.

Markets provide incentives for individuals to express their desires for private goods in the marketplace by offering to buy them since otherwise they cannot benefit. But markets provide no incentives for individuals to express their desires for public goods in the marketplace by offering to purchase them. Quite the contrary, in a market economy it is almost always foolish for individuals to buy public goods no matter how much they may value or want them. And therein lies the problem with *green consumerism* in market economies. The problem is not that when people choose to engage in green consumerism the world is not better off because of it. The problem is that markets penalize those who practice green consumerism and reward those who do not, which means that socially beneficial campaigns encouraging green consumption must always swim upstream in market economies.

There are a number of cheap detergents that get my wash very clean but cause considerable water pollution. "Green" detergents, on the other hand, are more expensive and leave my white bedsheets more gray than white, but cause less water pollution. *Whether or not I end up making the socially responsible choice*, because pollution reduction is a public good the market provides *too little incentive* for me to make the socially efficient choice. My own best interests are served by weighing the disadvantage of the extra cost and grayer sheets *to me* against the advantage *to me* of the diminution in water pollution that would result if I use the green detergent. But presumably there are many others besides me who also benefit from the cleaner water if I buy the green detergent—which is precisely why we think of "buying green" as socially responsible behavior. Unfortunately, the market provides no incentive for me to take *their* benefit into account. Worse still, if I suspect that other consumers consult only their own interests when they choose which detergent to buy—that is, if I think they will ignore the benefits to me and others if they choose the green detergent—by choosing to take their interests into account and consuming green myself,

Figure 4.2 **Public Good Provision If Left to the Market**

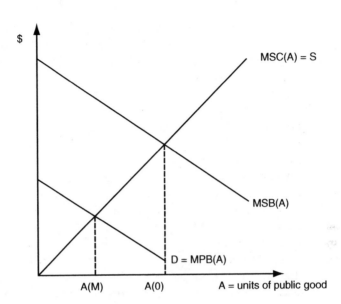

I risk not only making a choice that was detrimental to my own interests, I risk feeling like a sucker as well.[3]

This is not to say that many people will not choose to "do the right thing" and "consume green" in any case. Moreover, there may be incentives *other than the socially counterproductive market incentives* that may overcome the market disincentive to consume green. The fact that I teach environmental economics and fear my students would view me as a hypocrite if they saw me with a polluting detergent in my shopping basket in the checkout line at the supermarket is apparently a powerful enough incentive in my own case to lead me to buy a green detergent despite the market disincentive to do so. (Admittedly, I have only a slight preference for white over gray sheets, and who knows how long I will hold out if the price differential increases?) But the point is that because pollution reduction is a public good, market incentives are perverse, leading people to consume less "green" and more "dirty" than is socially efficient. The extent to which people ignore perverse market incentives and act on the basis of concern for the environment, concern for others, including future generations, or in response to nonmarket, social incentives such as fear of ostracism is important for the environment and the social interest, but does not make the market incentives any less perverse.

The Tragedy of the Commons

Much of the natural environment is what was traditionally called a common property resource, which nobody owns yet all are free to use. The term now preferred by many specialists is *common pool resource* (CPR), since the defining characteristic is that all have free access to use or exploit the "pool" or resource, whereas the term *property* indicates that some agent, even if not a private owner, may have the right to deny access to the pool. In any case, ocean fisheries, the upper atmosphere where greenhouse gases are stored, the lower atmosphere where smog and local pollutants accumulate, groundwater aquifers, and large tracts of land whose titles are either nonexistent or unenforced are examples of important common pool resources. Mainstream environmental economists often illustrate the problem Garrett Hardin (1968) made famous as the "tragedy of the commons" by exploring incentives for fishermen.

Imagine there are twelve salmon fishermen with boats moored at Friday Harbor on San Juan Island in Washington State. Suppose it costs $100 per day in fuel and wages to operate a salmon fishing boat and there are no other costs. For simplicity we assume the catch out of Friday Harbor is small compared to the total catch in the Salish Sea so the price of salmon is independent of the number caught by the twelve fishermen who fish off San Juan Island. But as more and more boats go out to fish in the same school of salmon, they get in each other's way and the number of salmon caught per boat declines. Suppose the revenues from selling the salmon catch depend on the number of boats that go out each day, as indicated in Table 4.1.

How many fishing boats will go out each day if all boats have free access—that is, if there is nothing preventing a boat captain from going out if he wants to? To answer this and further questions, we can complete Table 4.1 by calculating some additional columns. If every fisherman is equally equipped and competent, each would expect to catch the same amount as all others fishing that day and therefore expect to get the average revenue from the sale of the fish as his own expected revenue. We calculate the average revenue (AR) by dividing the total revenue (TR) by the number of boats fishing. What a profit-maximizing captain would compare this expected revenue to would be the cost of fishing for the day, which is $100 for each and every boat no matter how many other boats are fishing. In other words, the MPC, to a boat captain of fishing for the day is $100, and as long as the expected AR of fishing is at least as high as the MPC of fishing, we would expect profit-maximizing captains to go out if they have "free access" to the fishery.

When trying to think like a captain, imagine you have picked up your crew in your truck, and when you get to the dock you assume that everyone else who is going to fish that day has already gone out. You can count how many

Table 4.1

Total Revenues in the San Juan Island Fishery

Number of fishing boats	Total revenues from catch (in $)
1	200
2	375
3	525
4	650
5	750
6	825
7	875
8	900
9	900
10	875
11	825
12	750

boats are still there and therefore calculate how many have already gone out. For example, if you arrive and six boats are still at the dock, that means six boats have already set sail, and you assume that if you go out there will be seven boats fishing that day. Your decision is whether to go fish or walk back to the tavern with your crew and spend the day playing pool and telling fish stories. If you do not go out, you do not have to pay for fuel and you owe your crew nothing. Along with AR, MPC, and TR, Table 4.2 lists average cost (AC) and marginal revenue (MR), the change in TR because an additional boat went out fishing. The values of some of these variables change when the number of boats fishing changes while others do not.

The first captain will go out because he will expect to get $200 in revenues and spend only $100 in costs. The second captain to arrive at the dock will also go out because he will expect to get $187.50 for $100 in expenses. What about the captain who sees that seven boats are already out, meaning he would be the eighth? With eight boats fishing, he expects to get $112.50 for $100 in costs. If the next captain arriving at the dock thinks he is a little more skillful than the average captain, he will go out too because the expected revenue if he were only of average skill would be $100, which would pay for the $100 in costs. So the number of boats we expect to go fishing under free access is nine. The captain who arrives and sees that nine boats are already out fishing will head straight for the tavern that day since he cannot expect to cover $100 in fuel and labor costs with $87.50 in revenues—which is what each captain gets when there are ten boats fishing. The eleventh and twelfth late sleepers will turn back for the tavern even quicker.

Table 4.2

Average and Marginal Costs and Revenues in the San Juan Island Fishery
(in $)

Number of boats	Average revenue	Marginal private cost	Average cost	Marginal revenue	Total revenue
1	200	100	100	200	200
2	187.50	100	100	175	375
3	175	100	100	150	525
4	162.50	100	100	125	650
5	150	100	100	100	750
6	137.50	100	100	75	825
7	125	100	100	50	875
8	112.50	100	100	25	900
9	100	100	100	0	900
10	87.50	100	100	−25	875
11	75	100	100	−50	825
12	62.50	100	100	−75	750

But how much does the last boat that goes out fishing under free access increase TR from the catch? Economists call the change in TR when one more boat is added to the fishing fleet for the day the MR. MR is calculated in Table 4.2 by subtracting the TR in the previous row from the TR in the row we are looking at, since that is the change in revenues that came from adding another boat to the fishing fleet. So another way of asking the above question is to ask what MR was when the last boat went out fishing. The increase in TRs from the ninth boat is $0 since eight boats will catch $900 worth of fish just as nine boats do!—which illustrates the logic of overexploitation nicely. Clearly too many boats will fish each day.

If you have ever seen commercial fishermen racing each other to find the school of fish and cutting in on each other once the school is located, you will understand how at some point another boat does not increase the number of fish caught. This is true for grazing livestock, timber harvesting, and pumping oil in common pool resources as well. Notice that the ninth boat went out because its captain hoped to earn a small profit, even though the extra boat adds $100 in labor and fuel costs to the overall fishing effort while contributing nothing to benefits resulting from the overall fishing effort since $900 worth of salmon will be caught whether there are eight or nine boats fishing. If the cost of operating a fishing boat dropped to $85 per day, ten boats would go out under free access. Notice how counterproductive individual rationality is under free access in this case. The tenth boat will go out because the captain expects to get $87.50 while only spending $85. But by doing so he adds $100 to the overall cost of the fishing effort and *reduces* total fish revenues by $25!

Garrett Hardin (1968) called this outcome the "tragedy of the commons." Natural resource economists study this phenomenon as a "perverse incentive" that leads to "overexploitation" of the commons under a system of free access. If we apply cost-benefit analysis (CBA) to determine the efficient, or optimal, level of exploitation when MPC is $100, we would send out no more than five boats to fish every day because once five boats are fishing the additional revenue from sending more boats, MR, is less than the additional cost of sending more boats, MPC = $100. In conclusion, the socially rational level of exploitation is for five boats to fish every day, but under free access there is a perverse incentive that makes it individually rational for nine fishermen to go out every day, meaning that the fishery will be "overexploited" under free access.

In this overly simple model there is only one time period and consequently no future to worry about. In this case the only negative external effect of an additional boat fishing is that the other boats fishing that same day all catch less fish than before for a given amount of effort on their part. Since there is no incentive for individual captains to take this negative external effect into account, our model predicts that too many boats will fish on a given day—nine instead of five. But in the real world there is a future, and fish caught today are fish that are not available to be caught next year. Moreover, when more fish are caught today, there will be fewer fish to reproduce and therefore even fewer fish to catch in the future. When people think about overexploitation of fisheries, they naturally think of overfishing to extinction. It is noteworthy that even a single-period model, which does not account for negative external effects from fishing today that occur in the future, predicts overexploitation.

A more complicated and realistic model with two time periods and a fish reproduction rate would predict that overexploitation under free access is even more severe because such a model would account for three, instead of only one, negative external effects that each captain has no incentive to take into account: (1) The more fish any captain catches from a fishery, the fewer fish others will catch for a given amount of effort this year. This is the effect captured in our simple, one-time-period model, which leads to the conclusion of "overexploitation" in the sense that net benefits from fishing will be less this year than they would have been had fewer boats spent less time fishing. (2) The more fish any boat catches this year, the fewer fish will be available for all fishermen to catch next year. This negative external effect implies that net benefits during the two years together would have been higher had fewer fish been caught this year and more of these same fish caught next year. This effect would be captured in a two-time-period model. (3) The more fish any boat catches this year, the fewer fish will reproduce, and therefore the fewer fish will be available to be caught eventually. This negative external effect can be captured in a model with a multiperiod future, a reproduction rate, and a maturation rate. It implies that compared to the exploitation pattern from free access, net benefits over time would be higher if even fewer fish were caught in early time periods, thus allowing for more reproduction and larger catches in later time periods.

In Chapter 7 we explore policies to try to solve this problem. Besides privatization of CPRs, in this case having one fisherman buy up exclusive rights to the San Juan fishery, and regulation of CPRs, in this case having the Washington State or San Juan County government sell fishing licenses, we will explore the logic of a long ignored alternative—community self-management of CPRs.

Climate Change Preview

We take up the subject of climate change in great depth in Part IV. But it is instructive to pause here briefly and notice how all three of the above problems with market systems play an important role in causing climate change and obstructing its solution. Human economic activity over the past 100 years has led to dramatic increases in atmospheric concentrations of carbon dioxide. Between 1860 and 1990, global carbon emissions rose from less than 200 million to almost 6 billion metric tons per year. At the same time, deforestation has considerably reduced the recycling of carbon dioxide into oxygen. The result of increased carbon emissions and reduced sequestration—taking carbon dioxide out of the atmosphere by converting it to oxygen—is that the stock of greenhouse gases in the atmosphere has increased to the point where it is leading to climate change with serious adverse affects. At its old equilibrium level, the greenhouse effect was part of making the earth inhabitable, preventing the earth's mean temperature from falling well below freezing and reducing temperature fluctuation between day and night. But today's higher levels of greenhouse gases in the atmosphere mean global temperatures will rise and extreme climate conditions will intensify. Droughts will be longer, floods more severe, hurricanes and tornadoes more frequent, and melting polar ice caps will raise sea levels and threaten a large percentage of the world's population who live in coastal cities.

This is happening because businesses and households that burn fossil fuels are not charged for the adverse effects of their actions on the atmosphere— carbon emissions are a negative externality. It is happening because those who control tropical forests are not paid for the beneficial effect of carbon sequestration if they choose to preserve the forests—carbon sequestration is a positive externality. And as explained, markets create perverse incentives for businesses and households to engage in too many activities with negative external effects and too few activities with positive external effects. The upper atmosphere where greenhouse gases are stored is a CPR resource to which all have long had free access. As we have seen, there are perverse incentives for users to overexploit CPRs under free access. And, finally, those who reduce carbon emissions provide a public good, as do those who preserve forests that sequester and store carbon. But as explained, since no one can be excluded from benefiting from these public goods, and they do entail private sacrifices for those who provide them, all businesses, consumers, and nations wait for someone else to shoulder the burden of providing these public goods in hopes of riding for free on the sacrifices of others. Everyone wants to continue to enjoy the benefits associated with carbon-emitting activity and hopes that others will reduce their carbon emissions. For all these reasons, it should come as no surprise that too much burning of fossil fuel, too little preservation of forests, and too little reduction of carbon emissions goes on in market economies. Nor is it hard to see why international negotiations over ways to reduce greenhouse gas emissions and increase forest conservation keep getting stuck.

Resource Extraction and Rates of Time Preference

Decision-making by private owners of natural resources under the pressure of market competition often leads to decisions based on a rate of time discount that is higher than can be justified for social decision-making purposes. When this is the case, resources are extracted faster than would be socially efficient. But the reasons for this unfortunate outcome are not as simple as often believed.

When I decide how to weigh well-being now versus well-being next year, it is sensible for me to take into account the non-zero probability that I might be dead next year. What is more, there is a probability of one that I will be dead 100 years from now, so whatever benefits might be made possible 100 years hence by my forgoing benefits today would presumably not matter to me at all. These calculations imply that it is rational for a mortal being to *discount* well-being in the future compared to well-being now. For example, if I discount a dollar's worth of benefits next year by 10 percent compared to a dollar's worth of benefits right now, my personal *rate of time discount* is 10 percent.

On the other hand, there is a zero probability that there will be no human beings living next year. And while the probability that there will be no humans alive 100 years from now may not be zero, the probability is much less than one. So, unless we simply do not care as much about the well-being of future generations as we do about our own, there would seem to be no justifiable reason for society to discount human well-being in the future compared to human well-being now when making decisions about how to use the natural environment. Or so it first appears. Moreover, since mortal humans presumably make decisions based on their individual interests, it would also appear that the rate of time discount individuals will use when comparing present and future costs and benefits will be higher than the rate of time discount humans should use as a species that hopes to survive many generations.

But first appearances are sometimes deceiving. Suppose I own a mineral deposit that can be exploited this year or next year. If I know I will be alive both years and intend to exploit the deposit myself, I would be foolish to extract any ore this year that would be more valuable if extracted next year instead. But what if I do not expect to live past this year? Should I extract all the ore now since I will not be around to benefit from the profits from extraction next year? In a private enterprise market economy, the answer turns out to be "no." Suppose I am only interested in how much I can get from the deposit this year before I die. Rather than use an inefficient one-year extraction plan myself, I should sell the deposit to someone who will be alive for two years for a price that reflects the profits that can be earned from the deposit under a more efficient, two-year extraction plan. As we have just seen, if I do not own the deposit but only have user's rights, I will be tempted to overexploit it myself before I die. But if I own the deposit and can sell it to someone who will live two years and make the most profitable use of it, then individual mortality need not lead to overexploitation. By extension, since users today know there will be people who will pay for the ore indefinitely into the future, the price of the mineral asset should reflect its most valuable use over time, and whoever is the user should be forced to adopt the most socially useful pattern of exploitation in order to justify the price paid for the asset.

Thus, many natural resource economists argue that contrary to first appearances, even when natural resources are privately owned by mortals, as long as these assets can be bought and sold there is no perverse incentive to extract them faster than is efficient. The self-interest of resource owners protects the interests of future generations because the resource owners would earn lower profits by ignoring those who will be willing to pay for the resources tomorrow. In effect, today's market for natural resources gives unborn consumers as well as today's consumers votes about when to extract our natural resources.

So where is the problem? Why do decisions made in competitive market environments use a rate of time discount that is too high when deciding how fast to extract natural resources? Two reasons conspire to make the rate of time discount that is sensible for private resource owners to use when deciding how fast to extract the resources they own significantly higher than the rate of time discount that society can justify for itself on ethical grounds—future market failures, and profit rates in excess of the growth rate of net welfare per capita.

Future market failures: Since uncertainty is cumulative over time, there is a greater degree of market failure in markets for goods and services delivered in the future, or what are called "futures" markets, than there is in markets for goods and services now, or what we might call "present" markets. For example, finding a market for oil to be delivered twenty-five years from now is harder than finding a market for oil to be delivered this month, and if you do, the oil futures market is not likely to be as "well ordered." Futures markets tend to be "thinner"—have fewer participants—with wider and less predictable price fluctuations. But greater "market incompleteness" in futures markets means that, on average, you are more likely to be paid the full benefit of a good or service delivered today than the full benefit that will come from delivery of the same good or service in the future. In other words, the greater degree of market failure in futures markets means that market economies treat goods today as more valuable "birds in the hand" and goods in the future as less valuable "birds in the bush" even though future generations will value their birds as much as we value ours today.

A rate of time discount that is too high: Contrary to our preliminary conclusion above—that unless we favor present over future generations, the rate of time discount we use for social decision-making should be zero—a reasonable case can be made for discounting future net economic benefits compared to present net economic benefits if net *national welfare per capita* is growing. If we interpret intergenerational equity as an equal opportunity to enjoy economic welfare irrespective of generation, future welfare should be discounted by the expected rate of growth in per capita economic welfare. The idea is simple: If future generations are going to enjoy greater economic well-being than we do, then the same amount of economic well-being delivered now should count for more than if it is delivered later. According to this logic, a social rate of time discount equal to the rate of growth of per capita net national economic welfare is perfectly fair.

Eban Goodstein defines net national welfare (NNW) as the value of "both market and non-market goods and services produced *minus* the depreciation of capital, both natural and human made, used up in production, *minus* the total externality costs associated with these products" (1995, 63). At least in the first world, per capita net national product (NNP) has grown over the past 200 years. However, as discussed in Chapter 3, NNP per capita overestimates NNW per capita because it does not take into account the depreciation of natural capital or the production of harmful wastes as by-products of produc-

71

ing useful goods and services, both of which have been increasing. So using the growth rate of per capita NNP rather than NNW overdiscounts the future. Some empirical estimates of the rate of growth of per capita NNW compared to NNP are informative, even if they disagree to some extent. Nordhaus and Tobin (1972) estimate that per capita NNP in the United States had grown by 1.7 percent from 1929 to 1965 while per capita NNW had grown only by 1.0 percent. Daly and Cobb (1989) estimate a dramatic increase in the *difference* between the rate of growth of per capita NNP and NNW over the past forty years in the United States. For 1950–1960, Daly and Cobb estimate that per capita NNP grew by 1 percent per year while per capita NNW grew by 0.8 percent per year. And for 1960–1970, they estimate that per capita NNP grew by 2.6 percent per year while per capita NNW grew by 2.0 percent. However, for 1970–1980, they estimate that while per capita NNP grew by 2.0 percent per year, per capita NNW *fell* by 0.1 percent per year. And for 1980–1986, they estimate that per capita NNP grew by 1.8 percent per year while per capita NNW *fell* by 1.3 percent per year.

The possibility that per capita NNW may now be falling instead of rising is certainly alarming. If this is the case, it implies that instead of discounting future net benefits we should be discounting net benefits in the present when doing CBA or when calculating how fast to extract scarce natural resources. However, the relevant question with regard to resource extraction is how the rate of growth of NNW per capita compares to the average rate of profit in the economy, because the average rate of profit in the economy is the logical discount rate for private owners of natural resources to use when discounting future benefits from extraction compared to present benefits from extraction. If the average rate of profit is higher than the rate of increase of NNW per capita, then private resource owners will be driven by market competition to extract natural resources more quickly than is socially efficient.

During the past twenty-five years, profit rates on average have been two to three times higher than the growth rate of per capita NNP and four to five times higher than any estimates of the growth rate of per capita NNW. The reason is simple: The rate of profit is determined not only by how fast NNP—not NNW—grows, but also by how the net product is divided between employers and employees. The greater the bargaining power of employers versus employees, the more the rate of profit will exceed the growth rate of NNP.

This is easy to see by imagining a capitalist economy that is productive but not growing. An economy is "productive" if it is capable of replacing all the produced inputs it uses in production and still has a positive net product, or "surplus," left over. Unless the workers consume the entire net product, some of the surplus will be left over for employers as profits. So unless the workers are all-powerful and manage to keep all of the surplus, the ratio of the value of the net product left over for employers divided by the value of the goods capitalists advanced for the production process—that is, the rate of profit—must be positive, and greater than the rate of growth of NNP, which we stipulated by assumption to be zero. It can be shown that (1) there is a maximum rate of profit that corresponds to a wage rate of zero, (2) there is a maximum wage rate that gives workers the entire net product, which corresponds to a profit rate of zero, and (3) between these two extremes, the rate of profit is always positive and inversely related to the wage rate (Hahnel 2002, chapter 5). But all real-world capitalist economies must operate between the two extremes since workers would refuse to be workers in the first extreme, and capitalists would refuse to be capitalists in the second extreme. So profit rates would always be positive in capitalist economies even if the growth rate were zero. Analogous theorems for a growing economy prove that normal rates of profit will always exceed growth rates of NNP (Roemer 1981, chapter 4).

Since two of the most salient features of the global economy over the past thirty years are the escalating degradation of the natural environment and the increasing power of capitalists vis-à-vis workers on a world scale, the rate of growth of per capita NNW is declining relative to the rate of growth of NNP, and the normal rate of profit is rising compared to the rate of growth of NNP. Consequently, private owners of natural resources are not only discounting the benefits of leaving resources in the ground to be available for extraction in the future too much, but they have been overdiscounting to a greater and greater extent.

In sum, despite first impressions, the fact that individual humans are mortal while the human species is less so does not lead private owners to extract natural resources faster than can be ethically justified. However, because future markets are usually thinner and because the average rate of profit has been substantially higher than the rate of growth of net national economic welfare per capita, private owners of natural resources have been driven by competitive conditions to extract natural resources far faster than has been socially efficient for quite some time.

Notes

1. See Hunt and D'Arge (1973) for an eloquent criticism of the presumption that externalities are exceptions, rather than the rule.

2. People can, and sometimes do, vote with their feet by moving to states and localities that provide a mix of local public goods more to their liking. However, this does not solve the problem for public goods provided at the national level.

3. Most detergents call for a full cup per load of wash. Church & Dwight canceled a quarter-cup laundry detergent when consumer demand for this "green" product proved insufficient (Canning 1996).

Chapter 5

Where Mainstream Economics Dare Not Go

While the emphasis in Chapter 4 was on presenting insights from mainstream environmental economics clearly and in ways that help explain why the economic system puts the environment at risk, the emphasis in this chapter is on issues where mainstream economics provides little insight or obfuscates important causes of environmental distress. We explore why there is a counterproductive "growth imperative" in corporate capitalism, why salvation does not lie at the end of the environmental Kuznets curve, why the cure of Pigovian taxes is a pipe dream, and why the debate over "jobs versus the environment" is badly distorted.

The Growth Imperative: Beyond Assuming Conclusions

Mainstream economists have long regarded economic growth as something positive, and for many it continues to be their primary economic goal. On the other hand, many environmentalists increasingly view growth with suspicion, worrying that a *growth imperative* is at the bottom of our environmental problems. Growth is good . . . growth is bad . . . what are we to think?

As discussed in Chapter 4, when properly interpreted, mainstream analyses of perverse incentives created by externalities, public goods, open access to common pool resources, and rates of profit higher than a justifiable rate of time discount for environmental decisions all help explain important, systemic causes of environmental distress. But when people talk of a growth imperative, they usually mean something more than this. Unfortunately, the case that, above and beyond the perverse incentives discussed in the last chapter, an unhealthy growth imperative is putting the environment at risk is often not presented as well as it should be and therefore often fails to convince anyone who is skeptical to begin with.

What are we to make of statements like "On a finite planet infinite economic growth is impossible" from ecological economists? Or "Capitalism is a system that must continually expand. No-growth capitalism is an oxymoron" from Marxists? A good place to start is by asking precisely what it is that is growing, because often economists are not talking about the same thing at all.

Ecological Economics and Growth

As explained in Chapter 1, the growth of what ecological economists call *throughput* is limited. Supplies of different materials from the biosphere (and beneath) that we use as inputs in production are finite and limited, and the capacity of the biosphere (and the atmosphere above) to absorb material wastes is finite and limited as well. So infinite growth of throughput is impossible.

Nor is there any doubt that throughput has been growing mightily over the past few hundred years, and as a result we are nearing crucial limits on the ability of important components of throughput to continue to grow much longer. As mentioned in Chapter 1, contrary to what environmentalists believed in the early 1970s, the component of throughput that we seem to be exhausting most rapidly is the ability of the planet to absorb different kinds of physical waste products that are outputs of human economic activity, rather than the ability of the planet to continue to provide natural resources we use as inputs. Either way, there is strong evidence that we left the "frontier economy," where our impact on the natural environment was not yet significant, long ago, and we are now well into a "bull in the China closet economy" where we are a serious threat to ecosystem resilience, even if we have not yet reached a "spaceman" economy where every aspect of our natural environment must be meticulously managed.[1] Clearly we are pressing up against environmental limits to the growth of some components of throughput, and even if we are further away from reaching those limits than environmental alarmists claim, eventually if throughput continues to grow we will reach a limit.

However, *throughput is not gross domestic product* (GDP). And when mainstream economists talk about growth, they mean growth of GDP. As explained in Chapter 3, GDP is the *value* of final goods and services produced during a year. It is measured in dollars, not in the units we use to measure different kinds of physical matter throughput. "Real" GDP is measured in "constant" dollars in order to prevent inflation from deceiving us into thinking that the value of goods and services produced is rising when really all that is happening is the prices of goods and services are rising on average. As explained in Chapter 3, the process of correcting for inflation by using constant prices is inherently imperfect so that estimates of the rate of growth of real GDP depend arbitrarily on what base year is selected. But these complications are beside the point. The word *real* in front of GDP should not be taken to mean "physical" because it does not. The first question is: *Is it theoretically possible for real GDP to grow infinitely even though throughput cannot grow infinitely?* The answer is "yes." And that is the end of the all-too-facile claim that infinite growth is impossible on a finite planet, if what we are talking about growing is GDP.

Those who initially formulate an argument are often more careful than those who follow them. In this case, Herman Daly is aware of an important distinction, although his choice of words is partly responsible for the errors of his disciples. Daly acknowledges that "it is important to distinguish between the terms *growth* and *development*." He defines growth as "a *quantitative* increase in the scale of the physical dimensions of the economy, i.e., the rate of flow of matter and energy through the economy (from environment as raw material and back to the environment as waste), and the stock of human bodies and artifacts." Daly contrasts growth, so defined, to development, which he defines as the "*qualitative* improvement in the structure, design, and composition of physical stocks and flows, that result from greater human knowledge, both of technique and of purpose." He then concludes: "On a finite earth there are biophysical and ethicosocial limits to the growth of aggregate output, but there may not be any limits to development" (Daly 1995, 125; italics added).

Using Daly's definition of growth, infinite growth on a finite planet is impossible, as his disciples often quote him. However, Daly has defined growth in such a way that to all intents and purposes it is growth of throughput. It is certainly not growth of real GDP as defined by mainstream economists. The confusion arises where Daly draws a line between "quantitative" and "qualitative." When development is defined as something that is qualitative, it is easy to acknowledge that it may have no limits, whereas the growth that Daly defines as quantitative clearly must have limits as he has defined it. Since mainstream economists define GDP as something that is quantitative, and since many economists acknowledge that growth of GDP is not synonymous with economic development, which they also treat as a qualitative concept, it *appears* that Daly's definition of growth as something that is quantitative rather than qualitative must be the same as mainstream economists' definition of growth. But it is not. Nowhere in Daly's definitions of growth and development is there room for the *quantitative* concept, real GDP, which is what his opponents claim can, at least in theory, grow without limit.[2]

77

The phrase *aggregate output* adds to the confusion because almost everyone thinks of aggregate output in physical terms. As used by Daly, aggregate output is physical matter. As used by mainstream economists, aggregate output is an admittedly misleading phrase because it does give the impression that it is something measured in physical terms. But the fact is that for mainstream economists aggregate output is synonymous with real GDP, which, as we have seen, is a quantitative, aggregate value and not physical matter at all.[3]

The next question is: *Is it easy to imagine how real GDP could continue to grow even though throughput cannot?* Before we consider this question, let us clarify any ambiguity in the phrase *continue to grow*. Just how long are we talking about? At some point the solar system will no longer exist. Before that, planet Earth might well become as lifeless as Mars through nonhuman causes. But we generally assume that these endings are a long way off. Prominent founders of ecological economics such as Nicholas Georgescu-Roegen and Herman Daly have suggested that the second law of thermodynamics pro-vides a possible ending to our story that, unlike the end of our solar system, is worthy of consideration. This law states that the amount of energy available for work in a closed system necessarily decreases with use. This law is also known as the law of entropy, which is often stated as: In a closed system, if work is done, entropy necessarily increases. However, not only is the earth an open, not a closed system, since we get inputs of entropy-decreasing energy from the sun, but death by entropy would take place so far in the future that . . . what can I say? We should be so lucky as to last long enough to die from too much entropy![4]

Unfortunately, our problem is much more immediate. We are on track to render the biosphere uninhabitable long before entropy engulfs us. In any case, what "continue to grow" means in the question above is "can real GDP continue to grow long enough so the end comes from some other cause, not because an exhausted biosphere has stopped GDP from growing further." Now that we are clear about exactly what the question means, how do mainstream economists answer it? Most answer it in the affirmative, and many would add "no sweat" for emphasis.

Mainstream economists explain their answer by pointing out that the *value* of goods and particularly services people enjoy can increase even while the throughput used to produce them, and the throughput released as by-products in their production and consumption, do not increase and even decline. In the computer industry, throughput per unit of computing capacity has dropped dramatically since the 1940s. Suppose it had dropped by a factor of 10. This would mean that we could consume five times more computing capacity now than in 1940 while cutting throughput for computing services in half.

Many mainstream economists also answer yes because they believe that before we exhaust one kind of throughput, we can change production technologies to substitute a different input that is still plentiful or, if necessary, we can consume a different good or service instead. Sometimes called technological optimists by their critics, these mainstream economists point out that this is now the plan for energy inputs. We now know we must become carbon neutral before the end of the century in order to avoid risking cataclysmic climate change. That means those planning to prevent climate change believe it is possible to substitute renewable sources for fossil fuels before we run out of atmospheric storage space for greenhouse gases. Just as GDP can grow 10 percent a year without any increase in carbon emissions as long as carbon efficiency also grows at 10 percent a year, many mainstream economists argue this can be true for other kinds of throughput as well.

Instead of the above questions, however, what we need to be asking ourselves is this: *Is there something about our economic system that keeps us on a trajectory to produce the kinds and quantities of goods and services that will continue to increase throughput?* In other words, is there a growth imperative in our economic system that is environmentally unsustainable? In the words of Herman Daly, is there something about our economic system that generates *uneconomic growth*—growth that is environmentally destructive and fails to yield real economic development? If so, what are the causes of uneconomic growth, and what can be done to stop it? Of course, this is the question concerned environmentalists thought they were asking all along.

Marxism and Growth

Citing the master himself—"Accumulate, accumulate! That is Moses and the prophets!" (Marx [1867] 1967, 595)—Marxists have long argued that capitalism is nothing if it is not about accelerating economic growth. Whereas Marxists long emphasized what they called "internal contradictions" that render capitalist growth *economically* unsustainable,[5] some now argue that an even bigger problem arises when capitalism does sustain economic growth sufficiently to surpass critical environmental thresholds and become *environmentally* unsustainable. Four American Marxists who have written extensively on capitalism and the environment recently are James O'Connor (1998), John Bellamy Foster (1994, 2000, 2002, 2009), Joel Kovel (2003), and Paul Burkett (2006).

In a recent example, John Bellamy Foster and Fred Magdoff (2010) begin their essay "What Every Environmentalist Needs to Know About Capitalism" with an excellent summary of evidence indicating that we are experiencing a "planetary ecological crisis." They begin a subsequent section titled "Capitalism Is a System That Must Continually Expand" as follows: "No-growth capitalism is an oxymoron. . . . Capitalism's basic driving force and its whole reason for existence is the amassing of profits and wealth through the accumulation (savings and investment) process. It recognizes no limits to its own self-expansion." Foster and Magdoff go on to explain that because capitalism recognizes no limits to its self-expansion, environmental crises will continue to worsen until capitalism is replaced by socialism. We will consider system change in the conclusion of this book, but for now the question is whether the arguments offered by many Marxists that capitalist growth is *necessarily* incompatible with environmental limits are any more compelling than the reasons given by many ecological economists that infinite growth is impossible on a finite planet.

What Marx was at pains to explain was that capitalism drove capitalists relentlessly to appropriate and invest greater amounts of what he called *surplus value*. And just as mainstream economists do not measure the market value of goods and services produced in units of physical matter, Marx did not measure surplus value in units of physical matter either. Instead, he defined surplus value as the difference between the number of hours of labor needed to produce all goods and services minus the number of hours needed to produce the intermediate goods used up in the production process and the consumption goods purchased by the workers with their wages. In other words, the accumulation Marx referred to above is an accumulation of *hours* of labor expended, which he called exchange value, and the growth of surplus value is limited only by the total number of hours worked and by how many of those hours capitalists can manage to appropriate. Capitalist accumulation of surplus value is not necessarily limited by the availability of physical matter any more than the growth of GDP is.[6] Just because the planet has physical limits does not mean that capitalist accumulation of surplus value cannot increase indefinitely, any more than it means that the market value of goods and services produced, GDP, cannot increase indefinitely.

In conclusion, the claim that infinite growth of capitalist accumulation *of surplus value* is impossible on a finite planet is no more compelling than the claim that infinite growth *of GDP* is impossible on a finite planet. In both cases, those who make the claim, failing to realize that value is not matter, carelessly apply reasoning to value as if it were matter. Either conclusion may still be true, but would only follow if surplus value or GDP cannot grow *unless* throughput grows as well. Since this is precisely what is at dispute, and since neither facile argument addresses this issue, both ecological economists and Marxists who present the case that infinite growth is environmentally impossible in these ways are in effect guilty of assuming their conclusion.

However, this does not mean there is not an unhealthy and environmentally destructive growth imperative in today's capitalist economies and perhaps in any capitalist economy. It just means we must go beyond facile arguments that upon inspection prove not to be compelling.[7]

Biases Against Leisure and Collective Consumption

The problem is not that human beings have become more and more economically productive—which is what people *should* mean when they say that, at least in theory, human economic well-being can grow without limit. Infinite economic growth is a comment on the capacity of humans to continue to become more and more clever in how we go about our economic activities. It is an expression of faith that there is no inherent reason we cannot continue to satisfy our economic needs in an ever-shrinking portion of the twenty-four-hour day—if only we do not needlessly expand our economic needs! When understood in this way, the problem is not increasing productivity or an economic system that promotes energetic and creative pursuit of increasing economic productivity. Instead, the problem is (1) what we do with increases in our productivity, and (2) how we expand economic needs into desires whose satisfaction does little or nothing to increase economic well-being.

Why not more leisure? According to standard measures, productivity in the American economy increased fivefold between 1950 and 2000.[8] Yet the average American worked more hours per year at the end than at the midpoint of the century. This is amazing when you pause to think about it. It was this epiphany that led Juliet Schor (1992) to write her brilliant best seller, *The Overworked American*. In 1950 the United States was not a poor, underdeveloped economy where critical economic needs went unmet for an overwhelming portion of the population. It was the wealthiest country on the planet in 1950. Yet Americans "chose" to take 100 percent of their increase in productivity over the ensuing half-century in the form of increased consumption of material goods and services rather than in the form of increased leisure time. As a matter of fact, apparently not even that was sufficient as they dipped into their leisure time even deeper to get even more goodies! Had Americans instead taken all their increased productivity as leisure, their material standard of living would have been exactly the same in 2000 as it was in 1950, and the standard workweek, not workday, would have been eight hours instead of forty. In other words, working only one day a week instead of five, they could have been materially no worse off, and throughput would have been no greater in 2000 than in 1950. Clearly it is not endless increases in human economic productivity that threaten the environment.

Perhaps Americans chose to take so much of their increase in productivity in the form of consumption goods whose production and consumption required huge increases in throughput because they were unaware this was causing environmental problems. Maybe that old empty-world mind-set and mental lag time was the problem. No doubt this is partly true. Few Americans in the 1950s were aware that increasing throughput was rapidly creating a serious problem. And many since then who have come to environmental awareness have made a conscious choice to cut back on material consumption and place a higher priority on leisure. But however many people increased leisure at the expense of material consumption for environmental reasons, there were even more who worked more than before because on average Americans worked more hours per year in 2000 than they did in 1950. While environmental education and consciousness-raising no doubt help, it is hard to believe they suffice as a solution.

Perhaps the increase in productivity was captured mostly by people at the very top of the economic pyramid, leaving those at the bottom no choice but to keep working long hours to maintain their standard of living. Particularly during the last quarter of the century, when inequality of income and wealth accelerated dramatically, this explanation makes a great deal of sense. Since much of the productivity increase went to people who do not work at all, and little went to those who could work less, much of the productivity increase had to take the form of increases in consumption by the wealthy. In this case the solution is clear. We need to redistribute wealth and income to redirect productivity increases to those who have not already maxed out on leisure! But does the evidence suggest that once Americans reach middle-class status they typically begin to enjoy their productivity increases in the form of more leisure? After World War II, more of productivity increases took the form of longer vacations, earlier retirement, and more family leave in Western European countries than in the United States. But few would argue that *consumerism* among the middle classes has not flourished in Europe as well as in the United States, even if somewhat less so.

Concluding that Americans were overworked because they were overspent, Juliet Schor argued that the real question therefore was what drives them to consume more than they should. In *The Overspent American* (1998), Schor showed that middle-class Americans in particular were spending more than was fiscally prudent, more than they had in the past, and more than they realized. She fingered what she called *competitive consumption* as the chief culprit, placing herself in a heterodox tradition dating back to Thorstein Veblen that challenges how mainstream economic theory treats consumption. Veblen ([1899] 2008) identified the underlying mechanism as "invidious comparison," whereby people attempt to increase their stature relative to others in a social hierarchy. In capitalism he famously identified "conspicuous consumption" as a principle means of demonstrating status. The theory that people often seek social recognition, or status, rather than satisfaction of needs through consumption, later referred to as "keeping up with the Joneses," became the basis for James Duesenberry's "relative income hypothesis" in 1949.

Schor argued that two trends accelerated competitive consumption in the United States beginning in the mid-1970s. Most importantly, increasing income inequality put greater pressure on people, particularly those in the middle, to overspend to keep up with those toward the top. In an interview about her book published in the September 1998 issue of the *Multinational Monitor*, Schor explained:

> The lifestyle of the top 20 percent of the income distribution has come to be an important aspirational goal for people throughout society, many of whom earn far less than the roughly $100,000-a-year incomes that are represented by that group. That is part of how I understand the middle-class squeeze in this country: people in the $50,000 to $100,000 range, earning what in an earlier time would have been a comfortable income, now feel squeezed, as if they don't have enough, as if they are barely making it. And these are the people who have taken on the biggest increases in consumer debt in recent years and are feeling the pressure to upscale.

The second trend Schor identified was the increasing importance of television in defining status hierarchies in a society where "people know each other less and know television characters more." After controlling for other factors, she found that people who watch TV more spend more, and she hypothesized that this had more to do with the nature of the shows advertisers were paying for than with the advertising itself. "TV mainly shows people in the top 20 percent of the income distribution. A family that is supposed to be an ordinary middle-class family on TV has a six-figure lifestyle. TV inflates people's perceptions of what is normal and raises their consumption aspirations."

Stimulated to further investigation by Schor's book, sociologists have since offered competing hypotheses about why Americans do not take more of their productivity gains as leisure. In particular, researchers have concluded that time spent in work is not a voluntary decision by employees but is instead constrained by the demands of employers.[9] Recent research also suggests that increases in average income seem to have little positive effect on how happy people are on average, while increases in income inequality have a negative effect on most people's sense of well-being.[10] Many sociologists, environmentalists, and progressives, but few mainstream economists, now see a tragicomedy unfolding: A social species, hard-driven to compete for status in a hierarchical society, is fast becoming like the proverbial lemmings, trapped in an economy where the primary means of demonstrating social status is through competitive consumption that yields diminishing aggregate benefits even as it accelerates destruction of the environment we depend upon.

Why not more collective consumption? While productivity increases taken as leisure put far less strain on the environment, as people who have calculated their *ecological footprint* know, not all consumption is created equal as far as the environment is concerned.[11] Not only does eating a pound of hamburger tread more heavily on the environment than eating a pound of tofu, but individual consumption is more environmentally damaging than collective consumption, dollar for dollar.[12] So the problem is not only that we take too little of our productivity increases as leisure and too much as consumption; it is compounded by the fact that we engage in too much individual consumption and too little collective consumption.

As explained in Chapter 4, market economies predictably undersupply public goods because market demand for public goods grossly underrepresents their true social benefit due to the free-rider problem. Sometimes the inefficiency is so great that, in order to prevent it, we substitute an entirely different decision mechanism for the market. For example, no market economy leaves decisions about national defense to the market system because if it did there would be very little national defense, if any. Instead, governments supply the demand for defense spending that the market will not. But special interventions are always limited in number, leaving uncorrected many less striking inefficiencies in public good provision in market economies. Therefore, not only in a theoretical pure market system, but also in real-world market economies where some corrective action is taken, a perverse bias in favor of private over collective consumption remains. This bias generates an efficiency loss regardless of any environmental issues. However, because collective consumption is, on average, less environmentally damaging than individual consumption, this bias is also part of the reason we fail to use our productivity increases in ways that minimize throughput. Moreover, as explained below, there is every reason to expect this efficiency loss to grow over time once we recognize that people's preferences are endogenous to some degree.

Competition and Absentee Ownership

Executive officers of corporations whose stock is publicly owned—which actually means privately owned by absentee owners—have a legally binding fiduciary responsibility to maximize profits. Managers who fail to do so are likely to be dismissed by shareholders whose only interest is the size of their dividends and the market value of their shares. And finally, corporations that fall behind in the race to maximize profits will be replaced by more successful corporations as financial markets favor more profitable firms. In sum, competition and absentee ownership will relentlessly enforce profit maximization as the decision-making criterion in private enterprise market economies. It was Adam

Smith, not Karl Marx, who taught us that "it is not from the benevolence of the butcher, the brewer, or the baker that we expect our dinner, but from their regard to their own interest" ([1776] 1999, chapter 2). The question is not if the economic system is *driven* like no economic system before it. The question is not if the system is soulless. Smith knew that production is for profit and not for use in capitalist economies long before Marx was born. Smith knew capitalism for the heartless creature it is, but he argued that it serves us well nonetheless.

However, Adam Smith was unaware of many of the perverse incentives the system contains. Nor did he have before him the mounting evidence available to us that crucial ecosystems have been compromised. The question for us today, who do understand the perverse incentives and can see the environmental damage they have wrought, is whether our situation is all the more precarious because the system is designed to relentlessly follow a single rule, literally, come hell or high water. Those who make the crucial decisions about what we produce and how we produce it have been systematically rendered powerless to exercise discretionary judgment no matter how damaging the consequences of maximizing profits prove to be. And because we have been taught to defend the rule of profit maximization as our great benefactor against all detractors, timely reform becomes more difficult and therefore less likely.

The fact that the economic system is driven is not the problem per se. If the system were driven to maximize economic progress with regard to efficacy, equity, and economic democracy; if it were driven to achieve intergenerational equity; if it were driven to achieve social as well as environmental and economic sustainability, that would not be a problem but a godsend. It is not even necessarily a problem that the system is driven single-mindedly to maximize something that has nothing to do with our real goals if it were, without intending to do so, truly maximizing economic and social progress along all the dimensions we have identified as being worthy and important. The problem is that single-mindedly maximizing profits does not coincide with achieving all our goals and is, in fact, highly detrimental to achieving some of our most important goals, environmental sustainability among them. It is in this context that the single-minded, relentless energy of the system is part of the problem. We are like a racer who is programmed to run fast, but prone to racing off in a wrong direction. The problem is that we are running in the wrong direction, not our speed per se. But given the fact that we are running in the wrong direction, running fast does takes us farther afield and therefore is problematic as well.[13]

How Endogenous Preferences Matter

Mainstream economics always puts the blame on consumers for any problem regarding what the economy produces because it presumes that in

85

market economies producers will simply, only, and always supply whatever consumers want.[14] If developers build McMansions in what used to be farm fields, it is because that is what new homeowners and farmers want. Mainstream economics even has a name for this—*consumer sovereignty*. It is true that profit-maximizing corporations will not continue to produce goods and services they cannot sell. But this does not mean that consumers are the "sovereign" overlords over what is produced in private enterprise market systems.

First of all, as has often been pointed out, consumer sovereignty is a strange notion of economic democracy. Democracy usually means that everyone gets the same vote, or if some are much more affected by a particular decision than others, democratic "self-management" might mean voting in proportion to the degree one is affected.[15] But in market economies consumers get as many votes for the mix of products that will be produced as they have dollars to vote with. Unless we assume that the rich are affected more by the mix of goods the economy produces than the poor are, this is a very undemocratic election indeed. Even if consumers as a whole were sovereign, rich consumers are clearly "more sovereign" than poor ones.

Second, it is naive to deny that giant corporations have both an incentive and the capacity to influence consumers' desires considerably. Not all products are equally profitable, and businesses understand that steering consumers toward goods with higher profit margins is important to their bottom line even if mainstream economic theory does not.[16] Marketing would not be the most popular major in business schools and U.S. businesses would not spend over $250 billion a year on advertising if businesses did not want to influence what consumers buy or if consumers were beyond their influence and truly sovereign. And one thing that businesses do not want consumers to buy when their productivity as workers increases is "nothing"—because they choose to consume more leisure instead. "Nothing" is not at the top of the list of products with high profit margins that businesses have for sale.

However, there is a third reason that consumer sovereignty falls far short of what is advertised. As explained in Chapter 4, while markets minimize the transaction costs associated with expressing desires for individual consumption, they do not provide an institutional framework that helps people express their desires for collective consumption as easily, and they fail to register external effects on parties other than the buyer and seller. While market enthusiasts praise markets for allowing consumers to choose among different private goods, they fail to point out how markets infringe on consumer sovereignty by tilting the playing field in favor of private goods and against public goods, and in favor of private goods whose production or consumption generates negative external effects and against private goods whose production or consumption has positive external effects. This is a more subtle way to undermine consumer sovereignty than advertising, but it is no less important.

Once we recognize that markets are not neutral institutions that register different categories of preferences without prejudice, once we realize that markets do not provide an even playing field for public and private goods or for goods with associated positive and negative externalities, an interesting question arises regarding how people will respond to these *biases*. As we have seen, mainstream economic theory teaches that markets make it more difficult for people to acquire environmental protection and preservation than it should be and cheaper for people to buy goods whose production or consumption generates pollution than it should be. Mainstream theory also teaches that under free access it is easier for people to exploit common pool resources than it should be. If some things are harder to obtain or more expensive than they should be, while other things are easier to obtain or less expensive than they should be, how will people respond?

Anyone who has studied the substitution effect in a microeconomics class will recall that when price signals are wrong, they lead people who are attempting to maximize their satisfaction, given the preferences they have, to consume too little of things that are more expensive than they should be and too much of things that are less expensive than they should be. This means we will experience a degree of inefficiency whenever prices diverge from their true social opportunity costs. However, while this is where mainstream theory stops, this may not be the end of the story if people's preferences are not fixed, or what economists call *exogenous*. If instead people's preferences can change over time in ways they have some influence over—that is, if their preferences are *endogenous*—why would people not try to diminish their preference for things for which they are consistently charged more than their true social cost, and increase their preference for things that are cheaper than they should be?

A central tenet of evolutionary economics is that people's preferences do not fall from the sky but are instead formed and molded by social institutions, including our major economic institutions. Thorstein Veblen's famous caricature of the "hedonic calculus" was intended to drive this point home. The conviction that preferences and values are *formed* by social processes requiring analysis, and therefore should not be treated merely as *givens*, has played a central role in the contributions of luminaries like Gunnar Myrdal, John Kenneth Galbraith, and John Dewey to disparate fields of economic study.

In *Quiet Revolution in Welfare Economics* (1990), Michael Albert and I developed a formal model suitable to exploring the predictable consequences of what happens when economic institutions create biases in the terms upon which goods or services are made available when people's preferences are endogenous to some extent.[17] Recognizing that people's *environmental preferences* are influenced not only by information, but also by biases in our basic economic institutions deepens our understanding of why the environment remains at risk despite tremendous improvements in environmental education.

A model of endogenous preferences implies there are *two* effects of individual choice. (1) The *preference fulfillment effect* means that when an individual chooses a particular consumption/work bundle today, she will fulfill her present preferences to a greater or lesser extent. That is the effect of the choice on well-being in the present. (2) The *preference development effect* means that by choosing a particular consumption/work bundle today, to some extent the individual will affect the human characteristics she develops for the future. Since those future characteristics "parameterize" her future utility functions, changes in future characteristics will change the amount of satisfaction or utility she will receive from any given consumption/work bundle in the future. Any consequent change in well-being that results is the effect of today's choice of a consumption/work bundle on the individual's well-being in the future. Individual rationality requires considering *both* the preference fulfillment effect *and* the preference development effect on one's overall well-being when choosing consumption/work bundles in all time periods.

Once we have a model of endogenous preferences capable of tracking the preference development effects as well as preference fulfillment effects of people's choices, what remains is a way to model institutional pressures or biases. As already explained, particular institutions can be thought of as lowering the transaction costs of engaging in particular kinds of activities. For example, the transaction costs for nonfarmers of acquiring potatoes to consume are lowered by the existence of a market for potatoes. And the transaction costs of loaning savings are lowered by the existence of banks. On the other hand, the transaction costs of engaging in some activities remain high for lack of a facilitating institution. For example, in Chapter 6 we discover that multiple victims of pollution face free-rider problems when confronting a polluter in a free market environment. As a result, multiple victims of pollution often opt not to negotiate with polluters regarding pollution reductions because the transaction costs for individual victims are too high. So the transaction costs of coordinating pollution reduction are high in the absence of an appropriate facilitating institution, while the transaction costs of consuming potatoes and saving are lowered by the facilitating institutions of potato markets and banks. When we consider the entire set of economic institutions that constitute an economy, we can think of them as lowering the transaction costs for some kinds of activities or behaviors relative to the transaction costs of other kinds of activities or behaviors.

Through their effects on transaction costs, institutions affect the terms of availability of different kinds of economic activities that individuals choose from, which we can model as follows: If a set of economic institutions charges individuals who engage in an activity the *true* social cost of carrying out that activity, we say there is *no bias* in how the economic institutions make that activity available to people. But if a set of institutions charges those who choose an activity *more* than the true social cost for that activity, we say those institutions have a *bias against* that particular activity. And if a set of institutions charges *less* than the true social cost for an activity, we say those institutions have a *bias in favor* of that activity. The advantage of rigorous models is that they make it possible to prove theorems like the two below that illustrate the logical consequences of assumptions that may not be apparent.

Theorem 1: Snowballing inefficiency: In an economy that contains a bias in the relative terms of supply of two economic activities, and in which people have perfect knowledge about their endogenous preferences, (1) the divergence from the optimal, or efficient outcome will be greater than indicated by traditional welfare theory, which treats preferences as exogenous; and (2) the divergence from optimality will increase, or "snowball" over time.[18]

Theorem 1 is relevant to why the environment is increasingly at greater risk than mainstream economic theory leads us to expect because markets are biased in favor of goods whose production or consumption pollutes more, compared to those that pollute less; because markets are biased in favor of individual consumption, which generates more throughput as compared to collective consumption, which generates less; because markets are biased against environmental protection and pollution reduction because these are both public goods; and finally, because free access to common pool resources creates a bias in favor of their exploitation as compared to any procedure that charges users for the true social cost of using the common pool resource, which includes the negative effect their use has on other users. What theorem 1 tells us is to expect more pollution, less environmental protection, and more overexploitation than traditional economic theory predicts. But it also tells us something more disturbing. It tells us to expect the degree or extent of overpollution, underprotection, and overexploitation to grow over time.

While the proof of theorem 1 is not straightforward, the intuition behind the theorem is. Based on experience, individuals foresee the bias in the relative conditions of availability of activity choices they will face in the future. Recognizing that they can mold their preferences to some extent away from desiring activities for which they will be overcharged and toward activities for which they will be undercharged, rational individuals will take into account both the preference development effect as well as the preference fulfillment effect of their present activity choices. They thus select present activities

89

that tend to generate future human characteristics that in turn support future preference structures that permit them to attain greater future satisfaction than had they not adjusted their human characteristic trajectories appropriately. When faced with an overcharge in the future period, rational individuals will lower the quantity demanded to some extent simply by moving up along their future demand curve when they arrive in the future. But when afforded the opportunity to shift their future demand curve as well, rational individuals with endogenous preferences will avail themselves of a second means of adjusting to the biased conditions of availability: They will make consumption/work choices in the present that shift their future individual demand curve downward for the good for which they will be overcharged in the future.

Unfortunately, the effect of all individuals making these individually rational adjustments is to shift the future market demand curve downward for activities for which individuals are overcharged as compared to what it would have been in absence of such individually rational preference adjustments. In an economy in which production responds to market demand, this implies that the production of goods for which individuals are overcharged will be even less than had individuals not adjusted their preferences. As a result, the underproduction and consequent misallocation of scarce productive resources that would have occurred in any event due to the overcharge are *aggravated* by the process of rational individual adjustment. Individuals mold themselves to better cope with a bias in the economy, but the collective result is to move society farther away from the optimal production program than had people not engaged in individually rational preference adjustments. In other words, when people act in an individually rational way and take the preference development effects of their choices into account along with the preference fulfillment effects, their behavior is socially irrational because it generates a more inefficient use of society's scarce productive resources than would have occurred had people not adjusted their preferences in light of the bias in the economy. The more time people have to adjust, the greater the inefficiency becomes.

A second theorem predicts that environmental educators face a harder uphill battle than they may realize when they encourage people to develop stronger preferences for environmental protection and amenities based on a better understanding of their value.

Theorem 2: Warped human development: In an economy that contains a bias in the relative terms of supply of two economic activities, and in which people have perfect knowledge about their endogenous preferences, (1) individual human development patterns and the preferences that depend on them will be "warped" in a manner that can be rigorously defined; and (2) the "warping" will increase, or "snowball" over time.[19]

Theorem 2 reveals a principle mechanism through which institutional biases affect human characteristics and therefore preferences. When a set of economic institutions creates a bias in the terms on which different activities are available to people, it is individually rational for people to choose consumption/work activities that are different from those they would have chosen had there been no bias. Since different consumption/work choices lead people to develop different human characteristics and therefore preferences, the institutional bias has promoted development of some kinds of human characteristics and preferences at the expense of others.

It is appropriate to call this individual adjustment, or human self-molding process, "self-warping" even though we recognize it to be individually rational and caused by institutional bias. Individuals who did not make preference adjustments to economic biases would be irrational in the sense of failing to maximize personal well-being under the biased conditions of supply they face. However, the adjustments they engage in are *self-warping* in the sense that (1) they are freely and rationally chosen, but (2) nonetheless diverge from an optimal human development trajectory that is physically possible and would have afforded the individual greater well-being as she defines it.

So the problem is not only that people are unaware of all the benefits environmental protection brings and that therefore more education is required. The problem is also that it is rational in market economies for people to dampen their preference for leisure, which pollutes less, and enhance their preference for consumption, which pollutes more; to enhance their preferences for private goods, which pollute more, and dampen their preferences for public goods, which pollute less; to enhance their preferences for those private goods that cause more pollution and dampen their preferences for those private goods that cause less pollution; and to enhance their capacities to exploit common pool resources where access is unrestricted. The conclusion that the divergence from the optimal production program (theorem 1) and the rational self-warping of human characteristics and preferences (theorem 2) increase or snowball over time follows directly since the more time people have to adjust, the greater the self-warping and economic inefficiency that results will become.

Why the Kuznets Curve Will Not Save the Day

Simon Kuznets had even less to do with the "environmental Kuznets curve" than Jean-Baptiste Say did with "Say's Law"—whose principle architect was David Ricardo. In 1955 Kuznets published an article on the relationship between per capita income and income inequality. Measuring income inequality as the dependent variable on the vertical axis and per capita income as the independent variable on the horizontal axis, he found an empirical relationship that took the form of an inverted U. In other words, as per capita income grew, income inequality at first increased, but at some point the relationship between economic growth and inequality reversed, after which increasing per capita income was associated with a reduction in income inequality. Kuznets speculated about what might explain the inverted U-shaped relationship he had discovered in the data, and that was that. His article had nothing to do with the environment whatsoever, but the inverted U-shaped graph had caught the eye of economists.

Decades later, other economists, interested in what explains how much pollution economies generate, began with the same empirical approach Kuznets had used when studying income inequality (Grossman and Krueger 1995; Selden and Daquing 1994; Shafik 1994). When these economists plotted pollution of different kinds on the vertical axis and per capita income on the horizontal axis, they also found an empirical relationship that took the shape of an inverted U, suggesting an initial positive relationship between economic growth and pollution that at some point reversed, after which higher per capita income was associated with lower levels of pollution. *Their* inverted U-shaped curve is the famous, misnamed "environmental Kuznets curve," and these and many more economists have been speculating about how robust the empirical finding is and how to explain it ever since.

Just as proponents of trickle-down economics used Kuznets' own inverted U-shaped curve to argue against the need for policies designed to reduce economic inequality, others have cited the environmental Kuznets curve as evidence that environmental problems are merely a transitional phenomenon that economic growth will eventually resolve. And just as Kuznets cautioned against interpreting his findings as evidence that we could simply grow our way out of inequality, Grossman and Krueger, for example, issued a similar warning about growth and the environment, saying "there is no reason to believe the process is an automatic one" and opining that only when higher income "induced" a policy response did higher income reduce pollution (1995, 371). However, before evaluating the debate over the environmental Kuznets curve, it is worth considering a related equation that ecological economists often use to explain why they believe the relationship between growth and pollution is exactly the opposite of what the environmental Kuznets curve suggests it is.

Ecological economists like to begin with the equation $I = PAT$, where I stands for environmental *impact* (which ecological economists think of as throughput), P stands for *population*, A stands for *affluence* (which ecological economists define as per capita consumption, but we can think of as per capita income for purposes of comparison with the environmental Kuznets curve), and T stands for *technology*, meaning new technologies that increase "throughput efficiency," such as increases in "energy efficiency." In terms of growth rates, the $I = PAT$ equation says that throughput will grow at a rate equal to the sum of the population growth rate and the rate of growth of per capita GDP, minus the rate of growth of throughput efficiency. Ecological economists conclude that increasing the rate of growth of GDP per capita clearly has a positive effect on the rate of growth of throughput, or pollution, which is the component of throughput that those who study the Kuznets curve focus on.

This conclusion is beyond dispute, provided we add a phrase economists often use, *ceteris paribus*, which means holding all other things equal. But those who study the Kuznets curve understand this point because they acknowledge that what they call the *scale effect* of increasing per capita income increases pollution. However, the Kuznets curve literature also considers what they call the *composition effect* and the *technology effect* of increasing per capita GDP. When per capita income increases, the composition of output shifts between sectors that may differ in their pollution intensity. For example, the service sector may grow relative to the manufacturing sector, which would lower the pollution intensity of output. Or when per capita GDP increases, sectors may adopt new technologies because they conserve resources and lower costs or because some antipollution policy induces them to do so. So how does the Kuznets curve with its scale effect, composition effect, and technology effect really differ from $I = PAT$?

They do not differ regarding some key factors. According to $I = PAT$, throughput (pollution) will increase or decrease depending on whether the sum of the rates of growth of population and per capita income are higher or lower than the rate of growth of throughput (pollution) decreasing technological changes of one kind or another. According to the Kuznets curve, pollution (throughput) will increase or decrease depending on whether the scale effect is larger or smaller than the sum of the composition effect and the technology effect. But this does not mean there are not subtle differences between the two treatments.

If they are calculating properly, those who estimate environmental Kuznets curves for different categories of pollution measure pollution levels per capita, not simply pollution levels on their vertical axis. In that case they have implicitly held the P variable in $I = PAT$ constant. Environmentalists may find this misleading and therefore objectionable since population growth does impact the environment, *ceteris paribus*. But one could easily argue that the negative impact of population growth is taken for granted and certainly not disputed by those who think in terms of the environmental Kuznets curve. More importantly, the Kuznets curve analysis treats the composition and technology effects as associated with growth of GDP per capita. The thinking suggested is: as GDP per capita grows, this *causes* one bad thing to happen to the environment (the scale effect), but two good things to happen to the environment (the composition and technology effects.) The $I = PAT$ analysis, on the other hand, treats the good technology effect as distinct and independent from the bad scale effect. In this case, the thinking is: when GDP per capita grows, that is bad for the environment, whereas when technology becomes more throughput-efficient, that is good for the environment. Each effect is independent of the other. The Kuznets framework suggests that you can *only* lower T by raising A, whereas the I-PAT framework suggests that T can be lowered while holding A constant or even while reducing A.

So where does all this leave us? I suspect not much farther along than we were already. As far as the environment is concerned, only throughput matters. Even if we cannot measure aggregate throughput quantitatively, we can measure its important components quite well. The question is what causes helpful composition and technology effects and how fast we can enhance them—because growth of GDP per capita will increase throughput unless these effects are strong enough to offset the negative effects on the environment.

More recent empirical work has added two new findings of interest. James Boyce and Mariano Torras (2002) added several variables to the data used by Grossman and Krueger. They included a GINI coefficient to measure the degree of income inequality in a country, the literacy rate, and also the cube of per capita income to test for the possibility that the environmental Kuznets curve might start to rise again when GDP per capita passes a second threshold, taking on a sideways S-shape rather than simply an inverted U-shape. Boyce and Torras found that higher income inequality and lower literacy rates were strongly associated with higher levels of pollution, particularly in less developed countries, and that inclusion of these "power" variables diminished the significance of the per capita income coefficient. They also found that for some of the seven pollutants they studied, the cubic term was significant, indicating that after GDP per capita reaches a high level, pollution levels may well begin to rise again as GDP per capita rises further, casting further doubt on the hypothesis that countries can solve environmental problems simply by growing. Instead, Boyce and Torras conclude: "We believe, like Grossman and Krueger, that citizen demand and 'vigilance and advocacy' are often critical in inducing policies and technological changes which reduce pollution. However, we do not regard these as simple functions of average income. . . . We hypothesize that more equitable distributions of power tend, *ceteris paribus*, to result in better environmental quality. Our regression results are generally consistent with this hypothesis" (61).

How High Pigovian Taxes?

As explained in Chapter 4, early in the twentieth century A.C. Pigou proved that when there are negative external effects in a market, a corrective tax is required to eliminate the inefficiency, and when there are positive externalities, a corrective subsidy is indicated. Moreover, Pigou also taught us that the corrective tax or subsidy should be set equal to the magnitude of the external effect to fully correct for inefficiencies. So in theory we have long known how to use what are now called effluent taxes, green taxes, or pollution taxes, but are really just good old Pigovian taxes, to correct for inefficient environmental degradation from pollution.

But here is the rub: how are we to know what the size of the external effect is and therefore how high to set the tax? It is hard to calculate how high corrective Pigovian taxes and subsidies should be because there are no convenient or reliable procedures in market economies for estimating the magnitude of external effects. In this crucial regard, the market offers no assistance whatsoever because it does not contain what we might call a "pollution-damage-revealing mechanism."[20] As a matter of fact, as we discovered in Chapter 2, the problem arises precisely because the market ignores the effects on external parties entirely, so in market economies we are forced to resort to very imperfect and unsatisfying measures to try to estimate the magnitude of environmental damages and benefits. This situation hardly breeds confidence in the accuracy of the estimates economists come up with; rather, it provides interested parties with strong incentives and ample opportunities to object to estimates that disadvantage them and to finance alternative studies that yield widely different results. So the first problem with Pigovian taxes is that it is difficult to know how high to set a Pigovian tax or subsidy. The only thing we can predict with certainty is that interested parties will come up with very different estimates and be willing to devote a great deal of time, energy, and money to challenging each other's results.

The second problem is that because they are unevenly dispersed throughout the industrial matrix, the task of correcting the entire price system for the *direct and indirect* effects of externalities using Pigovian taxes and subsidies is much more daunting. Even if the external effects of producing or consuming a particular good were estimated accurately, if the external effects of producing or consuming goods that enter into the production of the good in question are not also accurate, the *theory of the second* best warns us that the Pigovian tax we place on the good in question may move us further away from an efficient use of our productive resources rather than closer. In other words, the improbability of setting Pigovian taxes correctly in many interconnected markets means it may not even be worthwhile trying to set the tax correctly in any individual market even if we could.

Finally, in the real world, where private interests and power take precedence over economic efficiency, the beneficiaries of accurate corrective taxes are all too often dispersed and powerless compared to those who would be harmed by an accurate corrective tax. As Mancur Olson explained in *The Logic of Collective Action* (1965), this makes it very unlikely that full Pigovian correctives would be enacted in most cases, even if they could be accurately calculated. More often than not, we will end up with no Pigovian tax or subsidy, and in the rare cases where we impose one it will predictably be much lower than necessary.

Jobs Versus the Environment Is Not the Problem

In the 1992 presidential campaign, President George H.W. Bush adamantly opposed the plan of candidate Bill Clinton to protect substantial tracts of old-growth timber on federal lands in the Pacific Northwest, claiming: "We'll be up to our neck in owls, and every mill worker will be out a job." Bush also justified his administration's opposition to a strong international agreement to reduce greenhouse gas emissions at the Earth Summit in Rio de Janeiro in 1992 as "protecting American jobs from environmental extremists." On the eve of negotiations in Kyoto in 1997, the U.S. Senate passed a resolution declaring that any treaty that did not require developing countries to adhere to the same timetable for greenhouse gas reductions as the industrialized countries was not acceptable. The vote was an astonishing 95 to 0 as a parade of Republican and Democratic senators predicted that the Kyoto treaty, which had been negotiated by the delegation President Clinton sent to Berlin in 1996, would cost between 1 and 2 million jobs and shut down manufacturing plants across the country. Not a single Democratic senator dared to challenge these claims even though the White House submitted a brief to the Senate explaining why it estimated that employment impacts from the Kyoto Protocol would be negligible. In the midst of the battle over amendments to the Clean Air Act in 1990, the *Wall Street Journal* reported that one out of three respondents in a national poll said that they personally felt they were likely to lose their job as a result of environmental regulation. Clearly not just politicians, but many citizens also believe the myth that protecting the environment is a threat to their jobs.

And it is a myth. Economists identify three kinds of unemployment: cyclical unemployment, frictional unemployment, and structural unemployment. Stricter environmental standards have nothing to do with cyclical unemployment, which is due to insufficient demand for goods and services in general and must be addressed by appropriate expansionary fiscal and monetary policies. Stricter environmental standards also have nothing to do with frictional unemployment, which results when people change jobs and spend a little time unemployed in between. However, stricter environmental standards do change the mix of goods and services produced and the technologies used to produce them and thus *can* cause structural unemployment, which results when those out of work do not have the skills necessary for the available jobs, or live where available jobs are located How serious is this threat?

First, we need to understand what is being accomplished by raising environmental standards at the price of creating some structural unemployment. Before the Clean Air Act tightened standards on sulfur dioxide emissions from power plants, the U.S. economy was producing an inefficient mix of goods and services and going about it in inefficient ways. We were producing too much electricity by burning too much high-sulfur coal. When the Clean Air Act put a price on sulfur dioxide emissions in 1990, economic efficiency was increased in four ways. The biggest efficiency gain came in the form of switching from high-sulfur coal mined mostly in eastern coalfields to coal with less sulfur mined principally in the West. A smaller efficiency gain came when a few electric utilities installed scrubbers in their smokestacks that captured not only sulfur dioxide before it was released but other harmful toxins as well. A less immediate efficiency gain came when a few utilities planned to eventually replace coal-fired plants with plants burning cleaner fossil fuels and to reconfigure grids to allow for greater use of renewable energy sources like wind power. And finally, to the extent that electricity prices became higher than they would have been otherwise, causing households and businesses to reduce energy consumption, the economy became more efficient for that reason as well.[21]

In other words, any structural unemployment caused by improving environmental standards is part of making the economy more efficient by moving resources, including labor, out of activities where the costs outweigh the benefits into activities where the benefits outweigh the costs when all the costs and benefits are correctly accounted for. So what we are talking about are short-run transition costs to achieve long-run efficiency gains. As long as the efficiency gains from the new, more efficient production mix and technologies are greater than the transition costs of getting there, it is in society's interest to make the change. In sum, the first problem is that those who argue against stricter environmental standards because they will cause structural unemployment seldom bother to point out that these standards create a substantial, permanent efficiency gain or that the unemployment is transitional and temporary.

The second problem is that those who wield the job loss argument against stricter environmental standards[22] seldom apply the same argument against other sources of structural unemployment where the argument is far more compelling. Tightening environmental standards may cause some structural unemployment, but it is by far the least important source of structural unemployment in the U.S. economy. Empirical evidence indicates that the amount of structural unemployment caused by efforts to better protect the environment in the United States over the past two decades is insignificant compared to the amount of structural unemployment caused by trade and capital liberalization, technological change, and corporate downsizing. Eban Goodstein (1999, chapter 3) estimates that during the 1990s more than 2 million workers per year were laid off due to import competition, shifts in demand, or corporate downsizing, while only 2,000 workers per year lost jobs due to environmental regulations.

Goodstein also debunks the myth that environmental regulations play a significant role in the relocation of new manufacturing investment overseas. So-called free trade agreements like the North American Free Trade Agreement (NAFTA), which are actually more about capital liberalization than trade liberalization, have encouraged firms to invest abroad, and this has cost U.S. workers millions of jobs. But all studies confirm that these firms did not relocate because of lax environmental regulations abroad, as much as environmentalists feared this might be the case. Goodstein explains that even in highly regulated industries, regulatory costs are still only a small percentage of total costs and therefore provide little incentive to relocate. Labor costs, on the other hand, are a significant portion of total costs, particularly for manufacturing industries, which is why multinational manufacturing firms have been relocating abroad where wages and labor standards are much lower. Put differently, the evidence does not suggest that lowering our environmental standards would be a good strategy for trying to bring jobs back to the United States!

Third, we need to ask if there are ways to share more equitably the transition costs of whatever structural unemployment stricter environmental standards do create. Pretending there are no transition costs when, in fact, there are, and showing little concern over who is paying those costs when the costs are distributed very unfairly, are mistakes many environmental organizations have made in the past. Letting the chips fall where they may is not only unfair; it is also unnecessary and politically self-defeating. There are policies that can relieve coal miners in West Virginia from bearing the cost of making the U.S. energy sector more efficient and placate their opposition to legislation like the Clean Air Act and climate bills, as well as to treaties like the Kyoto Protocol. The problem is that *readjustment assistance* and *economic conversion* policies are very underdeveloped in the United States compared to elsewhere.

In Sweden, victims of structural unemployment receive unemployment compensation that is far more generous than in the United States and lasts longer, when necessary. Laid-off workers also receive free retraining and education carefully tailored to suit them for employment in industries and occupations where employment is growing. And if moving to a different part of Sweden is necessary, relocation expenses are covered as well. Needless to say, Swedish workers and labor unions show little hostility to efficiency-enhancing changes in the mix of outputs produced in Sweden or the technologies and skills used to make them. In comparison, study after study has demonstrated that the underfunded, short-term approach to training under the U.S. Job Training Partnership Act (JTPA) has practically no positive impact on raising the earnings profiles of its graduates. But instead of dismissing programs like JTPA and the "Jobs in the Woods" program, aimed at providing living-wage jobs in forest restoration in the Northwest, what is needed is to increase their funding and competence. After all, there is every reason to believe they can be successful. By definition all the participants have already demonstrated that they are fully capable of doing hard, productive, steady work. That is the kind of selection bias any educator would give her right arm for!

Goodstein (1999) takes up the two worst cases of "environmental unemployment" in Chapter 4 of his excellent book. Considering timber workers versus old-growth forests in the Pacific Northwest and coal miners versus clean air in the southern Appalachians, he estimates that the number of direct layoffs was less than 10,000 and was spread out over several years and several states. As Goodstein points out that number is dwarfed by even one moderate corporate downsizing. But the important point is this is not a lot of people to "make whole," and when victims of direct layoffs are adequately taken care of, the number who are adversely affected indirectly shrinks dramatically as well.

For decades the U.S. labor movement has predictably lobbied for expanding and improving readjustment assistance programs. The problem is that it has received little support from other political circles. That is now changing as more and more environmental and labor leaders realize they can both accomplish more of their goals by working together. The unlikely sight of teamsters marching arm in arm with environmentalists in sea-turtle costumes at the demonstrations against the World Trade Organization in Seattle in 1999 has blossomed into the labor-environmental Apollo Alliance.

While adjustment assistance is an important palliative, the long-run cure for structural unemployment of any kind is a conversion program. The only reason it is no longer efficient for people to engage in their traditional line of work is because there is some other kind of work where they would be more socially useful. Creating whatever those industries of the future are at the same that declining industries are phasing out, and facilitating the movement of human resources from one to the other, is the way to minimize structural unemployment and its social costs as well as distribute those costs more fairly. While location may be crucial in real estate, timing is crucial in responding to structural unemployment. We need to be proactive about creating the new industries with new jobs as well as retraining the unemployed.

Notes

1. The metaphors of a frontier, bull in the China closet, and spaceman economy we owe to ecological economist Kenneth Boulding (1966). Along with important concepts such as empty-world and full-world mind-sets and throughput, these are all extremely helpful in reorienting our thinking about our relationship with the environment.

2. In one passage Daly does discuss gross national product (GNP) explicitly and acknowledges that it is a measure of value, whereas throughput is measured in physical units. "Although GNP is measured in value terms and cannot be reduced to a simple physical magnitude, it is nevertheless an index of an aggregate of things that all have irreducible physical dimensions. The relationship between real GNP and throughput is not fixed, but neither is its variability unlimited. And to the extent that one believes that GNP growth can be uncoupled from throughput growth, then all the more reason to be willing to accept limits on throughput growth. If the environmental protection achieved by limiting throughput costs little or nothing in terms of reduced GNP growth, then no one should oppose it. If GNP could grow forever with a constant throughput, then ecological economists would have no objection" (Daly and Farley 2003, 230). The question is to what extent GNP growth can, or cannot be "uncoupled" from throughput growth. Even in this passage Daly tries to rig the debate by asserting that GNP is "an index of an aggregate of things that all have irreducible physical dimensions"—implying that while the rate of growth of throughput need not be as great as the rate of growth of GNP, nonetheless GNP cannot grow without some increase in throughput. But this does not follow logically. With enough of what Daly calls "decoupling," at least in theory GNP can grow while throughput does not. However, Daly offers a peace treaty at the end of the passage quoted which decoupling pessimists and optimists would do well to accept: Limit growth of throughput, as protecting the environment requires, and then go ahead and grow GDP as much as you can.

3. At the risk of beating a dead horse, there is one last ironic twist in this Shakespearean tale of mistaken identities. Whereas many ecological economists believe it is difficult to quantify the benefits that come from all our economic activity in a meaningful way because different categories of benefits cannot or should not be measured on a single dimension, mainstream economists question whether it is possible to quantify throughput for the same reason. They point out that throughput comes in different components—top soil, oil, carbon emissions, and so on—and while each component can be quantified and measured in physical terms separately, there is no easy or meaningful way to aggregate them into a single quantitative measure of aggregate throughput. The two sides in this debate have not only talked past each other, they also have opposite views about what can and cannot be meaningfully and usefully quantified.

4. For an excellent explanation of why entropy is a red herring with regard to environmental problems, see Schwartzman (2008). Many ecological economists now admit that death by entropy is so far in the future that it is irrelevant to our present environmental problems. Nonetheless, many other ecological economists erroneously continue to cite the second law as the root source of environmental problems. This perceived need to continue to discuss entropy in ecological economics textbooks is disturbing since it only

serves to undermine the credibility of ecological economists on matters where they have a great deal to contribute (Costanza et al., 1997). Georgescu-Roegen and Daly are *great* economists who have provided us with many brilliant insights, but bringing entropy into discussions of our current environmental problems was not one of them. The best way to honor these founding fathers of ecological economics is to emphasize their insights and abandon their mistakes.

5. For a brief critique of the notion of "internal contradictions of capitalism" and traditional Marxist crisis theories, see Hahnel (2009b).

6. To be precise, Marx's argument was that competition would drive capitalists to seek to accumulate an even larger percentage of the exchange value produced. In theory, this percentage could continue to increase indefinitely as it approaches 100 percent in the limit.

7. I hasten to add that we have ecological economists like Herman Daly and Marxists like John Bellamy Foster to thank for pointing out many of the reasons reviewed below for why so much of our growth is uneconomic and environmentally destructive.

8. As explained in Chapter 3, the growth of per capita GDP overestimates how much productivity has truly increased in many ways. But whether productivity has increased fivefold or twofold, the point remains.

9. For a review of competing hypotheses and evidence, see Maume and Bellas (2001).

10. For an early example of this research, see Zoltas (1981).

11. The notion that people's consumption has an implicit "ecological footprint" is useful, even if measuring it is inherently more problematic than its supporters like to admit. In any case, anyone who has not done this exercise should do so. For more than ten years I have asked my students in environmental courses to take an ecological footprint quiz *twice*. First, I have them answer all questions as accurately as they can based on their actual lifestyles. Second, I have them answer the questions again after making a New Year's resolution to be as environmentally conscientious as possible. The results show how heavily or lightly students tread compared to their classmates, fellow Americans, or citizens in other countries. Some students are surprised at how much lighter their imprint could be if they tried harder. Many others are surprised to discover that no matter how hard they tried, given constraints they operate under such as not living near public transportation, there is very little they can do personally to reduce their footprint. The exercise invariably leads to interesting discussions about the limits of individual solutions and the importance of collective solutions. Redefining Progress is one organization that offers a footprint calculator online: www.myfootprint.org.

12. If we separate military spending from the rest of collective consumption, this difference would be even more dramatic.

13. Critics of capitalism are often challenged to deny that it has proven to be the most energetic and dynamic economic system humans have devised to date. Dynamism can be good, but when misapplied to produce *un*economic growth, this strong point only magnifies the damage.

14. The only exception is when few firms supply a product, in which case mainstream theory acknowledges that profit-maximizing firms in monopolistic and oligopolistic industries use their market power to produce less than consumers want in order to secure higher prices.

15. For a defense of this definition of economic democracy, see Hahnel (2005a, chapter 2; 2009c).

16. How anyone could believe that profit margins on all products are the same may seem strange to anyone who is not an economist. However, economists reason that, absent barriers, in the long run profit rates in different industries, profit rates of firms within in-

dustries, and profit margins on all products any firm produces will equalize. Unfortunately, as a famous economist once quipped, "in the long run we are all dead." In any case, in the real world there are barriers of many kinds and economic behavior invariably takes place in contexts where not all equilibrating dynamics have had time to work themselves out. Advertising to steer consumers to purchase products with higher profit margins is one such behavior.

17. See Hahnel and Albert (1990, chapter 6), and Hahnel (2001).

18. Proved as Theorem 6.6 in Hahnel and Albert (1990).

19. Proved as Theorem 6.7 in Hahnel and Albert (1990).

20. Lack of a pollution-damage-revealing mechanism in market economies is a critical blow to any hopes of sensible policy interventions to protect the environment. We return to this issue in the conclusion, which proposes a pollution-damage-revealing mechanism that is feasible in an egalitarian economy.

21. Not only is the efficiency gain from higher electricity prices generally ignored by opponents of stricter environmental standards, they almost always misinterpret the higher price as a sign that the economy has become less efficient at producing electricity. What this fallacious reasoning fails to take into account is that we were only deceiving ourselves about how efficiently we were producing electricity in the first place, because we were deceiving ourselves about how cheap it was to produce electricity with high sulfur content coal from eastern fields. Only because we ignored the damage from acid rain caused by sulfur dioxide emissions did we think the cost of producing a kilowatt-hour of electricity was as low as we did. Once we take this external cost into account, we discover that a cheaper way for society to produce coal is with low-sulfur coal from the West. However, since western coal must travel farther on trains to reach power plants in the East, it now costs more per kilowatt-hour to produce electricity in the East than we used to think it cost us. But what we used to think it cost us was wrong! When we correct our calculations to account for the external cost we mistakenly ignored, we discover that producing electricity in the East from low-sulfur coal mined in the West actually costs society less even though shipping costs are higher, and our electricity industry has therefore become more, not less efficient.

22. When relaxing environmental standards is recommended—as it often is these days—environmentalists should hasten to point out that if tightening environmental standards produced structural unemployment, then relaxing standards must also produce roughly the same amount of structural unemployment! If there are adjustment costs associated with changing technologies and the mix of outputs, there will be adjustment costs of moving in either direction—toward a "cleaner" economy or toward a "dirtier" economy. It also bears pointing out that the claim that capital and trade liberalization yield efficiency gains, even if they regrettably also create adjustment costs and job losses for some, is highly debatable. In many situations, trade and capital liberalization yield *global efficiency losses* for reasons that mainstream international economists fail to explain. See Hahnel (1999, 2005b).

Part III

Environmental Policy

Many non-economists, as well as some economists, suffer from fundamental confusions about how different environmental policies work. Part III equips environmentalists and progressives so they need not be brow beaten and can instead go toe-to-toe with professional economists who often do not share their values or priorities in debates over environmental policy.

Chapter 6

Free-Market
Environmentalism
Misinterpreting the Coase Theorem

In Part II we explored why the environment is endangered. In Chapter 4 we discovered that, to anyone who reviews mainstream theories carefully, the implications of externalities, public goods, free access to common property resources, and discrepancies between profit rates and the social rate of time discount reveal a great deal about why the environment is at risk. In Chapter 5 we confirmed that, above and beyond these problems, private enterprise market economies also contain an unhealthy *growth imperative* that is environmentally destructive, even if several heterodox schools of economic thought that make this argument fail to argue the case in a convincing way. We also discovered that the environmental Kuznets curve is not likely to solve our environmental problems for us. Having understood the nature of the problem, we are now ready in Part III to consider what can be done about it.

This chapter examines *free-market environmentalism*, a response with weak support elsewhere but strong support from conservative circles in the United States. According to this school of thought, government intervention to protect the environment is neither necessary nor desirable. Free-market environmentalists argue that government should limit itself to clarifying and enforcing property rights, leaving private parties to engage in negotiations without further government interference. According to free-market environmentalists, once property rights are clear, polluters and pollution victims can be relied on to reach agreements that lead to efficient levels of pollution through voluntary negotiations.

105

Free-market environmentalists base their laissez-faire policy on their interpretation of what is commonly referred to as the Coase theorem, after an article published by University of Chicago professor of economics Ronald Coase in 1960.[1] However, a careful examination of what the Coase theorem says, and does not say, reveals that free-market environmentalism rests on porous ground and that its hands-off policy would utterly fail to protect the environment.

The Coase Theorem: Standard Presentation

Microeconomics and environmental economics textbooks invariably present the Coase theorem using the diagram and explanations below. First, it is assumed that there is only one polluter and one pollution victim. Second, it is assumed that the "right to pollute" and the "right to be free from pollution" are clearly defined. Under these assumptions, the potential efficiency gain from negotiation is demonstrated using Figure 6.1.

The horizontal axis measures the number of units of pollution. The vertical axis measures the polluter's marginal profits from polluting and the victim's marginal damages from pollution in dollars—that is, how much additional profit the firm earns if it pollutes an additional unit and how much additional damage the victim suffers from an additional unit of pollution. Line BCD is the polluter's marginal-profits-from-pollution curve and it is assumed to slope downward. Line OCA is the pollution victim's marginal-damage-from-pollution curve and it is assumed to slope upward.

According to Figure 6.1, if the polluter has the legal right to pollute, the polluter will emit OD units. In this case the victim has an incentive to pay the polluter to reduce emissions. When the polluter emits OD units, the last unit of pollution emitted causes the victim DA in damages but profits the polluter practically nothing at all. The polluter would be better off reducing emissions by one unit in exchange for any positive payment, and the victim would be better off making any payment less than DA in exchange for a one-unit reduction in emissions. There are mutually beneficial deals to be struck as long as the polluter's marginal profit curve, BCD, lies below the victim's marginal damage curve, OCA. Only when emissions have been reduced to OE are mutually beneficial deals exhausted.

In the case where the victim has the legal right to live free from pollution, the victim will not allow the polluter to emit any units at all and the polluter will have an incentive to pay the victim for permission to increase emissions from zero. Again, there are mutually beneficial deals to be struck as long as the polluter's marginal profit curve, BCD, lies above the victim's marginal damage curve, OCA. Only when emissions have been increased to OE are mutually beneficial deals exhausted.

106

Figure 6.1 **Coase Theorem: Standard Presentation**

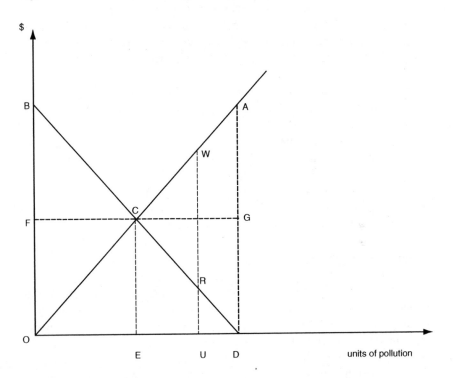

OE represents the socially efficient level of emissions. In this simple, hypothetical situation the only social benefits from pollution are profits received by the polluter, and the only costs to society are damages suffered by a single victim. Because OE is the level of emissions that equalizes marginal social benefits, BCD, and marginal social costs, OCA, OE is the level of emissions that maximizes net social benefits and therefore, according to the efficiency criterion, is the socially efficient level of pollution. Regardless of whether the polluter or pollution victim is assigned the property right, voluntary negotiation should yield the efficient outcome. This is the typical presentation of the Coase theorem in textbooks.

All textbooks acknowledge, as did Coase, that negotiations are likely to fail in the presence of high *transaction costs*, and more careful treatments of the Coase theorem acknowledge that the initial assignment of property rights not only affects who pays whom, and therefore how the efficiency gain from negotiation is distributed, but also might affect what the efficient level of pollution turns out to be.[2] However, the Coase theorem is widely interpreted, not only by free-market environmentalists but by the authors of economics textbooks as well, as "proving" that efficient outcomes can result even in the presence of externalities as long as property rights are clear, independent of who has them. For example, here are two passages by Thomas Tietenberg and Jonathan Harris, authors of two of the most widely used environmental economics texts and by no means conservative ideologues:

- "Ronald Coase held that as long as negotiation costs are negligible . . . the court could allocate the entitlement to either party, and the efficient allocation would result. The only effect of the court's decision would be to change the distribution of costs and benefits among the affected parties. This remarkable conclusion has come to be known as the Coase theorem" (Tietenberg 2003, 81).
- "The Coase theorem states that if property rights are well defined, and no significant transaction costs exist, an efficient allocation of resources will result even with externalities" (Harris 2002, 49).

There Is No Market!

Voluntary Coasian negotiations are often described as the free-market alternative to government regulation. Because the Coase theorem serves as the theoretical underpinning and intellectual predecessor of the free-market environmentalism movement, misrepresentation of Coasian negotiations as "market transactions" needs to be corrected. In the 2001 edition of the book that launched the free-market environmentalism movement, Terry Anderson and Donald Leal acknowledge their intellectual debt to Ronald Coase:

> The free market environmental approach to pollution is to establish property rights to the pollution disposal medium and allow owners of those rights to bargain over how the resource will be used. Following the lesson from Ronald Coase, the central questions are: who has the right to use the air, water, or land? For what uses? And what are the transaction costs for the owners of these rights to bargain over the uses of the resources? If the property rights are well defined and enforced and the bargaining costs are low, regulation . . . is unnecessary. (1960, 132)

Free-market environmentalists, however, are not the only ones to misrepresent Coasian negotiations as market processes. John Asafu-Adjaye is one example of a textbook author who mistakenly analyzes the movement from inefficient, initial levels of pollution to efficient levels of pollution during Coasian negotiations as if it were a market-driven process: "From the foregoing, it can be seen that, irrespective of who has the property right, *equilibrium* is achieved at the quantity of q* [OE in Figure 6.1] and a price of p* [OF in Figure 6.1]. The outcome of this *market* solution is an efficient allocation of resources and the removal of the Pareto-relevant externality" (2000, 82). Asafu-Adjaye leaves no doubt that he believes market forces are at work when he tells us that "the Coasian solution assumes a *perfectly competitive market*" (83; italics added).

It is reasonable to describe Coasian negotiations as the laissez-faire solution to the problem of externalities and as an alternative to government intervention. However, it is inaccurate and misleading to describe Coasian negotiation as a market process. Establishing property rights over externalities is not the same as creating a market for externalities. Establishing property rights is a necessary, but not sufficient condition for enabling market forces to emerge.

Coase was aware of problems that arise in the case of multiple pollution victims, and therefore he wisely confined his discussion to the case of a single polluter and a single victim. This means that Coasian negotiations are one-on-one negotiations between two parties. There is no market in Coase's scenario, much less a competitive market. Competitive markets are situations where there are many sellers and many buyers of a good. In competitive markets, individual actors do not negotiate price with each other at all, but instead take the market price as given and decide how much they are willing to buy or sell at that price. Even when markets are less than competitive, there are more than two parties involved. In a monopolistic (monopsonistic) market there are still many buyers (sellers) and it is assumed that the law of uniform price will determine a single selling price for all units of the good bought and sold in the market.[3] The process by which a polluter and a victim might negotiate a change from OD (or from zero, depending on the assignment of the property right) to OE is not a market process at all, but a one-on-one negotiation.[4] Before discussing what the literature tells us about bilateral negotiations of this kind, it is important to point out two erroneous conclusions that derive from treating Coasian negotiations as if they were a market process.

Misleading conclusions about payments: The first mistake relates to the size of the payment we expect would be necessary to induce both polluter and victim to agree to the efficient level of emissions. Authors who misinterpret the Coasian situation as a market process searching for an "equilibrium" price per unit of emissions are tempted to predict a definitive payment equal to the price where the marginal profits for the polluter are equal to the marginal damages of the victim, OF, times either the number of units abated if the polluter has the property right, OD – OE, or the number of units emitted if the victim has the property right, OE. It is easy to make this mistake. Assume the polluter has the property right. If we think of the victim as negotiating abatement with the polluter unit by unit, starting from OD and proceeding to OE, where all mutually beneficial deals have been exhausted, then the payment for the last unit of abatement would have to be OF. The victim would pay no more and the polluter would take no less than OF for the last unit of abatement to arrive at OE. If this were a market situation where the law of uniform price should apply, all units of abatement would have to sell for OF, and the victim would therefore have to pay the polluter an amount equal to OF times (OD − OE), or the area of the rectangle DECG, to induce the polluter to cut emissions from OD to OE. But there is no market, and therefore there are no market forces to secure the law of uniform price.

Moreover, if the victim negotiates abatement unit by unit, for every unit of abatement prior to the very last unit before OE, there is a range of prices that would leave both the victim and polluter better off. For example, if the victim wanted to negotiate a further unit of abatement starting from OU, any price less than UW and greater than UR would leave both the polluter and victim better off. It is not clear what price in that range they would agree on, and there is no reason to believe they would settle on OF for any other unit of abatement prior to the last.

In truth, there is no reason the polluter and victim must settle on a single price to be paid per unit of abatement at all. Once we realize that the traditional treatment of Coasian negotiations makes sense only if we imagine the polluter and the victim staring at Figure 6.1 together and negotiating how to share an efficiency gain whose size they both know, it becomes apparent there is no reason for them to negotiate abatement unit by unit at all and also no reason for them to agree on a single price to be paid for each unit of abatement.[5] In Coasian negotiations all the polluter and victim need to do is agree on how much the victim must pay the polluter—in grand sum total— to cut emissions from OD to OE. However, when seen in this light, it is far from obvious what size payment would be required to secure the deal. If the polluter and victim truly did have to agree on a single price per unit of abatement, the total payment would have to be equal to the area of the rectangle DECG to exhaust all mutually beneficial deals since no other price would secure the last unit of abatement. But since, in fact, they do *not* have to agree on a single price per unit, there are many different total payments the victim could make to the polluter to reduce emissions from OD to OE that would be mutually beneficial.

For example, if the victim paid the polluter an amount slightly less than the area of figure DECA, the polluter would capture almost the entire efficiency gain from negotiations and the victim would be only slightly better off. On the other hand, if the victim paid an amount only slightly larger than the area of triangle DEC, the victim would capture almost the entire efficiency gain and the polluter would be only slightly better off. Deducing the upper and lower bounds of the size of the payment is not difficult, but as we discover below, more definitive conclusions about how players would divide the efficiency gain depend very much on how bargaining is carried out.

The absurdity of the market interpretation of Coasian negotiations is further illustrated by considering what this line of reasoning implies about what would determine how the efficiency gain would be divided. As the marginal profit and damage lines are constructed in Figure 6.1, a payment equal to the area of DECG divides the efficiency gain, the area of DCA, equally between the polluter and victim. The victim's welfare improves by an amount equal to the area of GCA, while the polluter gains by an amount equal to the area of DCG. As long as the absolute value of the slope of the marginal profit line is equal to the absolute value of the slope of the marginal damage line, as it is in Figure 6.1, the areas of triangles DCG and GCA will be equal. However, if Figure 6.1 were redrawn so that the absolute value of the slope of the marginal profit line were less than the absolute value of the slope of the marginal damage line, the area of triangle DCG would be smaller than the area of triangle GCA and the victim would receive more of the efficiency gain than the polluter.[6] But there is no reason to believe that the division of the efficiency gain should depend on the relative slopes of the marginal profit and damage lines, much less that the efficiency gain would be divided equally if the absolute values of the slopes of the two lines happened to be the same. Instead, the division of any efficiency gain will depend on the relative bargaining power of the polluter and victim, as Coase (1960) himself remarked, and as game theory modeling of different bargaining procedures that advantage one player over another demonstrates, as discussed below. Assuming that Coasian negotiations are a market-driven process with a single price per unit of abatement that exhausts all efficiency gains leads to the erroneous conclusion that how efficiency gains are divided depends on the relative slopes of the marginal damage and profit curves.

Misleading conclusions about abatements: Independent of what size payment would be required to secure a deal, and most importantly for our purposes, misinterpreting Coasian negotiations as a market process also leads to unwarranted conclusions about the likelihood that parties will negotiate their way to an efficient level of pollution. When Coasian negotiations are misinterpreted as a market process, analysts can easily deceive themselves that the kind of forces that drive markets to their equilibrium will drive negotiations to OE units of pollution and a price per unit of abatement equal to OF. But just as there are no market forces to drive the price per unit to OF, there are no market forces to drive the level of emissions to OE. If the polluter and victim agree to a level of emissions equal to OE it must be for some other reason, not because there are market forces that drive the bargain to that outcome. It is clear why omniscient polluters would never reduce pollution below OE. It is also tautologically true that if polluters pollute more than OE, they will have failed to exhaust all mutually beneficial deals. But do protagonists always negotiate efficiently and leave no mutually beneficial deals unconsummated? It is time to consider what game theory has to tell us about these kinds of negotiations.

A Game of Divide-the-Pie

If Coasian negotiations are not a market process, what are they? The only way to make sense of the traditional analysis of the Coase theorem is to imagine the polluter and the pollution victim both staring at Figure 6.1 together and then negotiating how to divide the efficiency gain—the area of triangle DCA if the polluter has the property right, or the area of triangle OCB if the victim has the property right. In this case, the traditional analysis of Coasian negotiations is simply a two-person, noncooperative game called divide-the-pie. However, in this game the antagonists must both know the size of the pie they have to divide—that is, the true size of the potential efficiency gain from negotiations. And the only way Coasian negotiators could both know the true size of the pie would be if they both had what game theorists call *complete information.* In a game of complete information, each player knows not only her own payoffs in all possible outcomes, but also her opponent's payoffs in all possible outcomes as well. Moreover, each player knows that her opponent knows her payoffs, and each player knows her opponent knows she knows. In our context, this amounts to assuming that the polluter knows not only what her marginal profit curve looks like, but also what the victim's marginal damage curve looks like; and the victim knows not only what her marginal damage curve looks like, but also what the polluter's marginal profit curve looks like. Moreover, both the polluter and the victim know that they both know all of this information.[7]

When we relax the assumption of complete information below, we discover it is no longer likely that Coasian negotiations would lead to efficient outcomes, which means that only under the assumption of complete information is there any possibility of arriving at the conclusion that Coasian negotiations *may* yield efficient outcomes. However, even in this case the divide-the-pie game turns out to be more complicated than it first appears. A rich and complex *theoretical* literature, complemented by a growing *experimental* literature, reveals that even under the most favorable conditions we can imagine, the conclusion that Coasian negotiations will yield efficient outcomes is far from certain.

The theoretical literature: The theoretical literature on one-shot, bilateral, noncooperative, divide-the-pie games reveals that how the pie will be divided depends very much on how negotiations are organized. If offers are simultaneous, literally any division of the pie is a possible equilibrium.[8] Many games of alternating offers have a unique equilibrium, but what that equilibrium will be depends on key parameters in the structure of the game. In finite-horizon, alternating-offer games, changes in the number of offers permitted and changes in who makes the last offer can significantly change how the pie is divided. In infinite-horizon games, slight variations in discount rates, speeds of response, and penalties for rejecting offers can change how the pie is divided in surprising ways.[9]

Regarding the major issue at stake—will players agree to an efficient outcome, regardless of how they divide the efficiency gain—the theoretical literature on divide-the-pie games can be read as cautiously optimistic. Game theory rarely predicts inefficient outcomes *provided* (1) both parties care only about their own payoff, (2) both parties behave rationally, (3) neither party suspects the other may not behave rationally, and (4) neither player believes the outcome of an early game will become known to players in future games in which the player expects to participate. Joseph Farrell explains the intuition for this result: "If everyone knew all about everyone else, it is hard to envision how negotiation could drag on or break down" (Farrell 1987, 115). However, if any of these four assumptions fails to hold, the theoretical literature predicts it is quite possible for parties to fail to reach an agreement on how to divide the pie, resulting in an inefficient outcome. Robert Pindyck and Daniel Rubinfeld are unusual examples of textbook authors who acknowledge in their presentation of the Coase theorem that rational concerns for one's reputation as a bargainer can lead to inefficiencies: "bargaining can also break down even when communication and monitoring are costless. . . . One party makes a demand for a large share and refuses to bargain, assuming incorrectly that the other party will eventually concede. . . . An agreement may never be reached especially if one or both parties want to earn a reputation for tough bargaining" (Pindyck and Rubinfeld 2001, 640).

The experimental literature: The experimental literature, on the other hand, suggests reason to be pessimistic about achieving efficient outcomes in one-shot, divide-the-pie games. Ochs and Roth (1989) report that outcomes in alternating-offer, finite-horizon bargaining experiments they conducted were inconsistent with the predictions of theoretical models assuming mutually rational behavior. For example, notions of equity seem to intrude, often leading players to reject an offer they deemed unfair even though doing so left them with less than if they had accepted what they regarded as an unfair offer. Moreover, Ochs and Roth report that experiments in which players were first conditioned to expect a certain split and then matched with players who were conditioned to expect a different split often resulted in failures to reach an agreement and inefficient outcomes.[10] Based on an evaluation of both literatures, David Kreps hypothesizes that theoretically relevant factors such as "who has which discount rate and what is the precise protocol of bargaining will be swamped by expectations as to what one can expect to get and what one expects must be given in order to come to agreement" (1990, 568). In other words, Kreps cautions us not to always expect real people to reach an efficient outcome even if a Coasian negotiation were a one-shot, alternating-offer game with complete information.

Perfect Knowledge Is Not Complete Information

Economists are long accustomed to assuming *perfect knowledge* when analyzing the efficiency of market systems. This traditional perfect knowledge assumption is that each party knows "perfectly" what its own preferences or technologies are—that is, that no party is surprised to find that its choice affects it differently than it anticipated. In effect, this is an assumption about perfect *self*-knowledge. Traditionally, the only other "knowledge" actors are assumed to know "perfectly" are market prices, which they are assumed to take as givens if markets are competitive. Many critics have challenged the assumption of perfect self-knowledge as unrealistic. But many critics misconstrue the real purpose of this assumption.

Economists do not assume perfect self-knowledge because we really think people never mistake how they will actually be affected by an outcome. We assume it because otherwise it is impossible to use logic to *deduce* how people will behave in a given situation. Of course, there may be other ways to predict how people will actually behave, and they may prove to be better predictors than deducing what behavior would be in someone's self-interest. But if we wish to use logic to deduce behavior, we must assume actors know and act in their own best interest. More importantly, economists also assume perfect self-knowledge because if we want to know what kind of behavior particular institutional circumstances promote, the answer is found by deducing what individually rational behavior would be under those circumstances. Again, this is not to say that people always choose to act in their own self-interest. But it is true nonetheless that the kind of behavior any institution *promotes* is the behavior that would be in the self-interest of individuals who find themselves in that institutional situation.[11] In other words, the traditional assumption of perfect self-knowledge is less an assumption of conviction and more an assumption dictated by methodological considerations.

Of course, one of the great accomplishments of mainstream economic theory was the discovery that even when actors in an economy know nothing at all about other actors in the economy, if each actor is fully "self-aware" and also aware of the prices of goods and services, when all markets clear the outcome will be socially efficient—provided we make a number of important assumptions.[12] This grand discovery, which began as a vision in the mind of Adam Smith in the mid-eighteenth century, was refined over 200 years by economists such as Alfred Marshall and Leon Walras and was finally proved rigorously as the fundamental theorem of welfare economics by Kenneth Arrow and Gerard Debreu in the mid-twentieth century.

It is important to notice that it is *not* traditionally assumed that every actor has perfect knowledge about the preferences and technologies of all *other* actors in the economy. Not only is this more far-reaching assumption about what actors know far less plausible, but if it were required it would take the shine, so to speak, off the minor miracle contained in the fundamental theorem of welfare economics. How much more surprising and delightful that everything will work out for the best—at least as far as efficiency is concerned—when people are *not* assumed to know what others want or are capable of! However, as we have seen, hidden in standard presentations of Coasian negotiations is an implicit assumption that both actors know not only exactly how they are affected by pollution, but also exactly how their opponent is affected as well. In the language of game theory, traditional treatments of the Coase theorem assume "complete information"—even if most analysts seem unaware that this assumption is necessary to conclude that successful Coasian negotiations between a polluter and a single victim will lead to efficient levels of pollution, or that this necessary assumption is far more restrictive and less plausible than the traditional assumption of perfect self-knowledge.

Negotiations With Incomplete Information

What happens when we relax the highly implausible assumption of complete information—or mutual omniscience? How would Coasian negotiations proceed if one party has only perfect self-knowledge, leaving the other party with what game theorists call "private information"? In other words, what if one party knows the true size of the pie to be divided but the other party does not? We will let the polluter have the property right and assume that while the polluter knows the victim's marginal damage curve as well as her own marginal profit curve, the victim knows only what her marginal damage curve looks like and does *not* know what the polluter's true marginal profit curve looks like. For convenience of analysis, we will also assume that bargaining continues until the victim, believing all efficiency gains have been exhausted, pays the polluter an amount equal to the marginal damage of the last unit abated times the number of units abated. We can call this level of abatement and size of payment a "successful Coasian negotiation."

115

Figure 6.2 **Coasian Negotiations With Incomplete Information**

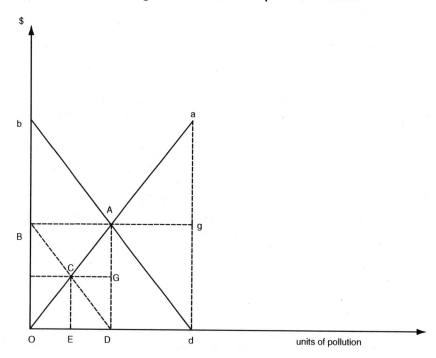

According to Figure 6.1 if the polluter reveals her true marginal profit curve, BCD, to the victim, as we have seen, a successful Coasian negotiation would have the polluter cutback on emissions from OD to OE in exchange for a payment from the victim equal to the area of rectangle DECG, and the polluter would gain the area of triangle DCG and the victim would gain the area of triangle GCA.

However, the polluter is in a position to pursue a more profitable negotiating strategy, as shown in Figure 6.2. Knowing that the victim does not know what her true marginal profit curve looks like, what if the polluter can convince the victim that her marginal profit curve looks like bAd? In this case the victim will negotiate based on Figure 6.2 where the true marginal profit curve, BCD, has been erased from her view, and she only sees the false marginal profit curve, bAd. In this situation, successful Coasian negotiations would lead the victim to pay the polluter an amount equal to the area of rectangle dDAg in exchange for a promise from the polluter to cut back emissions from Od to OD. From these negotiations the victim would *think* she had gained an amount equal to the area of the triangle gAa, and the victim would *think* the polluter had gained an amount equal to the area of triangle dAg. Of course, this is not the case. In truth, the victim has gained nothing in exchange for her large payment, and the polluter has been paid a great deal to do exactly what she would have done for no payment at all.

Clearly the polluter has much to gain if she can deceive the victim into thinking her marginal profit curve is higher than it truly is. If the polluter can substitute the false bargaining game above for the true bargaining game envisioned by Coase, she stands to gain considerably more than she could have hoped to gain from playing the true game. Moreover, only if the victim had complete information regarding the polluter's marginal profit curve as well as her own marginal damage curve would she be immune from this kind of deception. Clearly the consequences of dropping the implausible assumption of complete information, or omniscience, are profound. If the victim had the property right and the opportunity to deceive, she would stand to gain from exaggerating her damages, which would lead to less pollution than is socially efficient. In general, if the party with the property right also has private information, or a knowledge advantage, because her opponent does not know what her curve looks like, her rational strategy is to try to deceive her opponent into believing that her curve is higher than it truly is. The more successful her deception, the more she stands to gain and, what is more important for our purposes, the more inefficient the outcome will be. In light of the fact that complete information about the true situation of the other party is seldom the case in negotiations between polluters and pollution victims, it seems highly unlikely that Coasian negotiations will lead to efficient outcomes very often in the real world—even if negotiators behave rationally, even if they believe their negotiations will remain secret forever, even if there are no transaction costs, even if there is only a single pollution victim, and even if negotiations do not bog down and a successful deal is struck.

Joseph Farrell explained long ago how critical the assumption of complete information is: "The popular simple view of the Coase theorem is a tautology: that if bargaining and negotiation are perfect (that is, produce perfect outcomes) then the outcomes are perfect. Actually, negotiation is far from perfect, even in the simplest situations. . . . And it is especially imperfect in the hardest problems—those with private information" (1987, 125). Since Farrell first warned of the critical importance of "private information" in Coasian negotiations, game theory research on bilateral bargaining with incomplete information has confirmed his view. While theory predicts that parties will seldom fail to reach an agreement in one-shot, bilateral bargaining games of *complete* information provided both parties assume the other will behave rationally,[13] recent research in the theory of one-shot, bilateral bargaining with *incomplete* information yields a very different conclusion. When Ariel Rubinstein (1985) reexamined his classic,

117

infinite-horizon, alternating-offer, divide-the-pie game under the assumption that the discount rate of one player was private information, he discovered that truthful revelation was never a first best strategy. Martin Osborne warns that *in general* we should not expect the party with private information to reveal it truthfully: "When a receiver takes an action based on an unverifiable report about the state supplied by a sender, and the sender's and receiver's preferences differ, no equilibrium exists in which the sender accurately reports the state" (2004, 349). Colin Camerer explains why private information can lead players to fail to reach an agreement this way: "In theory, asymmetries in information fundamentally change the nature of how people bargain. Introducing asymmetries undermines efficiency because bargaining strategies then serve two different purposes: Players bargain both to get the most they can and to convey information. The two purposes usually conflict" (2003, 182).

Of course, in the traditional divide-the-pie game, deception and fear of deception only cause inefficiency if they prevent players from coming to an agreement on how to divide the pie, in which case the inefficiency is that neither player gets any pie. The theoretical literature on games with incomplete information focuses on this problem and concludes that because players are less likely to reach an agreement than when they have complete information, efficient outcomes can no longer be expected when there is private information. But as Figure 6.2 makes clear, in bargaining between a polluter and victim deception can lead to inefficiency in a different, more troubling way. In Coasian negotiations deception can lead to an inefficient outcome even when players *do* reach an agreement because it can lead them to play a false divide-the-pie game instead of playing the true divide-the-pie.

As demonstrated above, a polluter with the opportunity to deceive would find it in her interest to substitute a false bargaining game based on curves bAd and OCAa for the true bargaining game based on curves BCD and OCA envisioned by Coase. But while the true bargaining game contains an efficiency gain equal to the area of triangle DCA for the polluter and victim to divide, the false bargaining game contains no actual efficiency gain whatsoever.[14]

By assuming that Coasian negotiations would be "successful" in our analysis, we effectively assumed away the kind of inefficiency that results when incomplete information prevents players from reaching an agreement—the subject of most theoretical research in the theory of bilateral bargaining with incomplete information. However, this enabled us to focus on a more troubling inefficiency that results when the opportunity to deceive leads a rational player to trick her opponent into playing a different bargaining game with a smaller efficiency gain—or perhaps no efficiency gain at all—and thereby prevents them from playing the bargaining game with a larger efficiency gain envisioned by Coase.

Multiple Victims: More Than Transaction Costs

While incomplete information undermines the Coase theorem even when there is only a single polluter and a single victim, multiple victims make successful Coasian negotiations much more problematic. This problem has been widely acknowledged, but it is usually presented in a way that underestimates its severity. Beginning with Coase, most interpret the problem of multiple victims as one of high transaction costs. Though some critics have analyzed free-rider and holdout problems that arise in the case of multiple victims as problems of perverse incentives, the tendency within the economics profession has been to treat multiple victims as simply raising the costs of negotiation. However, this standard practice of treating incentive problems as transaction costs in the case of multiple victims is misleading because it trivializes problems created by perverse incentives.

It is perfectly reasonable to categorize not only lawyer fees but also the opportunity cost of time spent in negotiations between a polluter and her victims as transaction costs. Moreover, if the cost of time spent negotiating and lawyer fees exceeds the size of the efficiency gain from negotiations, it is clear we should not expect negotiations to yield efficient outcomes because there is no incentive to negotiate. Coase recognized this, and virtually everyone interpreting Coase has acknowledged it as well. It is universally referred to as the "zero transaction cost assumption" of the Coase theorem. But if the only reason we fail to get an efficient outcome is that the costs of negotiation are larger than the efficiency gain they would yield, the inefficiency cannot be very great in the first place! In other words, if transaction costs were the only problem introduced by multiple victims, it would not be terribly unreasonable for free market environmentalists to dismiss this objection as inconsequential.

Of course, multiple victims do presumably add to transaction costs because many more negotiations are necessary if the polluter must negotiate separately with each victim, or because there will be costs associated with identifying and inviting victims to join a coalition to negotiate with the polluter on behalf of all victims. But labeling these problems transaction costs prevents us from seeing that they are fundamentally different from lawyers' fees and opportunity costs of time spent in negotiations. The real problem with multiple victims is that because of perverse free-rider and holdout incentives, separate negotiations with individual victims will not occur, even if the potential efficiency gain is large, and because of perverse incentives for victims to misrepresent damages, negotiations with a victim's coalition will predictably yield inefficient outcomes as well. When multiple victims are improperly treated as merely increasing transaction costs, one is led to expect efficient outcomes as long as the potential efficiency gains from negotiations with multiple victims

119

are large compared to the additional costs of those negotiations. However, when properly understood as a problem of perverse incentives, it becomes apparent why relying on voluntary negotiations will not yield efficient outcomes when there are multiple victims even when potential efficiency gains are quite large. Why do multiple victims change the situation qualitatively and dramatically?

Separate negotiations: When there are multiple victims, we should not expect separate negotiations between the polluter and each individual victim to lead to an efficient outcome. If the polluter has the property right, each victim has an incentive to deny any harm in hopes that other victims will step forward and pay the polluter to abate—the free-rider problem. If the victims have the property right, each victim has an incentive to exaggerate harm and threaten to veto any deal unless she receives the entire payment the polluter is willing to offer all victims collectively—the holdout problem. In both cases, separate negotiations will end in failure, leading to too little abatement and too much pollution. But this is not because the transaction costs of multiple negotiations are prohibitive. It is because the existence of multiple victims creates perverse incentives for victims that will cause separate negotiations to quickly break down.

A coalition representing all victims: Therefore, when there are multiple victims, the only hope for successful negotiations lies in organizing a coalition of victims to negotiate with the polluter as a group. But there are two reasons why multiple victims of pollution are predictably unable to organize a coalition to negotiate effectively with a polluter—neither of which has anything to do with the transaction costs of identifying victims and issuing them invitations to join an organization. The first problem arises whenever there is no objective way to verify who is truly a victim and who is not, even when each true victim is damaged to the same extent. If the polluter has the property right, every victim has an incentive to deny her true status as a victim and hope other victims will join the coalition and contribute money to bribe the polluter to cut back on emissions. On the other hand, if the victims have the property right, everyone has an incentive to claim she is a victim even if she is not, in order to receive part of the payment the polluter will offer. In either case, there is an incentive for people to lie about whether they truly are victims. In one case, the victims' coalition will predictably contain many fewer victims than it should, and negotiations will therefore result in too little abatement because the coalition will lack funds to bribe the polluter sufficiently. In the other case, the victims' coalition will include many who are not truly victims, and negotiations will result in too much abatement as the polluter is compelled to pay more than is warranted.

Even if we could solve the problem of distinguishing between those who are victims and those who are not, there is a second problem. If victims are not affected to the same degree, but there is no objective way to determine who among them is more or less damaged, how can the coalition decide how much to collect from or pay to different victims? If victims are asked the extent of their damage, they have every reason to lie. If polluters have the property right and victims who are more damaged are expected to contribute more to bribe the polluter to abate, people will underreport their damage, which leads to too little abatement. If victims have the property right and victims who are more damaged expect to receive higher payments, people will overreport their damages, which leads to too much abatement. So even if we could accurately identify who are victims and who are not, when there is no way to know how much different victims are damaged there is no reason to believe negotiations between a coalition representing all victims and the polluter will lead to the efficient amount of abatement.

In most real-world situations, victims are damaged to different degrees and it is often difficult to distinguish those who are truly victims from those who are not. Therefore, when there are multiple victims, either separate negotiations between the polluter and individual victims will break down due to perverse free-rider or holdout incentives, or negotiations between a polluter and a voluntary coalition representing all victims will yield inefficient outcomes because of perverse incentives for victims to misrepresent their damages. Moreover, this problem is qualitatively different from inefficiencies that arise because the transaction cost of negotiations is greater than the benefit derived from correcting them. Perverse incentives to ride for free, to hold out, and to misrepresent are not transaction costs, and it is misleading to treat them as such.

The Myth of Free-Market Environmentalism

So where does all this leave us? As we have seen, what is called the Coase theorem is commonly interpreted as "proving" that if property rights are made clear, private negotiations between polluters and pollution victims will eliminate all inefficiencies larger than the transaction costs of necessary negotiations without need for government interference, provided people behave rationally. Careful examination reveals that this conclusion is false under any realistic conditions. Many have pointed out that the interpretation espoused by "property rights" or "free-market" environmentalists is wildly overoptimistic. But most critics emphasize inefficiencies that arise from practical and ethical complications of assigning property rights, irrational behavior, transaction costs of negotiation, and lack of financial means to secure agreements. Because of this failure to highlight the importance of perverse incentives, the main thrust of the Coase theorem has too often gone unchallenged. In the case of multiple victims, tying objections to positive transaction costs underplays fatal perverse free-rider, holdout, and misrepresentation incentive problems that have nothing to do with the opportunity costs of negotiations. And in the case of a single victim, the few critics who recognize that standard treatments hinge on an implicit and highly implausible assumption of complete information still fail to see that the real danger from private information lies not in obstructing agreement but in creating a perverse incentive to substitute a false bargaining game with a smaller efficiency gain for the true bargaining game with the maximum efficiency gain envisioned by Coase.

Ronald Coase deserves credit for challenging some misconceptions that plagued the profession before him. He pointed out that parties whose behaviors affect each other negatively might have an incentive to negotiate a more efficient modification of their behavior. He pointed out that if property rights are ambiguous, parties will be tempted to concentrate their energies on winning the ambiguous property right through litigation rather than on negotiating efficiency gains. He also pointed out—to everyone's surprise at the time—that *regarding efficiency* it may not be important which party has the property right. However, an accurate summary of the issues raised by the Coase theorem should read as follows:

(1) *Even if* there is only a single polluter and a single victim, *even if* it is clear who has the property right, *even if* there are zero transaction costs to negotiations, *even if* both parties have "complete information" (i.e., they know not only their own marginal profit or damage curve but the marginal profit or damage curve of the other party as well), *even if* both parties know that the other knows all this as well, *even if* both parties play rationally and know the other party will do likewise, *even if* players care only about the absolute size of their own payoffs, and *even if* the bargaining procedure is carefully structured, it is still quite possible that a polluter and victim might fail to reach an efficient outcome if either has reason to be concerned for her bargaining "reputation."

(2) However, it is highly unlikely that Coasian negotiators would have "complete information." In this case the party with the property right can exaggerate her profits or damages because her opponent has no way to know what they truly are, and when this occurs it is predictable that even "successful" Coasian negotiations will lead to grossly inefficient outcomes. If the polluter has the property right and the victim does not know what the polluter's marginal profit curve looks like, the polluter has an incentive to exaggerate her profits from pollution, and "successful" Coasian negotiations will lead to more pollution than is socially efficient. If the victim has the property right and the polluter does not know what the victim's damage curve looks like, the victim can gain by exaggerating her damages, and "successful" Coasian negotiations will lead

to more abatement than is efficient. While this conclusion derives from an absence of complete information, the kind of omniscience that is necessary to conclude that negotiations will tend toward efficient levels of pollution is highly unrealistic for polluters and their victims, going considerably beyond the kind of perfect *self*-knowledge necessary to assume that competitive markets will lead to efficient outcomes. Moreover, the most important way that incomplete or private information causes inefficiencies is not by preventing polluters and victims from coming to agreements, but by permitting the party with private information to substitute a false bargaining game with less or no efficiency gain for the true bargaining game with a larger efficiency gain envisioned by Coase. In that case, inefficiency arises not from failure to reach agreements but from inefficient agreements that are reached.

(3) If there are multiple victims of pollution, perverse free-rider and holdout incentive problems will doom separate negotiations between the polluter and each victim to failure. But if victims attempt to negotiate collectively, perverse incentives to misrepresent damages will lead to inefficient outcomes. In either case it is highly unlikely that voluntary negotiations when there are multiple victims will achieve efficient levels of pollution. To his credit, Professor Coase was aware of this limitation to his "theorem," although he initiated the unfortunate practice of trivializing problems introduced by multiple victims as transaction cost problems when, in truth, they are far more fundamental problems of incentive incompatibility. A reasonable assessment of a host of perverse incentives that are likely to impact voluntary negotiations between polluters and multiple victims should lead us to expect failure, not success, even if the "transaction costs" of identifying potential victims and issuing them invitations to join a victim's coalition are low.

(4) Finally, a common conclusion regarding the size of the payment required to secure a successful agreement to Coasian negotiations is completely inaccurate. It is common to interpret Coasian negotiations as if they were a market process, which they are not. When the Coasian situation is properly understood as a two-person game of divide-the-pie with complete information, it becomes clear that bargaining protocol and asymmetries in players' situations determine how the pie will be divided. In this case it also becomes clear that the size payment we would expect from successful Coasian negotiations has nothing to do with a per-unit price that equates marginal benefits and marginal damages. Instead, it simply depends on the relative bargaining power of the two parties, modified by any notions of equity the parties may bring to their negotiations.

In conclusion, the main reasons voluntary negotiations between polluters and their victims will not lead to efficient outcomes are not because of positive transaction costs or irrational behavior, but because negotiators seldom know their opponent's true situation, which leads to perverse incentives to dissimulate, and because the existence of multiple victims creates perverse incentives for victims to free ride, hold out, and misrepresent the extent of damages. To treat the first problem as a lack of perfect knowledge is disingenuous because it is not the traditional assumption of perfect *self*-knowledge that is required, but instead a far more implausible assumption of "complete information" that is tantamount to social omniscience. Moreover, to treat the problem of incomplete information merely as an obstacle to reaching agreements misses a far more significant problem: If information about the situation of the party with the property right is private, that party will have both the motive and opportunity to replace the positive sum game of negotiations envisioned by Coase with a smaller or zero sum game whose "successful" outcome is inefficient. To treat problems that arise when there are multiple victims as just more transaction costs trivializes serious incentive problems that go far beyond the time and expense of identifying and contacting multiple victims. Perverse incentives to free ride, hold out, and misrepresent are fatal to any hopes of achieving efficient outcomes through voluntary negotiations between polluters and multiple victims even when potential efficiency gains are quite large compared to the true transaction costs of achieving them.

How careless interpretations of the so-called Coase theorem can be easily manipulated to undermine the case for government regulation is not hard to see. Even if the Coase theorem does not always apply because some premise is unmet, leaving the impression that it *may* apply, and implying that only inefficiencies in excess of the transaction costs of negotiating their elimination will occur, means that one can always argue that "voluntary" solutions to environmental problems should be explored first before "second-best," "command and control" policies be considered. Given the enthusiasm for "market-based solutions" and the antipathy for regulation in the neoliberal era, it is hardly surprising that free-market environmentalism wields more influence on policy than is justified by its theoretical underpinnings. What is surprising is that after Coase drew attention to the all-important subject of incentives in the case of externalities, discussion of important *perverse* incentives that externalities generate has played only a limited role in the ensuing debate among professional economists for so many years. Lack of precision regarding "transaction costs" has served to hide perverse free-rider and holdout incentives from view in the case of multiple victims. A similar lack of precision regarding what information Coasian negotiators are presumed to have has disguised perverse incentives that arise even in the case of a single pollution victim.

Hopefully, the admittedly tedious argument presented in this chapter demonstrates why the realm of real-world situations where voluntary negotiations could be reasonably expected to provide efficient solutions to environmental problems is so small that free-market environmentalism no more deserves a seat at the policy table than miracles deserve a role in the operating room.

Notes

1. It is worthy of note that Coase did not use the word *theorem* in his article, much less provide a formal proof of any proposition. Nonetheless, the argument is universally called the Coase theorem.

2. This is often referred to as the difference between the "weak" and "strong" version of the Coase theorem. In the weak version, no matter who has the property right, the level of pollution that results from Coasian negotiations is efficient but not necessarily the same if the wealth effect of changing the property right changes the location of either party's marginal curve. In the strong version, the outcome is not only efficient but the same because it is assumed there is no wealth effect on either curve from assigning the property right.

3. Only a discriminating monopolist (monopsonist) negotiates different prices separately with each buyer (seller), and this is only possible if buyers (sellers) cannot trade the good among themselves. Conceivably we could interpret the Coasian situation as a "market" that is both a perfect monopoly, with only one seller, and a perfect monopsony, with only one buyer. But this is no help since outcomes in this situation—where, in truth, there is no market—can only be analyzed using game-theory tools, as discussed below.

4. Below it is argued that the traditional analysis of Coasian negotiations makes sense only when understood as a two-person, noncooperative game called "divide-the-pie," which can *only* be the case if the polluter and the victim are both assumed to have what game theorists call complete information.

5. This scenario assumes that the polluter and victim have complete information, a point we return to below.

6. If the absolute value of the slope of the marginal profit line were greater than the absolute value of the slope of the marginal damage line, the area of triangle DCG would be larger than the area of triangle GCA and the victim would supposedly receive less of the efficiency gain than the polluter.

7. Games of complete information can be thought of as situations where actors are presumed to be omniscient (i.e., they know everything about everybody) and not merely "self-aware" (i.e., they know everything only about themselves).

8. The word *equilibrium* in game theory should not be confused with the concept of a market equilibrium. The concept of an equilibrium solution to a game does not mean that there is a market or that market forces are at work.

9. For the initial analyses, see Stahl (1972) for finite-horizon alternating models and Rubinstein (1982) for infinite-horizon alternating models. However, in no case is there reason to believe the victim would necessarily pay the polluter an amount equal to the area of rectangle DECG to cut emissions from OD to OE, which is what interpreting Coasian negotiations as a market-driven process misleads one to expect.

10. See Roth (1997) and Camerer (2003, chapter 4) for two excellent evaluations of what the experimental literature on bilateral bargaining reveals. Of particular interest is that both authors conclude that failure to reach agreement—and therefore inefficient outcomes—occurs more often in experiments than theory predicts.

11. For a more extensive discussion of different assumptions about what kind of information actors are assumed to have or not have, and situations in which one or another assumption is more appropriate and useful, see Hahnel (2001).

12. Why the necessary assumptions of the fundamental theorem of welfare econom-

ics for private enterprise market economies are more numerous and less plausible than usually admitted, and how this leads to misleading conclusions, is explored in depth in Hahnel and Albert (1990).

13. What varies greatly depending on how complete information games are structured is who will capture more of the efficiency gain from bargaining. See Osborne and Rubinstein (1994) and Ishiguro (2003).

14. Since there is no efficiency gain in the false game analyzed above, the false game is a zero sum game. So when the victim pays the polluter an amount equal to the area of rectangle dDAg, this is simply a redistribution of a constant pie—the inefficient pie that results when the polluter emits OD units of pollution. If the polluter can only convince the victim that her marginal profit curve is higher than BCD but not as high as bAd, then "successful" Coasian negotiations will lead to an inefficient level of emissions somewhere between OE and OD, and the false game would be a positive sum game, but a smaller positive sum than the true game Coase envisioned.

Chapter 7

Real-World Environmental Policy

Once we are free from the illusion that free-market environmentalism will protect the environment, we are free to explore the pros and cons of different policies that can. This chapter seeks to provide environmentalists and progressives who are not economists with the necessary information to correct common misunderstandings about what different policies do, and do not do. Hopefully this knowledge will render environmentalists and progressives immune from intimidation at the hands of technocratic economists who often do not share their values and priorities.

While mainstream economists argue that the choice of environmental policy should be based on technical merits and guided by traditional cost-benefit analysis (CBA), environmentalists and progressives sense that often CBA is not the appropriate methodology and that policy choices both are and should be based on other concerns as well. This chapter validates common concerns of progressives and environmentalists by exploring complications and real-world issues regarding environmental policies that mainstream economists do not like to talk about.

First we explore the basic logic of regulation, taxes, and tradable permit programs; dispel common myths about monitoring and enforcement; and explain how to analyze the distributive effects of policy options. Next we explore property rights, zoning, and how a little-known policy called transfer development rights can help overcome political resistance to anti-sprawl initiatives. Then we discuss community management as an alternative to both privatization and government regulation of common pool resources (CPR) to prevent the tragedy of the commons. Finally, we evaluate fears about permit markets and Wall Street machinations and discuss the practical implications of tax-phobia.

A Policy Primer

We begin by exploring the logic and implications of three different ways to reduce carbon dioxide emissions in a market economy. Suppose the U.S. government decides it wants to reduce national emissions by 10 percent next year. This could be done in three ways: (1) a regulation approach mandating a 10 percent reduction in emissions from every source; (2) a carbon tax set at a level that achieves a 10 percent overall reduction in emissions; (3) or a cap-and-trade program where the number of permits printed allows for only 90 percent of last year's total emissions. Since all three policies reduce emissions by the same amount they are called *equivalent*, but as we will discover this does not mean their consequences are the same in other regards.[1]

Regulation: The regulatory approach would be to order every source inside the United States emitting carbon dioxide to reduce its own emissions by 10 percent. Many economists object to this approach for two sensible reasons: (1) This policy fails to minimize the cost to society of achieving a 10 percent reduction in overall emissions if there are differences in abatement costs among sources.[2] For example, suppose one source emitting carbon dioxide can reduce emissions for half what it costs another source to reduce its emissions. It is inefficient to require the second source, for whom abatement costs are higher, to reduce emissions by the same percentage as the first source, for whom abatement costs are lower. Because there are significant differences in abatement costs among different sources, this criticism of the regulatory approach to reducing carbon dioxide emissions is well taken. (2) Ordering all sources to reduce emissions by 10 percent provides no incentive for any source to search for new technologies that could reduce its emissions by more than 10 percent—no matter how cheap it might be.

There is an additional problem with the regulatory approach that mainstream economists seldom point out, but that should be of concern to anyone concerned with equity. The regulatory approach does not require sources who, in our example, continue to emit 90 percent of the carbon dioxide they emitted the previous year to pay for the costs their emissions continue to impose on the rest of us. In other words, the regulatory approach does not implement the "polluter pays" principle, which many environmentalists and progressives champion with good reason. In effect, the regulatory approach draws an arbitrary line. It says that the last 10 percent of emissions from each source is so damaging that it must be outlawed completely, whereas the first 90 percent of emissions costs society nothing, and therefore sources should be free to emit 90 percent of their previous levels without payment or apology. But this is not consistent with the facts. The fact is that as long as sources wish to emit more carbon dioxide in the aggregate than is consistent with climate stability, whenever anyone emits any carbon dioxide it imposes a cost on society. In effect, the regulatory policy excuses 90 percent of socially costly emissions.

Another way to look at the issue is that the regulatory approach implicitly grants sources a legal property right to emit 90 percent of what they were emitting previously, but cancels what had been their de facto property right to emit the last 10 percent. In other words, regulation creates a valuable new legal property right, gives 90 percent of this property right to those emitting carbon dioxide, reserves only 10 percent of the new property right for the rest of us, and bars everyone—both emitters and the public—from selling their new property right, no matter how beneficial a deal they might be able to find.

A second kind of regulation mandates use of particular technologies and outlaws use of other technologies. For example, all new coal-burning power plants could be required to include a new process that captures and stores carbon emissions, and existing plants might be given a specified time to acquire this new technology. Or buildings could be required to include more insulation or sealants for energy conservation. When the best response takes a particular form that the government can easily determine or when businesses fail to make changes that reduce emissions even though these changes will prove profitable over time, this kind of regulation can be very effective. As a matter of fact, many of the most successful environmental policies to date, like the Clean Water Act and Clean Air Act, have been of this kind.

However, the fact that those who claim technological expertise with regard to alternative technologies for producing and consuming energy often disagree on what they recommend—or at least disagree on which changes should be prioritized and mandated first—suggests that technological regulation with regard to energy production and consumption may not be as obvious as its supporters often assume. Since there are many different ways to produce and conserve energy, since least-cost means are often different for different sources, since least-cost means are particularly difficult for outsiders to identify, and since businesses often do respond more or less sensibly to price signals, using a price mechanism to induce businesses to find their own least-cost means of compliance has obvious advantages.

Tax: An alternative way to achieve a 10 percent reduction is to impose a tax on carbon dioxide emissions. The government would have to use trial and error to find the level to set a carbon tax in order to achieve an overall reduction in emissions of 10 percent. However, there is a carbon tax—some number of dollars per ton of carbon dioxide emitted—that would achieve a 10 percent overall reduction in carbon dioxide emissions in the United States.

The logic of a carbon tax is to force producers to take into account the cost to society of their carbon dioxide emissions, just as they have to take into account the cost of using labor and scarce raw materials. Labor and resource markets make producers pay for the labor and raw materials they use, but unless the government levies a carbon tax nobody has to pay for the damage their emissions cause. Consequently, in the absence of a carbon tax, producers ignore the social cost of their emissions in order to maximize their profits, and households have no incentive to consider the damage their emissions cause. A carbon tax seeks to "internalize" this otherwise neglected, negative "external" effect so businesses and households will take it into account.[3]

When all who emit carbon dioxide pay the same tax per unit of emission, those with lower abatement costs will find it in their interest to reduce emissions by more than those with higher abatement costs. Sources will find it in their interest to reduce their emissions as long as their reduction costs are less than the tax they must pay if they fail to reduce emissions. Sources with high reduction costs will reduce their emissions by less, while sources with low reduction costs will reduce their emissions by more. This means a carbon tax distributes reductions among emitters in a way that minimizes the cost of achieving the overall 10 percent reduction—sources with low abatement costs will do more of the total reduction and sources with high abatement costs will do less. It also means all sources have an incentive to develop new technologies to further reductions no matter how much they have already abated.

So a carbon tax minimizes the overall cost of achieving a 10 percent reduction in aggregate emissions. A carbon tax also explicitly makes polluters pay. It forces those who wish to emit greenhouse gases to pay the rest of us (in the form of a carbon tax) for using a scarce, valuable resource—space in the upper atmosphere where too much carbon is already stored. At least in theory, each citizen of the United States has an equal claim on the tax revenues of the federal government. So implicitly a carbon tax awards 100 percent of what was formerly an ambiguous property right that was habitually appropriated by polluters without asking permission—the right to release carbon dioxide into the atmosphere—to all citizens on an equal basis.

Tradable emission permits: While commonly misunderstood, each part of this policy is quite simple. *Emission permits:* Anyone emitting carbon dioxide is required by law to own permits to do so. If I am emitting 246 tons, and if a permit allows me to emit one ton, then I must acquire 246 permits. If I have 246 permits but emit more than 246 tons, I am in violation of the law—just as I would be if I caught six trout when my fishing permit only allowed me to catch five trout—and I am subject to whatever punishment for violation is established as part of the carbon permit law. *Tradable:* Anyone who owns a permit is free to sell it to anyone she chooses, and anyone who wants to buy a permit is free to buy it from anyone who is willing to sell it. In other words, there is a free market for the permits to emit carbon where everyone is free to strike any mutually agreeable deals they wish.

So if the U.S. government wants to reduce carbon emissions by 10 percent, all it has to do is print up 10 percent fewer permits than the number of tons of carbon emitted in the United States last year. However, declaring these permits to be tradable in a free market is not the same as deciding how to distribute the permits in the first place. Many assume that when the government says there will be a market for emission permits, it means the government will sell the permits at an auction where all are free to come to buy. But this is not the only possibility and unfortunately has seldom been the case. Prior to 2008 the bulk of pollution permits were given away free of charge to firms emitting the pollutant.[4] The procedure usually used is called the "grandfather system," which awards permits for free to polluters based on their share of past emissions. Under the grandfather system, for example, if a company was responsible for 28 percent of all carbon emissions last year, it would receive without charge 28 percent of all the permits printed this year. Another way to think about the grandfather system is that every source of carbon emissions would receive, without charge, permits sufficient to cover 90 percent of whatever amount it had emitted the previous year. That would be its windfall wealth gain, which it is free to use as it pleases. Companies, for example, could use all their permits themselves, or sell some of them on the permit market if they decide to reduce emissions by more than 10 percent, or add to the permits they received free of charge in the initial grandfather distribution through purchases in the permit market if they decide to emit more than 90 percent of what they emitted last year.

In many respects, tradable carbon permits will lead sources to behave in the same way a carbon tax does. If I want to emit more carbon dioxide, I need to have more permits. If I do not own enough permits, I have to buy more in the permit market—which is costly. But even if I own enough permits to pollute as much as I want, it is still costly for me to emit carbon dioxide because the more I emit, the fewer carbon permits I can sell for a profit to others in the permit market. Under both a carbon tax and a cap-and-trade permit program, there is an opportunity cost when sources emit carbon dioxide. And if the price of a permit to emit one ton of carbon dioxide is the same as the tax on a ton of carbon dioxide, as it will be if the programs are *equivalent*, the opportunity cost of emitting a ton of carbon dioxide is the same in both cases and therefore induces the same behavioral response. In other words, at least in theory, tradable carbon permits yield the same efficiency advantages as carbon taxes—they minimize the overall cost of achieving a 10 percent reduction in carbon dioxide emissions–because they induce sources with lower reduction costs to reduce their emissions by more than sources with higher reduction costs.[5] Like a carbon tax, a tradable carbon permit program also provides incentives to develop cleaner technologies to reduce a company's carbon footprint since lower emissions leave fewer carbon permits to buy or more permits to sell.[6]

Like a carbon tax, cap-and-trade permit programs *where all permits are auctioned* also implements the "polluter pays" principle and distributes new property rights on an equal basis to all citizens. Anyone who wants to emit carbon dioxide must pay for that privilege by purchasing a permit to do so at a government auction. A carbon cap-and-trade program takes an ambiguous property right—the right to release carbon dioxide into the atmosphere—and explicitly transforms it into a legal property right. Whereas this "right" was formerly appropriated by any who wished because nobody (who mattered) objected, under a cap-and-trade program the property right is encapsulated in carbon permits. If 100 percent of the permits are sold at auction, the property right is explicitly awarded to all citizens on an equal basis since all citizens, at least in theory, have an equal claim on the revenues of the federal government.

However, if permits are given away free of charge—as they always have been with the single exception of the recent North East Regional Greenhouse Gas Initiative—the new, legal property right is awarded to whoever receives them. Under the grandfather system, the new property rights are awarded to those who are emitting carbon in proportion to their share of past emissions. The fact that those who receive the permits under the grandfather system may choose to sell them or buy more of them on the permit market simply means that those who have been explicitly awarded this new wealth are legally free to do with it as they please.

Monitoring and enforcement: Critics sometimes argue that if monitoring and enforcement are inadequate, permit programs will fail to deliver expected reductions. This is true. However, this is equally true for regulatory and tax policies. If sources can get away with underreporting emissions so they do not have to purchase as many permits as they should, we obviously have a problem. But if they can get away with it, sources will underreport emissions to avoid fines under a regulatory program, and sources will underreport emissions to reduce tax liability in the case of a carbon tax. In other words, all three policies require authorities to know how much sources have emitted and establish effective penalties for violations. All three policies face the same practical problems with regard to devising an effective system for measuring, monitoring, and enforcing compliance. And contrary to the claims of some free-market environmentalists, none of these policies, including cap-and-trade, is "self-monitoring." With regard to monitoring and enforcing, we could say all three policies are "created equal."

Incidence, Progressivity, and Rebates

Incidence: Any policy that reduces carbon emissions will raise the price of carbon emissions and thereby change the price structure in the economy, which will in turn change income distribution as well. This is true if we regulate carbon emissions by ordering an across-the-board cutback of 10 percent for all sources, if we impose a tax, or if we "put a price on carbon" through a cap-and-trade program. The distributive impact of raising the price of anything has long been studied by economists with regard to sales taxes imposed on particular commodities under the label "tax incidence." It turns out that in a market economy it is far from obvious who will end up paying how much of a sales tax. For example, whether the tax is collected from sellers or from buyers turns out not to affect who ends up paying the tax. Instead, the relative *elasticities*[7] of market demand and supply for a commodity determine how much sellers and buyers end up paying. If the tax is imposed on an *intermediate good*—a commodity that enters into the production of other commodities, as fossil fuels and the energy they are used to produce do—the tax will affect the relative prices of goods it is used to produce, raising the prices of goods whose production is more fossil-fuel-and-energy-*intensive* relative to the prices of goods that are less fossil-fuel-and-energy-intensive. Since people in different income categories spend different percentages of their income on different goods, this means that any policy that raises the price of energy reduces the purchasing power and therefore the real income of poor and rich to different extents. Fortunately, many empirical studies of tax incidence largely agree on the distributive effects of putting a price on carbon regardless of how we do it. Unfortunately, it turns out that the poorer you are, the larger will be the drop in your real income if the price of carbon emissions is raised through regulation, taxes, or a permit program.

Progressive versus regressive taxes: When a tax is *progressive*, the higher your income is, the higher *percentage* of your income is spent on the tax. For example, before deductions the federal income tax is progressive since the tax rate for people in high-income brackets is higher than for people in lower income brackets. When a tax is *regressive*, the higher your income is, the lower *percentage* of your income is spent on the tax. For example, sales taxes on cigarettes are regressive because (1) low-income people consume more (and save less) of their income in general, and because (2) out of their consumption expenditures, low-income people spend a higher percentage on cigarettes than wealthier people—even when a low-income person buys the same number of packs per week as a higher-income person. When a tax is *proportional*, everyone pays the same *percentage* of their income on the tax, regardless of whether they are rich or poor. Few existing taxes are exactly proportional, although not long ago some economists called for replacing all existing federal taxes with what they called a *flat tax* of 19 percent on all income, which they calculated would be *revenue-neutral*—that is, it would raise the same amount of revenue as the taxes it replaced. In sum, a progressive tax makes after-tax income distribution more equal than the pre-tax distribution, a regressive tax makes after-tax income distribution more unequal than the pre-tax distribution, and a proportional tax keeps after-tax income distribution the same as the pre-tax distribution.

What kind of tax is more or less *fair?* Support for making the tax system more progressive on grounds that this would make it fairer has long been a hallmark of "progressive" politics. The most common reason given is that the rich are more able to pay taxes than the poor—in effect, that the rich can afford to be more charitable. A less common reason given is that government programs and services, which include protecting property rights, benefit the rich more than the poor, so those who benefit more should pay more. Strangely, the best reason why progressive taxes are fair is the least articulated: A higher percentage of the income of the rich, as compared to the poor, is *un*deserved, making a progressive tax necessary to reduce economic injustice.

Those who argue for progressive taxes as a means to reduce economic injustice could stipulate that in every income bracket there are some who deserve what they get as well as some who do not. All one has to believe is that a *smaller percentage* of poor people do not deserve even the smaller amounts they receive than the percentage of rich people who do not deserve the far larger amounts they receive. Not only does this strike most people as plausible, but also it is virtually a statistical certainty! If we break income down into a "deserved" and an "undeserved" component, then in groups with a higher-than-average observed income we should expect to find a disproportionately large number of people with higher-than-average "undeserved" income.[8] Whereas the noblesse oblige argument for progressive taxation implicitly sanctions pre-tax income distribution as fair but requires the wealthy to be more charitable, this argument for progressive taxation forces people to confront how labor and capital markets distribute income unfairly in the first place.

Unfortunately, it is a well-known fact that carbon taxes are regressive. Since the poor save a lower percentage and consume a higher percentage of their income, carbon taxes, like most consumption taxes, are regressive. And while wealthy households have a higher carbon footprint because they consume so much more in absolute terms, per dollar of expenditure poorer households have a higher carbon footprint, which also makes carbon taxes regressive.[9] One remedy for the unfortunate fact that carbon taxes are regressive is to substitute revenues from the carbon tax for revenues from an even more regressive tax, such as the employee share of the FICA (social security) tax. However, while such substituting on a dollar-for-dollar basis would be revenue-neutral and make the overall tax system less regressive, it does not change the fact that in and of itself the carbon tax is regressive. Raising the price of carbon emissions through mandatory reductions or a carbon cap-and-trade policy also has a regressive effect on income distribution for the same reasons.

Rebates: Since neither regulation nor grandfather cap-and-trade programs collect any revenues, they provide no direct means to redress the regressive effects of putting a price on carbon. However, taxing carbon and a cap-and-trade program where permits are auctioned both generate new revenues that can be used to offset the regressive effects of raising the price of carbon emissions. "Tax and dividend" has been discussed in policy circles for some time, and Senators Cantwell and Collins introduced a cap-and-dividend bill during the 111th session of Congress that unfortunately was never even brought to the floor for discussion. Their Carbon Limits and Energy for America's Renewal (CLEAR) Act would have auctioned 100 percent of carbon permits and used 75 percent of the revenues to give every legal resident of the United States an equal rebate, or what the bill called a "dividend." Due to the high inequality of income in the United States, rebating an equal amount to every resident is so progressive that it more than overcomes the regressive effect of raising the price of carbon. Studies estimated that under the Cantwell-Collins bill the rebate would have paid all households up through the 70th income percentile more than what they would have lost because the cap on fossil fuels entering the economy raised energy prices; the higher prices would have cost only the top 30 percent of households more than their rebate. Of course, in theory, the revenues from a carbon tax could be rebated in exactly the same way.

Zoning and Sprawl

It has been a long time since owning a piece of property in the United States meant you could do absolutely anything you wanted with it. Special laws and regulations about land use have been with us for centuries. In 1860 a New York State statute prohibited all commercial activities along Eastern Parkway in Brooklyn. Today this statute would be considered a necessary "downzoning" for urban planning by city officials, but criticized as a "taking" by property rights activists since it reduced the market value of property along the parkway. In response to public displeasure with construction of the Equitable Building on Broadway, which blocked views and sunlight from reaching adjacent residents, the City of New York adopted citywide zoning regulations in 1916. The author of these regulations, Edward Bassett, went on to write the Standard State Zone Enabling Act, which became the blueprint for zoning in most states and empowered local governments to establish their own zoning laws.

In the 1920s a landlord in Ohio challenged the Village of Euclid zoning ordinance on grounds that by restricting use of his property it violated his rights under the Fourteenth Amendment to the U.S. Constitution. While lower courts ruled in favor of the landlord and declared the zoning ordinance unconstitutional, the U.S. Supreme Court overruled the lower courts and upheld the ordinance in 1926 in the case of *Village of Euclid, Ohio v. Ambler Realty Co.* The Supreme Court based its decision on two arguments: (1) that zoning extended and improved on nuisance law by providing advance warning of what would be considered a nuisance; and (2) that zoning was a necessary instrument for municipal planning. To this day "Euclidean zoning," named after the Village of Euclid, which segregates land uses into districts where the type and degree of development is specified, is by far the most prevalent zoning in U.S. cities and municipalities. Typical categories of land use are single family residential, multifamily residential, commercial, and industrial; and typical "dimensional standards" include minimum lot sizes, maximum densities, maximum heights for buildings, and minimum setbacks from public roadways and sidewalks.

One of the most politically contentious environmental issues in the United States is urban sprawl. A great deal of local politics revolves around this issue. The flip side of abandoning poor, inner-city neighborhoods is environmentally destructive growth, or "sprawl," in outlying areas. But while it may be profitable for developers to spread new homes for upper- and middle-class families indiscriminately over farmland, this is not what is best for either people or the environment. It is an environmental disaster because it needlessly replaces green space with concrete and asphalt. It is a fiscal disaster because, since new residents are spread over a large area lacking in existing services, for every new dollar in local taxes collected from new residents, it costs local governments roughly a dollar and a half to provide them with the streets, schools, libraries, and utilities they are entitled to. And it has a disastrous effect on people's lifestyles as the "rural character of life" in outlying areas is destroyed for longtime residents, and those moving into bedroom communities spend more and more of their time on gridlocked roads commuting to work and driving to schools and strip malls at considerable distances from their homes.[10] Nor does sprawl even address the nation's most pressing housing need—a scandalous shortfall of "affordable" housing.

Typically rural land is initially zoned in a way that allows for subdividing farms into many lots for new houses—which is how sprawl happens. The way to prevent this is to downzone land outside cities and town centers. For example, whereas a 100-acre farm might have been zoned to allow for 100 houses, it could be downzoned to allow for only two dwellings. This prevents houses from sprouting in farm fields where they are not wanted and forces new residential construction inside growth boundaries, where "upzoning" to permit greater density can absorb residential growth where it is more desirable. But environmentalists and urban planners are sadly mistaken if they think their jobs are done once they demonstrate that zoning changes like these to prevent sprawl produce large positive net benefits. While changes in zoning to promote *smart growth* often yield a large efficiency gain in the form of better protection for the environment and a reduction in the cost of providing public services, changes in zoning also change the market value of land, which means there will be losers as well as winners. Ignoring these distributive effects has prevented environmentalists from winning many local battles against sprawl.

Farmers usually strongly oppose downzoning because it dramatically decreases the price they can sell their land for if they decide to give up on farming. In some ways this is ironic because farmers can wax poetic over how much they personally enjoy rural life and how much they hate to see subdivisions sprouting up where their neighbors' farms used to be. As former chair of a special task force appointed by the Commissioners of St. Mary's County, Maryland, to recommend ways to protect the county's rural preservation district, I can assert that farmers there seldom took kindly to urban refugees moving in—particularly when their kids drove all-terrain-vehicle toys across fields that looked unused to them and when their parents threatened lawsuits over noxious smells and allergies caused by fertilizers and pesticides, leading to retaliatory "right to farm" ordinances. But the psychic pain of seeing neighbors' farms turn into housing developments apparently does not compare to seeing the market value of your own farm drop to a fraction of what it had been before downzoning because developers no longer knock on your door. In effect, farmers want all their neighbors' land downzoned but not their own. The conflict over who will sell out first to the despised developers, combined with a great deal of self-rationalization, makes for very confusing testimony at public hearings but a solid block of votes against downzoning land in "agricultural preserves" by those who claim to love living there. In any case, the downzoning is clearly a "taking" because it creates a significant financial loss for rural property owners. Developers traditionally oppose downzoning farmland as well because it is cheaper than buying land inside growth boundaries to build on, and also because profit margins on larger homes with larger lots are higher on average than on smaller houses on smaller lots.

A policy called *transfer development rights*, or TDRs, can change the calculus of self-interest for landowners near urban growth areas by compensating the traditional losers from zoning changes necessary to promote smart growth. One reason to do this might be because it is unfair to expect farmers who are often not particularly wealthy to bear the burden of preventing sprawl. But even if landowners are better off than others, it might be wise to support TDR programs that provide financial compensation for landowners because otherwise their political opposition to smart growth may prove strong enough to stall smart growth initiatives.

The problem is that the farmer owns two assets that are unfortunately tied together into a single commodity. The actual land has a certain value when used for agricultural purposes, which may be higher or lower depending on soil quality, rainfall, demand for crops the land is suitable for, and so on. Because farming near growing metropolitan areas has become less and less profitable for a variety of reasons, the value of the land for this purpose has generally been falling. But the farmer also owns the development rights that the current zoning of the land permits. And as metropolitan populations grow, the demand for residential development rights increases and the development rights the farmer owns become more valuable as a result. As a matter of fact, unless taxing authorities tax land in agricultural use at a lower rate, the growth in the value of the development rights inflates farmers' property taxes and is part of the reason farmers near urban areas have a hard time making ends meet. TDRs allow farmers to break their commodity into two parts and sell them separately from each other and, most importantly, sell them at different times.[11]

How does a well-designed TDR program work? First, farmland in an agricultural or rural preservation district must be downzoned. This prevents sprawl. In exchange for taking away the development rights on his own land, the farmer is given development rights that can be used only to build new living units elsewhere, inside *growth boundaries*: hence the name TDR. Finally, what gives the TDRs a market value is that developers are required to buy TDRs to build additional units inside growth boundaries or *development zones*. This is why developers will continue to knock on farmers' doors. But now, instead of offering to buy the farm to secure its development rights, developers will only be interested in buying farmers' TDRs. Because it cannot be built on, developers no longer want the farmland itself. But developers need farmers' TDRs or else they cannot build additional units inside development districts where upzoning has increased permissible densities—provided a developer has TDRs.

Environmentalists and urban planners anxious to replace inefficient sprawl with more efficient smart growth get what they want. Farmers not only get to cash in on their development rights, they can do it whenever they wish and continue to farm as long as they want, secure in the knowledge that they will remain surrounded by farming neighbors. Developers now have to pay for TDRs to build more units inside growth boundaries, but they were paying for the same development rights before when they purchased farmland along with its development rights to build in rural areas. Ignoring differences on profit margins for different kinds of housing, developers are no worse or better off than before. And finally, once development rights are stripped from farmland, it becomes cheaper for a new generation of organic farmers to buy land near urban areas when older farmers growing traditional crops go out of business. Young, idealistic organic farmers no longer have to outbid developers for land to use. Just as the developers really only wanted the farmers' development rights and not the land, new farmers really only want the land, not the development rights, which are a financial barrier to entry for them. The TDR program means that nobody has to pay for more than what they want to use, just as it means that landowners can sell their development rights separately from their land.[12]

As with any policy, there are devils in details that require careful attention. And as with most policies, it is possible to tilt the policy to the advantage of different constituencies. For example, if developers are required to purchase more than one TDR to build an additional residential unit inside growth boundaries, this will increase the demand for TDRs and therefore their price, to the advantage of farmers and the disadvantage of developers and new home buyers to the extent that developers can pass on their increased cost. And while TDRs are designed primarily to make the pattern of development more concentrated and efficient, they can also be used to change the overall rate of development by creating more or fewer TDRs than the number of development rights that are lost when rural areas are downzoned. Finally, TDRs are no guarantee to untie all Gordian political knots that prevent communities from engaging in smart growth. At least for now, the efforts I participated in to create an effective rural preservation district in St. Mary's County by fixing a dysfunctional TDR program there have failed, and as a result not only agricultural land but also forest and wetlands crucial to restoring water quality in the Chesapeake Bay, which surrounds the county on three sides, remain at risk.

Community Management: The Neglected
Alternative for CPRs

Until recently, the only answers considered worthy of discussion to the problem Garrett Hardin made famous as "the tragedy of the commons" were government regulation and privatization. In 1990 Elinor Ostrom introduced a third policy response into the public debate with publication of *Governing the Commons: The Evolution of Institutions for Collective Action.*

In *Governing the Commons* Ostrom demonstrates that a review of the literature covering many historical case studies where CPRs were managed by communities of users revealed that while overexploitation was sometimes the result, in many cases overexploitation did not occur. In chapter 3, "Analyzing Long-Enduring, Self-Organized, and Self-Governing CPRs," she presents case studies of communities that proved successful in avoiding the tragedy of the commons so widely predicted. In chapter 5, "Analyzing Institutional Failures and Fragilities," she examines other cases where communities failed to prevent overexploitation. Ever since, Ostrom and many others working in what is now known as the institutional analysis and development (IAD) framework have continued to add more case studies to their database and refine theoretical tools helpful in the search for key factors that determine success or failure when communities *self-manage* access to CPRs without resort to privatization or government involvement. Ostrom was awarded the Nobel Prize in Economics in 2009 for her pathbreaking work.[13]

We return to our example from Chapter 4 of a salmon fishery on San Juan Island to illustrate the logic of regulation, privatization, and community self-management of a CPR. Under free access, we discovered that as many as nine fishing boats would go out each day even though nine boats would catch no more fish than eight while adding $100 to the cost of fishing. We also discovered that CBA reveals the optimal number of boats to be five since a sixth boat would raise revenues (social benefits) by only $75 while adding $100 to both private and social costs.

Privatization: Free-market environmentalists recommend privatizing CPR to prevent the tragedy of the commons. How would this work in the San Juan salmon fishery? If one of the fishing boat captains bought out the other eleven, he would only send out five of what are now his boats each day because sending out more or fewer would only lower his profits. In the view of free-market environmentalists, the problem lies in the ambiguous property rights inherent in CPRs, and the solution lies in eliminating any ambiguity by converting CPRs into privately owned resources to realign the profit criterion with the efficiency criterion. In this case, the benefit from using the fishery will go to its private owner, who presumably can be better trusted to manage it efficiently and will receive $250 in profits per day for doing so.[14] In sum, the tragedy of the commons has been solved by turning a CPR into private property and awarding the benefit from its use to a single fishing company.

It is important to note that to implement this policy the State of Washington would have to back up the legal right of the owner to deny all others access to the fishery, which is now his private property. Otherwise, even if he has purchased the boats of the other eleven fishermen, there is nothing to prevent any of them from buying new boats and fishing again, or to prevent others from fishing in the owner's private property, for that matter. Moreover, by restricting his own use to five boats per day, he has created an incentive for all others to poach because any sixth boat that manages to fish in his private property can expect to earn a profit of $37.50 per day. So he will need the State of Washington to protect his property rights, which, of course, is not a problem for free-market environmentalists, who are only too happy to restrict the role of government precisely to this and only this.

Regulation: Opponents like to label regulation "command and control" and treat it as a "taking" by "clumsy Big Brother." If we go beyond sound bites, what does regulation actually look like? Suppose the State of Washington eliminated any ambiguity about ownership of the CPR by declaring it to be public property that nobody can access without permission from the Washington State Department of Fisheries. The Department of Fisheries could solve the problem of overexploitation by limiting fishing to only five boats per day. The Department of Fisheries would have to decide which five of the twelve captains were allowed to fish on any given day. This could be done in a variety of ways, including drawing five names out of a hat with all twelve names in it every evening or following a fixed rotation.

While the CPR has been converted into public property, in this case the fishing captains are still the ones who benefit from its use. It is now all twelve captains who benefit rather than only a single fishing company who receives the benefit under privatization, but it is only fishermen who are beneficiaries nonetheless. As a matter of fact, the State of Washington has just done the fishermen a big favor! Under free access, expected profits from fishing are zero when nine boats fish. If the Department of Fisheries restricts access to five boats, average profits are $50 for each of the five boats fishing on any day.[15] If each captain can expect to fish five out of every twelve days, this means average expected daily profits are now 5/12 times $50 or $20.83 rather than zero. As a CPR the fishery was overexploited, and the users barely broke even. Now the resource is public property, but the benefits from its use go entirely to the twelve captains as profits—five boats times $50 profit per boat, or $250 per day. Citizens of the State of Washington might want to ask why they should not also benefit from a resource if it is now explicitly owned by the public at large. The answer, of course, is that they can.

Suppose the Department of Fisheries required fishermen to buy a license to fish in what is now public property, charging $50 per day for a commercial salmon fishing license. This would raise the daily cost of fishing from $100 (for gas and wages) to $150 (for gas, wages, and license). Now if there were already five boats out fishing, no captain who arrived later at the dock would go out to fish that day because he would expect to earn only \$137.50—or even less, if others arriving after him foolishly went out as well. In this case, regulation has converted a CPR into public property, but the benefit from its use will go to the general public. What was before \$250 in fishing profits per day has now become \$250 a day of revenue for the State of Washington and all its citizens as five captains pay \$50 each for a daily fishing license. James Boyce (2002) might suggest at this point that in the real world, if regulation is chosen as the answer to the tragedy of the commons for fisheries, whether regulation takes the form of fishing licenses or limits on the size of catch will be determined largely by who has more power—the fishing industry or ordinary citizens. But as Mancur Olson taught us, it would be naive to assume that just because there are more citizens than there are fishing captains, the citizens will prevail. As Olson famously explained, precisely because they are greater in number, each citizen individually has little to gain from lobbying legislators on state fishing policy, while each fishing captain has a great deal at stake (Olson 1965).

Community self-management: Elinor Ostrom and now many others ask why communities cannot restrict their use of CPRs themselves without resort to privatization or government intervention. After all, our twelve fishing captains are killing themselves when nine of them go out to fish every day. Why don't they wake up, smell the coffee burning, and do themselves a favor by agreeing to send out only five boats a day? If they can manage to agree to a certain amount of self-restraint, their expected profit will increase from zero to \$20.83 per day, and they will have 44 percent more leisure time as well![16]

In this case, the CPR has become what some call community property to distinguish it from private property and public property. It would be more accurate to call it "user common property," although users frequently coincide, or at least strongly overlap, with those who live in communities adjacent to CPRs. As we have seen, if traditional users restrict their own exploitation of user common property, they will generate the same efficiency gain we observed under privatization and regulation, and they will be able to appropriate these benefits all for themselves. While progressives criticize privatization of CPRs on equity grounds with good reason, many progressives fail to consider the possibility that community self-management may also be objectionable on equity grounds. If user communities are poor, then allowing them to appropriate the benefits from restricting access through self-management increases equity. On the other hand, if our twelve salmon captains are wealthy compared to other residents, their fellow Washingtonians may find the distributive effect of this policy that converts a CPR into user common property objectionable on equity grounds.

But why would users ever fail to do what is clearly in their self-interest?

The problem is that it may not be easy for users to come to an agreement on how to restrict their own use, particularly if they will find it difficult to deny access to outsiders. If traditional users can get over the first hurdle and mutually agree to restrict their own use, they increase incentives for others to crash their party if they cannot successfully deny outsiders access to their user common property. And unlike private property and public property, where property rights are clear-cut and legal enforcement is generally reliable, user common property is often more tacit than legal and requires self-enforcement against poachers besides self-restraint among traditional users.

We can begin to think about problems that prevent users from successfully managing to restrict their use of CPRs by asking why our twelve captains might fail to organize themselves into a fishing cooperative to decide how many boats to send out each day. Any actual or perceived inequalities between the captains in equipment, skill, experience, and so on make it more likely that some would refuse to join an organization that restricts access because they believe they can do better than average under free access. Also, if there are variations in catches, negotiating a deal where some captains get one-tenth the profits and others get one-fifteenth, for example, makes the bargaining more prone to hassle and therefore less likely to result in a successful agreement to form a cooperative than if it is obvious why cooperative profits should be split equally among all twelve members. But most importantly, stability among potential users is crucial to achieve and maintain restricted access. If, after the twelve captains from Friday Harbor have formed a cooperative that maximizes cooperative profits they have agreed to share by sending out five boats per day, a new, thirteenth fishing boat can come over from an adjacent island—or worse still, a larger fishing boat can easily reach San Juan waters from harbors on the mainland—there is little incentive for the twelve Friday Harbor captains to restrain themselves. If other boats can fish every day and ride for free on the self-restraint of the Friday Harbor captains, it is hard to imagine they would be able to organize and keep a cooperative intact.

Of course, discovering what real-world conditions are likely to make CPR users more or less successful at organizing either a formal or what amounts to an informal producers' cooperative is what Ostrom began to tease out by comparing the successful historical cases with the unsuccessful ones in *Governing the Commons*. Based on a great deal of further empirical and theoretical investigation since then, IAD researchers now feel confident about a list of factors Ostrom identified on a provisional basis back in 1990 as critical for successful community self-management of CPRs. Whenever one or more of these conditions is not present, the tragedy of the commons becomes more likely.

1. Who has rights to withdraw resources from the common pool must be identified, and the boundary of the resource itself must be clearly defined.
2. Rules regarding appropriation must be well suited to local conditions.
3. Users must be able to participate in elaborating and modifying the rules of use.
4. Those who monitor use must come from the ranks of the appropriators and/or be clearly accountable to them.
5. There must be effective but graduated sanctions against those who violate rules of appropriation.
6. There must be quick, easy, and cheap mechanisms available to appropriators and officials to resolve conflicts.
7. The right of the community to self-manage the CPR must be acknowledged by higher authorities.

In sum, community self-management is now widely recognized as one possible solution to overexploitation of at least some CPRs. When there is good reason to believe that most of the above conditions hold, there may be no reason to resort to privatization or government regulation to prevent the tragedy of a commons. While neither Ostrom herself nor most IAD researchers argue that community self-management is always the best policy, they do recommend exploring the possibility of creating the missing conditions before jumping to the conclusion that privatization and outside regulation are the only alternatives to the tragedy of the commons. One issue many who jump on the community self-management bandwagon would do well to think more about is the equity implications of allowing traditional users to appropriate the benefits of user common property. As always, progressives need to ask if the distributive effects of a policy ameliorate or aggravate existing inequities, which means that careful attention should be paid to whether traditional users are better or worse off than the public at large.

Permit Markets: Dream or Nightmare?

Before the financial crisis of 2008, many people reacted positively to the idea of creating a new market for carbon. Mainstream economists, politicians, and the mass media—particularly in the United States—were inclined to assume that markets were the best solution to any and all economic problems and could be relied on to behave in a predictable and desirable way. In Part II we discovered that because of perverse incentives resulting from externalities and free riders, markets are often the root source of environmental problems and that private enterprise market economies are, indeed, plagued by an unhealthy growth imperative. And in Chapter 6 we discovered that free-market environmentalism was based on a gross misinterpretation of the Coase theorem and that there was every reason to believe that, if matters were left to voluntary negotiations between polluters and pollution victims, grossly inefficient levels of pollution would be the result. But before 2008, not only were well-established theories about "market failure" widely ignored, but a literature documenting inefficiencies that result from disequilibrium dynamics in markets went ignored as well, as did concerns about pernicious effects of marketization on preference formation raised by economists outside the mainstream of the profession.[17] In sum, until recently only a few people worried that a market for carbon emission permits might prove problematic.

However, the havoc unleashed by the crash of financial markets in 2008 and the "great recession" that swept around the world in its aftermath has dramatically altered popular attitudes about markets. Now when people hear that a policy requires creating a new commodity that can be traded in a new market, many react with trepidation, fearing that the new market may not behave like the ideal markets in economic textbooks or may even "go postal" on us. Complacency about serious problems with markets prior to 2008 was, to put it mildly, naive. Hopefully a greater awareness of potential problems triggered by the collapse of financial markets in 2008 will facilitate a more judicious examination of (1) how a carbon market might malfunction, (2) what, if anything, can reduce the likelihood of this happening, and (3) what would and what would not be affected if a carbon market did behave badly.

The first point that cannot be over-emphasized is that *in the real world* there are both efficiency and equity reasons to prefer a carbon tax, which does not create a new commodity and market, over an equivalent cap-and-trade carbon permit program, which does. A carbon cap-and-trade program can yield the same efficiency gains as an equivalent carbon tax only if the carbon permit market achieves its equilibrium price instantaneously—that is, only if the permit market behaves perfectly. A carbon tax does not require a market for carbon emission permits to behave more perfectly than any real market ever has or will in order to deliver the maximum efficiency gain possible, whereas a cap-and-trade policy does. A carbon tax also has an important practical advantage over a cap-and-trade policy with regard to equity. As explained above, a tax automatically awards the property right to emit carbon to "we, the people." For a cap-and-trade policy to do the same, we must first win the political fight to auction all carbon emission permits rather than give any away for free.

However, sometimes circumstances may favor a cap-and-trade program over a tax, so it is important to be neither naive nor paranoid about what kind of problems real permit markets can create.[18] In the short run, the problems with permit markets derive from what economists call "false trading." However, there are larger potential problems in the long run if speculators become involved in the permit market. Because price volatility magnifies uncertainty with adverse effects on investment decisions, any bubbles or crashes in the market for carbon allowances would be counterproductive. And if a poorly regulated financial sector allows speculators in the carbon market to profit from bubbles and crashes at the expense of the rest of us, as they were permitted to profit from the recent bubble and crash in real estate markets, the economy would become even more unfair than it already is.

We need to put a price on carbon. The price should be as close as possible to the magnitude of the negative consequences that a ton of carbon emission generates. And this price signal needs to be steady and predictable in order for it to affect behavior in desirable ways. If the price of carbon permits is way below or above what it should be, if the price fluctuates wildly, or if the permit market experiences bubbles and crashes, both efficiency and equity will be adversely affected.

False trading: In a cap-and-auction program that is equivalent to a particular carbon tax, the price of a permit sold at the auction should, in theory, turn out to be the same as the tax. But what if some sources underestimate their need for emission permits and either do not attend the auction or buy too few permits? This means that those who do buy at the auction will pay a lower price for permits than had everyone demanded as many as they should have. In other words, the price that clears the auction market will be too low because not all of what we might call "fully informed demand" showed up. One of two things will happen: If no postauction trading of permits is allowed among sources, those who bought lots of cheap permits will fail to reduce their emissions as much as is efficient given their emission reduction costs compared to others, and those who failed to buy as many permits as they should have will have to reduce their emissions more than is efficient given their relative emission reduction costs. On the other hand, if postauction trading of permits among sources is allowed, presumably the wise, early birds will be able to sell some of their permits at a higher price than they paid for them at the auction to those who were caught sleeping, and the postauction price will rise toward the price that would have cleared the auction had everyone correctly estimated their situations in the first place. By allowing the wise (or lucky) to benefit at the expense of the dimwitted (or unlucky), postauction trading reduces the inefficiency that occurs when early birds who could have reduced emissions more cheaply than sleepyheads fail to do so. But here is the important point: Any behavior committed to and carried out while the price signal is wrong—which includes the auction price that was too low by hypothesis, and any of the prices that are climbing, but still below the eventual postauction equilibrium price if postauction trading is permitted—will be inefficient to some degree. In the language of theoretical economics, behavior induced by trading at "false prices" is inefficient.

In this example, the question reduces to how much false trading will take place, how much inefficiency this false trading will generate, and how unfair we think it is for the wise and lucky to profit at the expense of those who are less so. In the real world there will always be some false trading, and whatever inefficiency and inequity results is a measure of how much more inefficient a cap-and-trade program will be as compared to an equivalent tax program where nothing is ever traded. If permits are good only for the year they are printed the time frame for false trading will be limited to one year. However, if permits can be "banked" and used at any time over a number of years, as is often the case, the time frame for false trading will be longer and the inefficiency caused by false trading can be much greater as well.

Speculation: Much of the behavioral change we want to induce requires major investments in energy production, storage, and distribution from renewable sources, as well as massive investments in energy conservation. Decision-makers will weigh benefits that stretch decades into the future against very large sunk costs in the present. What if the price signal from the carbon permit market that tells them how large those benefits will be is not loud and clear? What if there is a great deal of volatility in the price signal, or what if investors have reason to believe there may be a carbon permit bubble followed by a crash, so the price of emitting carbon will yo-yo out of control? This, of course, is exactly the wrong kind of price signal to send investors. What are the chances that a cap-and-trade program will send a much less effective price signal to investors than a carbon tax that can be set for as many years into the future as we wish?

If speculation enters into the auction or postauction trading, the problem of false trading can expand into a much bigger problem. Despite hundreds of years of empirical evidence to the contrary, mainstream economists prefer to believe that equilibrating forces can be relied on to push nonequilibrium prices toward their equilibrium, and therefore false trading occurs only because these adjustments may take time during which transactions will be inefficient to some degree. Most economists regard market bubbles and crashes—where prices "inexplicably" diverge farther and farther from their equilibria—as rare exceptions, blaming these aberrations on those they call "speculators" whose "herd behavior" they characterize as "irrational." However, standard treatments of market bubbles and crashes are badly misinformed and misleading. Not only are bubbles and crashes far more common and serious problems than market enthusiasts want to admit, but they are the result of very rational behavior on the part of market participants who cannot be nicely partitioned

147

into "good" buyers and sellers whose only interest is how useful the commodity is to them, and "evil" speculators who have no use for the commodity themselves but seek only to profit from trading.

The famous "laws" of supply and demand, which predict that when market price rises, quantity supplied will increase and quantity demanded will decrease, leading markets toward their equilibria, are based on a questionable, implicit assumption about how market participants interpret price changes. Standard analysis implicitly assumes that sellers and buyers believe that when the market price rises, the new higher price is the new stable price. Or, more precisely, standard reasoning assumes that when a market price rises, buyers and sellers assume that price is just as likely to fall from this new higher price as it is to rise further. If this is truly the case, then it *is* sensible when market price rises for sellers to offer to sell more than before and for buyers to offer to buy less than before—as the "laws" of supply and demand say they will.

However, sometimes buyers and sellers quite sensibly interpret price changes as indications of *further* price movements in the same direction. In this case, it is rational for buyers to respond to an increase in price by increasing the quantity they demand before the price rises even higher, and for sellers to reduce the quantity they offer to sell while waiting for even higher prices to come. When buyers and sellers behave in this way, they create greater excess demand and drive the price even higher, leading to a market bubble. When buyers and sellers interpret a decrease in price as an indication that the price is headed down, it is rational for buyers to decrease the quantity they demand, waiting for even lower prices, and for sellers to increase the quantity they offer to sell before the price goes even lower. In this case, their behavior creates even greater excess supply and drives the price even lower, leading to a market crash. This means that if market participants interpret changes in price as *signals* about the likely direction of further price changes, and if they behave rationally, they will not only fail to behave in the way the "laws" of supply and demand would lead us to expect, but rather behave in exactly the opposite way from what these "laws" predict.[19]

We have had more than enough reminders recently that market bubbles and crashes are alive and well. The U.S. housing bubble was the largest bubble in history, and the Great Financial Crisis that began in 2008 is only the most recent and serious financial crisis to occur over the past few decades. The Mexican "tequila" crisis of 1995 was followed by the far bigger East Asian financial crisis of 1997, which was followed by smaller financial crises in Russia, Turkey, and Brazil, and finally by the disastrous Argentine financial crisis of 2001. It is therefore sensible to ask if creating a market for carbon emission allowances may lay the groundwork for the next big financial bubble and crash. A domestic cap-and-trade program could create a hundred billion dollar annual carbon market in the United States alone. A post-Kyoto cap-and-trade climate treaty could generate half a trillion dollars of carbon trading a year.

Keeping Wall Street at Bay

There are only two ways to prevent the financial industry from ripping off sizable chunks of economic output while creating conditions that give rise to financial crises. The best way is to declare the entire financial industry too important to be allowed to fail—repeatedly—and so replace private with public finance. Accepting deposits and making loans to creditworthy consumers and businesses with sound investment plans is not terribly complicated. Only if one is trying to turn a simple industry into one that will make obscene fortunes for its investors and executives are complicated financial instruments and esoteric ways to increase leverage necessary. Where did the wizards of Wall Street steer investment resources over the past few decades? Did they wisely steer investment into renewable energy and energy conservation technologies and projects? Have they deftly orchestrated a massive conversion program to transform our fossil-fuel-based economy into a carbon-neutral system in time to avert climate change? Or did the private financial sector steer savings into a stock market bubble followed by a housing bubble and into the production of more energy-guzzling, big-ticket items such as SUVs and McMansions? A very high percentage of all the global savings that were sucked into the U.S. financial system over the past two decades was funneled into counterproductive activities that took us farther down an unsustainable dead-end road. In the words of Herman Daly, much of the investment chosen by the private financial sector went into promoting *un*economic growth. A public financial sector not only would be much more immune from crisis, but could do a much better job of channeling savings into the kinds of productive investments we really need rather than asset bubbles—investments that lead to better products and technologies, investments that increase our physical, human, and natural capital.

The only other way to protect the rest of us from Wall Street excesses is to restructure the financial industry and subject its various parts to regulations that are appropriate and competent. This is a second-best policy because, as history has just demonstrated once again, (1) the financial industry is very adept at figuring out ways around existing regulations—regulating finance is like hunting a moving target that has every incentive and means to stay one step ahead of its pursuers; (2) the financial sector will relentlessly lobby politicians to remove and relax regulations, and even if the industry's profits were less bloated it would still have sizable financial resources to devote to such efforts; and (3) there is little reason to believe that in private hands the financial sector, even if competently regulated, would steer investments as aggressively as a public credit system could into the kinds of projects desperately needed at this critical juncture in history when we must mobilize to avert climate change.

In any case, if we replace private with public finance or if we subject private finance to competent regulation, we need not fear that carbon allowances will become part of the next toxic financial cocktail. Moreover, if we fail to reform finance in one of these two ways, it is almost certain there will be more financial cocktail crises, whether or not carbon allowances are one of its ingredients. In other words, we cannot prevent future financial crises by refusing to create certified carbon emission reduction credits. Future financial crises can only be prevented by successful financial reform.

However, consider a worst-case scenario. Suppose we create a global market for carbon allowances and offsets that climbs above half a trillion dollars a year. Suppose financial regulatory reform never happens. Suppose Wall Street does create a horrible cocktail of subsidiary markets around the carbon market—including carbon futures markets, markets for carbon swaps, derivatives based on fluctuations in the price of carbon, and whatever financial "innovation" Wall Street comes up with next. Suppose all these carbon futures, swaps, derivatives, and so on are packaged together with other opaque securitized financial instruments, based on other commodities, which nobody understands but eventually everyone comes to mistrust. In other words, suppose Wall Street mixes carbon allowances into a terrible, toxic, financial potion, and suppose this new asset bubble does burst with a vengeance.

This would be dreadful indeed. And if the financial crash were worse than the one that just occurred, it would lead to even more awful consequences for all of us who live on Main Street. But this is the important point: The financial collapse would not diminish the reduction in global carbon emissions one iota. Fluctuations in the price of carbon allowances and any derivatives based on those prices would redistribute income and wealth in mostly undesirable ways. And the price volatility for allowances that results would fail to send the steady, reliable price signal desired. But as long as laws and treaties requiring those who emit carbon to have the appropriate number of permits were enforced, the effort to reduce emissions and avert climate change would not be undermined.

In this worst-case scenario, what would happen is Wall Street would siphon off a big chunk of world product—first by trading in toxic assets that include carbon allowances as a bubble built, and then by shifting the cost of the financial cleanup onto the rest of us when the bubble burst. But this has nothing to do with the number of carbon permits in existence, and therefore nothing to do with how much carbon can be emitted. Moreover, such a financial crisis would not be the fault of the carbon market. This tragedy would be due entirely to the failure to either nationalize or subject the financial sector to competent regulation. It is highly implausible that denying Wall Street access to one new commodity, carbon allowances, would prevent future financial crises if the financial industry remains free from competent regulation.

The United States: A Very Special Country Indeed

There are strong reasons for progressives to prefer a carbon tax over a domestic cap-and-trade program. As explained above, a tax is simpler and easier to administer. With a tax there is no carbon market to go haywire. With a tax the government collects the revenue automatically, whereas in a cap-and-trade program progressives always have to fight for 100 percent of the permits to be sold at auction so the government gets the revenue instead of giving away the new wealth the cap creates for free to polluters. For all these reasons, most progressive economists, including me, generally prefer a domestic carbon tax over an equivalent cap-and-trade program—that is, one that achieves the same overall emission reduction. However, there are some very compelling reasons to favor cap-and-trade over a carbon tax in the United States right now.

Unfortunately, in the United States a great deal of the electorate suffers from acute *tax-phobia*. While it is often irrational for low- and middle-income people to fear taxes, the fact is that raising taxes is extremely difficult in the United States. Apparently it is much easier to remind people of the pain taxes cause them, and how much they dislike how their taxes are often spent, than to remind them that sometimes they like the programs their taxes go to pay for. In any case, the bottom line is that even if we could get a carbon tax passed in the United States, there is no way it would be high enough to generate nearly as large a reduction in emissions as the reductions we can achieve through a cap-and-trade policy.

Of course, there are better and worse versions of domestic cap-and-trade programs, and as every day passed during the spring and summer of 2010 the chances of the U.S. Congress passing an effective, fair, and efficient cap-and-trade domestic climate bill diminished to the point where no climate legislation was ever voted on, much less passed. Due to successful industry lobbying, the Waxman-Markey bill, which was passed by the House of Representatives but left to die by the Senate, was a cap-and-trade disaster. It was ineffective because it allowed generous offsets in agriculture where emissions were not capped without adequate provisions to ensure that agricultural offsets would be "additional" and therefore not puncture large holes in the bill's emission cap.[20] It was unfair because it gave 85 percent of permits away free of charge to large sellers of carbon fuels and utilities and failed to compensate working- and middle-class households for higher energy bills. It was inefficient because it compensated very low-income households for higher energy prices by subsidizing their utility bills rather than giving them a rebate they could spend as they wished, thereby failing to provide them with any incentive to reduce their energy consumption.

The Cantwell-Collins CLEAR Act was a *much* better bill. This bill, which was introduced in the Senate would have auctioned 100 percent of the permits and rebated 75 percent of the revenues on a per household basis. As mentioned above, it is estimated that the bottom 70 percent of households would have been more than compensated for higher energy prices, and only the top 30 percent would have paid more in higher energy prices than their rebate. By compensating for higher energy prices through rebates, which could be spent however people wished, the incentive provided by higher energy prices for all consumers to reduce their energy consumption would have been preserved. The Cantwell-Collins bill would have required the other 25 percent of revenues to be used to stimulate investment in renewable energy and energy conservation programs, which are desperately needed if we are to jump-start conversion to a carbon-neutral economy before it is too late. The bill permitted no offsets, which meant that the bill's emission cap was firm. Because fossil fuels would have been capped as they entered the economy at mine sites, oil and gas heads, and ports of entry, only a few thousand businesses would have had to be monitored. Finally, Cantwell-Collins contained provisions designed to reduce the dangers of speculative activity in the market for carbon permits.

Unfortunately, under pressure from industry lobbyists and the Obama administration, the Democratic Party Senate leadership opted to champion a far worse bill, the American Power Act, sponsored by Senators Kerry and Lieberman, not the Cantwell-Collins bill. Some environmental organizations denounced the Kerry-Lieberman American Power Act, pointing out its many deficiencies that would have taken us backward, not forward. Other environmental groups, fearing that prospects for passing a better bill after the November 2010 elections would have been even worse, reluctantly endorsed the bill, arguing that it was better than no climate bill at all. In the end none of the debates over pros and cons in any proposed bills mattered. Decades of lobbying for legislation to address climate change and hundreds of millions of dollars environmental organizations poured into these efforts all went for naught as the U.S. Senate adjourned for the summer with its two-decade record of never passing a single piece of legislation to address the climate change crisis still intact.

Notes

1. In theory it is the harmful activity that the government would want to regulate, tax, or limit through permit—which in this case is the act of releasing carbon dioxide into the atmosphere. For this reason we analyze different ways to reduce carbon emissions as applied to sources of emission. However, the number of emission sources for carbon dioxide in the United States is very large and includes homeowners, operators of automobiles, most farmers, and virtually all businesses and industries, which would make monitoring and enforcing any carbon reduction policy applied to all emitters exceedingly burdensome. Instead, what is usually recommended is applying any of these policies as far "upstream" as possible in order to reduce the number of actors one must monitor. Since a very high percentage of all carbon emissions derives from burning fossil fuels, which enter the economy from a relatively small number of sources—domestic oil and gas heads and coal mines, and imports of fossil fuels at ports of entry—it is more practical to apply any of the above policies to these sources only. Companies that extract or import oil, gas, and coal are referred to as "first sellers," and most legislation currently under discussion in the U.S. Congress proposes regulating, taxing, or permitting only the roughly 2,000 first sellers based on the amount of carbon dioxide that will be released by a barrel of oil, a cubic foot of natural gas, or a ton of coal when it is burned.

2. The cost of reducing emissions is commonly referred to as the *abatement* cost, and *abatement* is the common way to refer to the activity of reducing emissions.

3. As already explained, A.C. Pigou was the first to propose taxes to correct for negative external effects in market economies, and economists traditionally refer to these kinds of corrective taxes as *Pigovian taxes*, although they are more commonly called pollution taxes, emission taxes, effluent taxes, or green taxes. Unlike sales taxes on goods where no externalities are involved, which cause what economists call "dead weight efficiency losses," Pigovian taxes correct for an existing inefficiency in the market system and therefore yield an efficiency gain.

4. The first exception was the North East Regional Greenhouse Gas Initiative, under which virtually all permits were sold at auction. But selling permits at auction is, unfortunately, not the new norm. In its current draft the Western Climate Initiative still calls for giving a large percentage of permits away free of charge to major carbon users. Europe still gives away most carbon permits free of charge to sources. And even though presidential candidate Barack Obama called for a 100 percent auction, the Waxman-Markey bill passed by the House of Representatives would have given away 85 percent of permits for free, and the Kerry-Lieberman Senate bill would also have given away a significant number of permits free of charge in the early years of the program. Clearly we are far from winning the political battle to stop giving permits away free of charge.

5. Only if the actual permit market functioned like the ideal market in mainstream economic textbooks would a cap-and-trade policy be as efficient as an equivalent pollution tax. We discuss the implications of possible problems in real-world permit markets later in this chapter.

6. There is one version of tradable carbon permits that in theory yields exactly the same results as an equivalent carbon tax. If the government auctioned off 100 percent of the carbon permits and if the permit market reached its equilibrium price instantaneously, the results of the two policies would be not only *equivalent* but also *identical* in every way. In both cases every source would reduce its emissions by exactly the same amount because the opportunity cost of failing to reduce emissions would be the same—pay a tax or buy a permit for the same amount as the tax. In both cases every source would pay the government exactly the same amount—in one case in taxes and in the other case by purchasing permits at the government auction. And in both cases the government would

collect the same amount of total revenue—in one case as tax revenue and in the other case as proceeds from a permit auction.

7. Elasticity is a useful concept that measures how sensitive demand or supply is to a change in price. If, for whatever reason, demand is more sensitive than supply to a change in price, sellers will pay more of any tax imposed on the good than buyers. If supply is more sensitive than demand to changes in price, buyers will pay more of the tax than sellers.

8. A delightful irony that should not escape economists is that the above argument is analogous to the one made by Milton Friedman half a century ago in support of his famous theory of "permanent" consumption based on the concepts of "permanent" versus "transitory" income and consumption.

9. A host of empirical studies of the incidence of carbon taxes confirm this finding. The explanation lies in the fact that low-income families tend to spend a high percentage of their income on transportation, utility bills, and energy-intensive manufactured products. The only exception may be for the very poor who do not own cars.

10. An excellent documentary film on the harmful effects of sprawl and what can be done about it is *Save Our Land, Save Our Towns*, produced by Thomas Hylton and available from Bullfrog Films.

11. The idea of breaking land titles into separable commodities when convenient is not original to TDRs. Long before TDRs were invented in the 1970s, coal and oil companies purchased mineral rights and oil and natural gas rights to what lies underneath land while leaving farmers and ranchers free to continue to own and use the land surface.

12. In my new home state of Oregon, long famous for land use planning and growth boundaries, rural landowners and developers have battled environmentalists and urban planners repeatedly over the past few years. In 2004, ballot measure 37 gave property owners the right to claim compensation from state or local governments if their property values were adversely affected by land use or environmental regulations. In 2007, ballot measure 49 reversed many of the provisions of ballot measure 37. If either "49ers" or "37ers" wanted to negotiate an end to their civil war, they might consider offering TDRs as a peace initiative.

13. Elinor Ostrom, whose PhD is in political science, not economics, was the first woman to win a Nobel Prize in economics.

14. When five boats fish, total revenues are $750 while total costs are only $500, leaving $250 in profits. Note that here we are concerned *only* with the perverse incentive that arises from free access to a CPR. Other perverse incentives might still lead the private owner of the fishery to exploit it inefficiently. As discussed in Chapter 4, if the owner's rate of profit were higher than the social rate of time discount, as is quite likely, he would still overexploit the resource, but for a different reason than the one examined here.

15. When five boats are fishing, average revenue is $150 while average cost is only $100, which leaves $50 per boat per day as profit.

16. Under free access, each captain goes out nine out of every twelve days on average. If they agree to restrict access, each goes out only five days out of twelve. Cutting back from nine to five days saves four workdays out of nine, which means 44 percent less fishing time and 44 percent more leisure time.

17. For a full treatment of a long list of problems that markets create and reasons to search for alternatives to market economies, see Hahnel (2007a).

18. In Part IV we explore why an international treaty that places caps on national emissions and allows trading is a better approach than chasing the illusion of an international carbon tax, and later in this chapter we discuss why cap-and-trade domestic policies can achieve much greater emission reductions in countries plagued by tax-phobia.

19. Standard textbook treatments try to salvage the "laws" of supply and demand in face of these seemingly anomalous outcomes by interpreting them as the result of changes

in the "expectations" of buyers and sellers that *shift* the supply and demand curves. In the standard explanation, both before and after the shift, the supply curve slopes upward and the demand curve slopes downward—that is, at all times the curves obey the "laws" of supply and demand. It is the shift that causes the seemingly anomalous result that the quantity actually demanded responds positively to changes in price while the quantity actually supplied responds negatively to changes in price. It is certainly true that the anomalous behavior results from changes in expectations, but what textbooks invariably fail to point out is that the standard interpretation renders the "laws" of supply and demand unfalsifiable. In any case, however we choose to interpret the phenomenon, it is clear that market bubbles and crashes can result from behavior on the part of individual buyers and sellers that is perfectly rational when they interpret a change in price as an indication of the direction the price is headed, and that this behavior leads to movement away from, rather than toward the market equilibrium.

20. In Part IV, problems caused by offsets from sectors (or countries) without caps are discussed at great length.

Part IV

Climate Change

Part IV applies our new understanding to climate change, the greatest environmental problem humanity has ever faced. We review the history of climate negotiations, identify important lessons to be learned, and apply those lessons to designing an effective, efficient, and fair post-Kyoto treaty.

Chapter 8

A Brief History of
Climate Negotiations

Meetings to discuss an international treaty to combat climate change began in earnest in 1992 at the Earth Summit held in Rio de Janeiro. Understanding the history of how we became aware of the problem of climate change and how international negotiations about responding to climate change have proceeded over the past eighteen years is crucial if we are to figure out how best to proceed from here.[1]

The Road to Copenhagen

Early discoveries: French physicist Joseph Fourier first described a "greenhouse effect" in a paper delivered to the Royal Academy of the Sciences of Paris in 1824. In the 1860s research by Irish physicist John Tyndall demonstrated that carbon dioxide changes the atmospheric quality to admit entrance of solar heat but block its exit. In 1896 Swedish chemist Svante Arrhenius was the first to propose the idea of an artificial greenhouse effect caused by burning coal—which he speculated would be desirable since future generations would live under "a milder sky." In the 1930s British engineer Guy Stewart Callendar collected temperature statistics from around the world and concluded that the mean global temperature had risen markedly in the previous century, which he attributed to an increase in carbon dioxide levels of 10 percent over the same period. In the 1950s work by Gilbert Plass at Johns Hopkins University and Hans Suess and Roger Revelle at the Scripps Institute

159

of Oceanography led to a seminal article published by Revelle and Suess in 1957 warning that "humans are now carrying on a large-scale geophysical experiment." In 1958 Revelle and Suess employed geochemist Charles Keeling to continuously monitor carbon dioxide levels in the atmosphere, leading to the famous "Keeling curve," which charts annual increases in carbon concentrations right up to today. In 1963 the Conservation Foundation estimated that a doubling of the carbon dioxide content of the atmosphere would raise mean global temperatures by close to 4 degrees Celsius, and in 1979 NASA went on record saying: "There is no reason to doubt that climate change will result from human carbon dioxide emissions, and no reason to believe that these changes will be negligible."

But there is a difference between (1) awareness among a few researchers working in an obscure scientific subfield, (2) concern on the part of a large group of scientists specializing in the officially recognized scientific field of climatology, (3) virtual consensus within the entire scientific community that there is a potentially big problem, (4) popular awareness of a looming climate crisis, (5) discussion of remedies by political leaders, and finally (6) international meetings to address climate change attended by official delegations from most countries as well as experts and groups of concerned citizens.

Preliminary meetings: The first World Climate Conference in 1979 was attended mostly by scientists who warned of the threat of climate change and called on nations to anticipate and guard against dangers. This was followed by a meeting in Villach, Austria, in 1985 and the famous 1987 Brundtland Commission report, *Our Common Future*, discussed in Chapter 3. Scientists attending workshops sponsored by the Beijer Institute decided that the scientific issues must be clarified before a political response would be forthcoming, and an interdisciplinary group of scientists from all parts of the world, including physicists, atmospheric scientists, biologists, and economists, began work as part of the Intergovernmental Panel on Climate Change (IPCC), created in 1988 by the World Meteorological Organization and by the United Nations Environment Program. Ever since, the IPCC has provided reports based on scientific evidence that reflect the dominant viewpoints of the global scientific community.

In 1988 Dr. James Hansen of the NASA Goddard Institute for Space Studies at Columbia University testified before the U.S. Senate that based on computer models and temperature measurements he was 99 percent sure that the greenhouse effect was already changing the climate. The Second World Climate Conference in Geneva in 1989 included representatives from many governments who called for creation of an international convention on climate change. The United Nations responded by creating the United Nations Framework Convention on Climate Change (UNFCCC), which became the international body charged with negotiations to address climate change. In 1990 the IPCC's first report predicted that average global temperatures would increase faster over the ensuing 100 years than during any century in the previous 10,000 years.

The Earth Summit in Rio: However, international negotiations about how to respond to the threat of climate change only began in earnest in Rio de Janeiro in 1992 at the United Nations Conference on Environment and Development, popularly known as the Earth Summit. The Earth Summit is where the UNFCCC was signed by 154 nations (now more than 190 countries have signed). The document contains a number of important principles including a commitment to preserve the climate system for the benefit of present and future generations, recognition of the precautionary principle as the defining reason for global action to prevent climate change, and identification of "sustainable development"—defined as policies that satisfy the basic needs of the present without jeopardizing the rights of future generations to satisfy their needs—as our economic goal. But most importantly, Article 4 of the 1992 UNFCCC establishes the *principle of common but differentiated responsibilities* for mitigating climate change based on countries' contribution to the buildup of greenhouse gases (GHGs) in the atmosphere and ability to afford reductions. Article 4 further stipulates that industrial nations must take the lead in emissions reduction and that developing nations would not be asked to reduce their emissions without compensation.

However, after much discussion, country delegations in Rio were unable to agree on mandatory reduction targets for industrial countries. Instead, countries were strongly encouraged to make voluntary reductions according to "responsibility" and "capability," and more developed countries (MDCs) were encouraged to help less developed countries (LDCs) reduce emissions by providing technological and financial aid. In Rio the Conference of the Parties to the Convention (COP) was created to organize future meetings and make whatever decisions were necessary to secure UNFCCC objectives: stabilize GHG concentrations to prevent dangerous interference with the climate system and enable sustainable economic development to proceed.

The UNFCCC entered into force in 1994 and the IPCC became the official scientific advisory board to the COP. In 1995 the IPCC stated for the first time in an official report that it found a "discernable effect of human carbon emissions on the earth's climate." However, it became quickly apparent that most countries were not on track to meet their nonbinding reduction goals and that the principle reason was not doubts about the danger of climate change. Instead, the chief obstacle was fear of incurring significant economic costs to reduce emissions with no guarantee that others would do their fair share, and therefore that one's sacrifices would prove unfruitful. Discussion gravitated around this dilemma at COP meetings held in Berlin and Geneva between the 1992 meetings in Rio and the 1997 meetings in Kyoto, and also at important meetings of other organizations like the Organization of Economic Cooperation and Development (OECD), which hosted a conference on this subject in 1993.

The Kyoto Protocol: On December 11, 1997, after difficult negotiations that until the last minute seemed destined to break down, very much as negotiations would break down twelve years later in Copenhagen, 160 nations voted at COP 3 to approve a document known as the Kyoto Protocol.

The agreement requires industrialized countries, classified as Annex-1 signatories, to cut their emissions of six major GHGs by an average of 5.2 percent below their 1990 emission levels by the period 2008–2012. However, for equity reasons and because of some special circumstances the percentage reductions for Annex-1 countries differ. For example, the mandated reduction for the European Union is 8 percent, for the United States (had it signed) is 7 percent, and for Canada is 6 percent. Iceland, on the other hand, is allowed to increase emissions by 10 percent, Australia by 8 percent, and Norway by 1 percent. Russia, Ukraine, and New Zealand were simply required to maintain emissions at 1990 levels—that is, a 0 percent change. LDCs, designated as non-Annex-1 signatories, were assigned no mandatory reductions to be achieved by 2012, but were asked to reduce their emissions voluntarily with technological and financial help from MDCs.

At the insistence of U.S. negotiators, European delegations at COP 3 in Kyoto agreed at the last moment to permit "carbon trading"—although key details remained to be worked out at subsequent COP meetings. While the Kyoto Protocol called on Annex-1 countries to meet their commitments "predominantly" from domestic reductions, it sanctioned three kinds of carbon trading: (1) Annex-1 governments that fail to meet their national caps can purchase emission rights from other Annex-1 governments emitting less than their national caps allow; (2) individual sources in Annex-1 countries can buy emission rights—referred to variously as offsets, credits, or allowances—from sources in other Annex-1 countries; and (3) individual sources in Annex-1 countries can purchase emission rights from projects located in non-Annex-1 countries that are certified by the executive board of the Clean Development Mechanism (CDM) as reducing emissions in the non-Annex-1 country above and beyond what would have occurred had the project not been undertaken. Finally, the Kyoto Protocol contained a trigger mechanism stating that the agreement would not go into effect as a binding treaty until enough Annex-1 countries had ratified the agreement to account for at least 55 percent of total emissions from all Annex-1 countries in 1990.

From Kyoto to Copenhagen: Even as the Kyoto Protocol was being approved by delegations from 160 countries in Kyoto, the U.S. Senate ominously passed a resolution 95 to 0 against any treaty that did not require developing countries to make "meaningful" cuts in emissions. In 2001 President George W. Bush officially renounced the protocol and the United States withdrew from participation. Nonetheless, the European Union ratified the treaty in 2002, and after Russia ratified in November 2004, the Kyoto Protocol became a legally binding treaty on February 16, 2005. Australia ratified the treaty in 2007, leaving the United States as the sole country not to have done so.

Final rules regarding carbon trading were worked on at the COP 7 meetings in Marrakech. The Marrakech Accords set no quantitative limits on emissions trading and allowed significant credits for forest and cropland management, but set caps on CDM and sequestration credits and allowed no credits for forest preservation. At subsequent COP meetings in Bali and Poland, new provisions to discourage deforestation and forest degradation known as REDD (which are reviewed in Chapter 9) were prepared to be voted on in Copenhagen.

The Free-Rider Problem

The most crucial change in the history of thinking about how to avert climate change was understanding the free-rider problem when different actors are responsible for providing a public good. When any country reduces carbon emissions, its citizens bear the entire cost of doing so, while most of the benefit from those reductions is enjoyed by citizens of other countries. This is not to say that a country's own citizens do not benefit when domestic emission reductions help avoid climate change. But since everyone benefits from averting climate change, this means that even for China, where roughly 1 billion of the 6 billion people on earth live, five-sixths of the benefits from reducing GHG emissions in China are enjoyed by non-Chinese citizens. For every other country, the fraction of the total benefit that comes from their own emission reductions is even smaller. Because there is little incentive for countries to take into account benefits from their behavior for citizens of other countries, this means that when comparing the costs to their own citizens with the benefits to their own citizens, countries will predictably reduce carbon emissions by far less than is warranted when we compare the costs to *all* of the benefits. This in turn means that global reductions, the sum of all national reductions, will predictably be far less than scientists say are necessary to stabilize atmospheric concentrations at levels that are safe. Economists' shorthand way of summarizing this problem is to point out that all countries have a perverse incentive not to reduce their own emissions, but instead hope to "ride for free" on the reductions of other countries.

At the Earth Summit in Rio in 1992, too few participants appreciated the severity of the free-rider problem or were willing to take difficult but necessary steps to do something about it. But after watching emissions continue to climb despite nonbinding promises to the contrary made by MDC delegations in Rio, a majority of delegations arriving at Kyoto in 1997 realized that they could no longer avoid hammering out an agreement that set binding caps on national emissions. They realized that the only way to change outcomes was to change the calculus of national self-interest. And they realized that this is what an international treaty can and must do. When binding caps are *mutually agreed to*, this can change the calculus of national self-interest to better align with the global interest of achieving sufficient global reductions to avert cataclysmic climate change. When national reductions are mutually agreed to, the benefits each country achieves for its own citizens by agreeing to reduce its own emissions are expanded manyfold because this commitment wins its citizens the additional benefits from all the reductions made by other countries as well. We might say this difference "makes all the difference in the world," but it requires mutual agreement on binding reductions. When negotiators sat down in Kyoto in 1997, they finally realized they had to bite the bullet and secure an agreement on binding caps.

Reconciling Effectiveness, Equity, and Efficiency

After overcoming inevitable resistance to the loss of sovereign power over GHG emissions implied by a treaty that imposes binding caps on national emissions, negotiators in Kyoto still faced three major problems: (1) how to make the treaty *effective*—that is, guarantee sufficient global reductions to reduce the risk of cataclysmic climate change to an acceptable level; (2) how to distribute the costs of averting climate change fairly, or *equitably* among countries; and (3) how to make the treaty *efficient*—that is, how to minimize the global cost of averting climate change.

Effectiveness: Most negotiators at Kyoto probably realized that a 5.2 percent reduction in emissions by 2012 was not likely to be enough to do what scientists were insisting even then was necessary. Of course, since the 5.2 percent reduction was only to be imposed on emissions from MDCs, this was even less likely to prove effective even though MDCs accounted for 60 percent of global emissions. A little over 5 percent is what delegations agreed to because no higher reduction target was deemed politically feasible since many of their governments faced domestic opposition to ratifying a treaty that required greater reductions. It was also invariably described as a first step, which some defended as a significant and worthy first step and others criticized as woefully inadequate.

Equity: Even if all countries could be expected to benefit to the same degree from averting climate change—which is not the case—is it reasonable and fair to expect all countries to shoulder the burden of doing so to the same extent—that is, to reduce their national emissions by the same percentage? Article 4 of the UNFCCC approved in Rio in 1992 established the principle of "common but differentiated responsibilities and capabilities." As explained above, negotiators in Kyoto implemented this mandate and addressed the problem of equity by dividing countries into two groups, MDCs and LDCs, and assigning mandatory caps only to MDCs.

As mentioned above, not all Annex-1 countries were assigned the same percentage reductions. Negotiators in Kyoto had to consider reasons for any differences among Annex-1 countries on a case-by-case basis, but regardless of the ad hoc nature of this process, the reductions for each Annex-1 country were mutually agreed to by 160 countries who signed the protocol. All other countries were assigned no mandatory emissions reductions on grounds that reducing emissions, at least initially, would detract from their ability to accomplish what should be their primary task of economic development.

Efficiency: Once caps were agreed to for different Annex-1 countries, negotiators at Kyoto faced the dilemma of whether to require countries to meet their caps entirely through internal reductions or to allow some kind of trading of "emission rights." Proponents of emissions trading—the U.S. delegation chief among them—presented a strong case that, absent opportunities to trade, the global pattern of emission reductions agreed to as (at least roughly) fair was likely to be very inefficient—that is, the global cost of achieving the reductions was likely to be much higher than necessary. Any method for assigning caps equitably without allowing trading will leave the cost of the last ton of emissions reduced in some countries much higher than in other countries. This means that by relocating the last ton reduced in a country where the cost is higher to a country where the cost is lower instead, we can lower the global cost of reductions. Proponents argued that self-interested trading in emission rights could achieve these efficiency-enhancing relocations while retaining an equitable distribution of emission rights by separating who pays for a reduction from where the reduction is located. If LDCs without caps are also permitted to sell emission rights, as they are through the CDM of the Kyoto Protocol, trading will also generate a predictable flow of income from MDCs purchasing emission rights to sources in LDCs where abatement is cheaper.

As explained above, the 1997 Kyoto Protocol accepted trading in principle with some limitations, leaving details to be hammered out later during negotiations in Marrakesh and Bali. Controversies surrounding the Kyoto Protocol and emissions trading are discussed at length immediately below and in Chapters 9 and 10 as well. However, interested readers would do well at this point to read the Appendix to Part IV, *Exercise on Climate Control Trea-*

ties (see page 215), which graphically illustrates the interplay of efficiency and equity in an international cap-and-trade climate treaty, with and without different kinds of emissions trading.

Kyoto: Myth Versus Reality

In a true cap-and-trade program, aggregate emissions from all sources are capped. The Kyoto Protocol is not a true cap-and-trade program because emissions are capped only for Annex-1 countries, the MDCs, but not for non-Annex-1 countries, the LDCs, and therefore global emissions are not capped under Kyoto. Critics complain that this feature of Kyoto is highly problematic because it means carbon trading can undermine the treaty's ability to reduce overall global emissions. It is important to examine carefully this claim that carbon trading punctures holes in the global emissions cap and that therefore Kyoto deceives people into thinking we are addressing climate change when in fact we are not.

Trading between Annex-1 governments: Under the Kyoto Protocol, each Annex-1 country has agreed to reduce annual emissions from within its territory in 2012 by a specified percentage as compared to its annual emissions in 1990. This implies a cap on the number of tons each Annex-1 country is permitted to emit in 2012.

Suppose the government of Japan exceeds its cap by 10 million tons. If Canada comes in under its cap by 10 million tons, then Canada can sell "credits" for 10 million tons to Japan, which Japan can use to meet its cap. As long as Canada actually reduced its emissions by 10 million tons more than required by Kyoto, then total emissions reduction in Canada and Japan together is obviously exactly what it would have been had each country met its Kyoto quota through internal reductions. Moreover, as will be discussed in Chapter 9, monitoring to make sure this is the case requires only the ability to verify national emissions, which is necessary even if Annex-1 countries were not permitted to trade credits with each other.

So if Annex-1 governments meet their treaty obligations, it is impossible for any trading between Annex-1 governments, by which a country that exceeds its cap buys credits from a country that comes in under its cap, to undermine the overall emissions reductions those countries agreed to.

Trading between individual sources in different Annex-1 countries: Suppose a Japanese power company buys certified emissions reductions (CERs) for 100 tons of carbon emissions from a Canadian power company. This allows Japan to exceed its national emissions under Kyoto by 100 tons because after counting actual reductions in Japanese emissions any CERs *purchased* by sources inside Japan from sources outside Japan are *added* to Japan's measured, national reductions, just as any credits purchased by the Japanese government from other Annex-1 governments are added to Japanese measured reductions. However—and this is the crucial point—when a source within Canada sells CERs for 100 tons to a source outside Canada, Canada must now reduce emissions by 100 tons more than its Kyoto reduction quota because after counting reductions from within Canada any CERs *sold* by sources inside Canada to sources outside Canada are *subtracted* from measured Canadian reductions, just as any credits sold by the Canadian government to other Annex-1 governments are subtracted from measured Canadian reductions.

If the CERs sold by the Canadian power company are legitimate—that is, the Canadian power company actually reduced its emissions by 100 tons more than it would have otherwise, thus actually lowering Canadian emissions by 100 tons, then it is easy to see that trading CERs did not reduce total emissions reductions in Canada and Japan combined. The 100 tons the Japanese power company did not reduce is made up for by the 100 additional tons the Canadian power company did reduce. But what if CERs are not legitimate? What if the Canadian seller of CERs is cheating?

A great deal of criticism has been focused on private parties who buy CERs that are not legitimate in lieu of reductions in their own emissions. These bogus CERs may not deserve certification because no actual reduction on the part of the seller took place or because the actual reduction was less than the amount certified. They may not be legitimate because the reduction would have taken place anyway—that is, it was not "additional" to what the seller would have achieved in any case. Or the bogus CERs may not deserve certification because the additional reduction that took place allowed an increase in emissions somewhere else in the country that would not have been possible otherwise.

Moreover, critics point out correctly that the Japanese power company buying the CERs has no reason to care if the CERs are legitimate or not. The market for CERs is not like the market for apples, where the buyer can generally be relied on to monitor the integrity of the exchange by refusing to pay for rotten apples. The piece of paper certifying the CERs is the only thing that matters to the Japanese power company because that is all it is required to present to the Japanese government in lieu of a 100-ton reduction in its own emissions. What really did or did not take place in Canada is of no concern to the Japanese buyer of the CERs. Nor does the Japanese government care if the CERs it will accept without question from the Japanese power company is legitimate. The Japanese government will present those CERs for a 100-ton reduction to those in charge of verifying that Japan has met its treaty obligations, who will simply add those CERs for 100 tons to the measured reductions from within Japan, also with no questions asked.

Much of the literature criticizing carbon trading consists of exposés of cases where certification and sales have taken place when the reductions were not legitimate in one of these ways. But what critics fail to understand is that if the seller of a bogus CER is located within an Annex-1 country, this does *not* erode overall emission reductions as long as the seller's Annex-1 country is forced to comply with its national obligations under Kyoto.

Suppose the CERs for a 100-ton reduction sold by the Canadian power company to the Japanese power company are completely bogus—a pure hoax. Under Kyoto, Japan can now emit 100 tons more than it would have been permitted to otherwise. The Canadian power company, by assumption, will not emit any less than it would have in any case. However, the country of Canada will now be required to emit 100 tons less than it would have been required to otherwise because a source within Canada sold CERs for 100 tons to a source outside Canada, and those responsible for verifying that Canada has met its Kyoto treaty obligations will add 100 tons to the reductions Canada is required to make. So actual global reductions will be exactly equal to the global reductions agreed to by Canada and Japan even if the CERs are totally bogus, as long as the Canadian government is forced to meet its obligations under Kyoto.[2]

In other words, the effort to avert climate change is not "cheated" when sources in Annex-1 countries sell bogus CERs to sources in other Annex-1 countries. But if not the environment, then who has the devious Canadian power company cheated by accepting a handsome payment for doing nothing? Usually when a seller cheats—for example, by selling a rotten apple—it is the buyer who is cheated. However, in this case the Japanese power company got exactly what it wanted—the CERs for 100 tons that allowed it to emit 100 tons more than it could have otherwise. But if neither the environment nor the buyer of the bogus CERs were cheated by the Canadian power company scam, then who was cheated? Could this be one of those so-called crimes without victims? Unfortunately not.

The Canadian power company has cheated its fellow Canadians. By selling bogus CERs, it has forced Canada to reduce its emissions by 100 more tons than it would have had to otherwise. Somebody *else* in Canada is going to have to reduce its emissions by 100 more tons than it should have had to. Or somebody *else* in Canada is going to have to buy CERs for 100 tons from a source outside Canada it should not have had to buy. Or the Canadian government is going to have to buy credits for 100 tons from another Annex-1 government that it should not have had to buy to avoid being in violation of the Kyoto Treaty. The cap on Canadian national emissions will force some other Canadians to make up the difference and plug the hole the devious Canadian power company punctured in the global cap when it sold a bogus CER to the Japanese power company. It is these other Canadians who are the victims when a source in Canada sells bogus CERs to someone in another country.

This means that governments of Annex-1 countries have good reason to try to prevent private parties located in their national territory from selling bogus CERs to foreigners because this will harm other citizens and make it more difficult for the government to meet its treaty obligations. But even if CERs sold by sources in Annex-1 countries are completely bogus, this cannot erode the cap on aggregate emissions from all Annex-1 countries that Kyoto has established.

The key is that the international treaty organization must be able to measure aggregate, annual emissions from Canadian territory in 2012. Once this is done, any Canadian government sales of credits to other Annex-1 governments, and any private sales of CERs by parties within Canada to parties outside Canada, are added to measured emissions, and any Canadian government purchases of credits and any private purchases of CERs by parties within Canada from parties outside Canada are subtracted from Canadian measured emissions. Those verifying Canadian compliance with its obligations under Kyoto simply compare the resulting number to the cap Canada committed to when it agreed to (1) its percentage reduction by 2012, and (2) a figure for Canadian emissions in 1990. If measured emissions in Canada, plus credits and CERs sold to outsiders, minus credits and CERs purchased from abroad, are higher than Canada's cap, the government of Canada is in violation of its treaty obligations and subject to whatever sanctions have been established. Moreover, the treaty must be able to measure national emissions from Canada in 2012 and force Canada to comply with its treaty obligations in any case, whether or not carbon trading takes place.

In Chapter 9 we discuss measurement issues at length. But the important point for present purposes is that while Canada may question the initial estimate of its 2012 emissions and petition for adjustments, most observers believe that arriving at an agreement between countries and those charged with verifying national compliance with the treaty about what the countries' actual national emissions are in 2012 will not be overly difficult. In other words, in Chapter 9 we will discover a second counterintuitive truth that is also responsible for a great deal of misunderstanding: Measuring annual national emissions is far easier and less controversial than measuring how much a particular project reduced emissions and therefore how many CERs the project should be awarded.

In conclusion, if Annex-1 governments meet their treaty obligations, then it is *impossible* for any trading between individual sources in Annex-1 countries to undermine the overall emissions reductions those countries agreed to—no matter how much chicanery is involved in the certification and trading process. This is an important point that many critics fail to understand.

Trading between Annex-1 and non-Annex-1 countries: Critics point out that Kyoto allows governments and private parties in Annex-1 countries that are capped to purchase CERs from projects located in non-Annex-1 countries where emissions are not capped through the CDM. Critics argue that carbon trading between Annex-1 and non-Annex-1 countries through the CDM undermines the effort to reduce global emissions since countries with caps can avoid domestic reductions by purchasing CERs from countries that are permitted to increase emissions without limit. In this case critics have a valid argument—but only if the CDM accreditation process fails to work as it is supposed to. Whether this is likely to be the case we consider below. However, first it is important to understand that if the accreditation process accomplishes its mission, carbon trading through the CDM mechanism does not diminish global reductions and can generate very large transfers of income from MDCs to LDCs.

The CDM executive board is supposed to grant CERs to projects in non-Annex-1 countries only if the project represents a real reduction in GHG emissions, if the reduction is beyond what would have occurred had the project not taken place, and if the project does not cause an increase in emissions elsewhere in the country. As we will discover in Chapter 9, this is not an easy task since it requires establishing a hypothetical scenario of what would have happened had the project never occurred—which can be problematic. However, if the CDM executive board evaluates projects accurately, carbon trading through the CDM does not undermine global emission reduction targets. Instead, it merely lowers the cost of reductions and distributes the efficiency gain from doing so between MDC purchasers and LDC sellers of CERs.

Under Kyoto there is a cap on Canadian emissions but not on Mexican emissions. Suppose a company in Mexico sells a CER to a company in Canada. Further suppose the CDM executive board did its job and the reduction is real, additional, and causes no leakage. So far the trade reduces global emissions by the same amount as if the Canadian company had reduced emissions itself and the project in Mexico had never occurred. The only difference is that the reduction took place in Mexico.[3] However, since there is no cap on emissions in Mexico, it is possible that Mexican emissions will increase. Rather than achieving a reduction in global emissions by mandating a reduction inside Canada, instead we get no reduction in emissions in Canada because the Canadian company instead bought an allowance from Mexico, and even though the Mexican company that sold the CER did reduce its emissions more than it would have otherwise, and even though this did not cause an increase in emissions somewhere else in Mexico, nonetheless, other sources in Mexico might increase emissions, leaving us with no reduction or even an increase in global emissions.

With no cap on Mexican emissions, this could happen. However, when CERs are legitimate, it is not trading that causes this problem; rather, it is the lack of a cap on Mexican emissions that makes it possible for emissions in Mexico to increase. Since so many critics have misunderstood this issue, it warrants more careful scrutiny at risk of belaboring the obvious. For those who are still not convinced that permitting trading between countries with caps and countries without caps does not erode global reductions as long as CERs are legitimate and in accord with CDM guidelines, consider what would happen if no trading were allowed between sources of emissions in Canada and Mexico. Mandated reductions for wealthy, industrialized countries, no mandated reductions for developing economies, and no trading is what some critics who want to shut down the CDM favor.

Under such a program where no trading is allowed, we would get reductions in emissions from sources in Canada, but there would be no reason for sources in Mexico to do anything different from what they were going to do anyway. If sources in Mexico were going to reduce emissions, they would still reduce them. If they were going to increase emissions, they would still increase them. It is possible that global emissions would fail to decline because emissions in Mexico might increase by more than emissions decline in Canada. But this is obviously not because we allowed trading—since we did not allow trading in this scenario. Instead, it is because we failed to cap emissions in Mexico. Moreover, both Mexico and Canada would be worse off because trading was prohibited. Sources in Canada would have to pay more to reduce their own emissions than it would cost them to buy legitimate CERs from Mexico. And sources in Mexico would be unable to profit from selling legitimate CERs for more than it cost them to reduce their emissions. In sum, no useful purpose is served by prohibiting trading as long as CERs are "real," "additional," and do not cause "leakage." [4]

But some CERs approved by the executive board of the CDM clearly have not been legitimate. It is not easy to establish a hypothetical baseline scenario or determine how much more a project reduced emissions than emissions would have fallen anyway, much less be sure the project did not allow for an increase in emissions someplace else in the country. And if CERs are not legitimate—that is, if the accreditation process fails to carry out its admittedly challenging mandate successfully—then criticisms that trading through the CDM punctures holes in Kyoto's cap on aggregate emissions from all Annex-1 countries are valid. If the CDM awards more credits than are warranted, trading will cause global reductions to be less than planned since non-Annex-1 countries without caps do not have to make up for any shortfall due to sales of illegitimate CERs with real reductions elsewhere in their countries. Moreover, since governments of non-Annex-1 countries selling CERs have no incentive to police the legitimacy of CERs sold by their residents, and since the buyers and sellers of CERs never have any incentive to guarantee that the CER represents a real, additional emission reduction, there is every reason to be concerned.

In conclusion, a great deal has been written criticizing carbon trading under the CDM of the Kyoto treaty. Most of the valid criticisms expose cases where CDM authorities failed to ensure that reductions were additional and without leakage, in which case the failure of the executive board to carry out its mandate does puncture holes in the aggregate cap on Annex-1 emissions and undermines our ability to achieve the global emissions reduction planned under Kyoto. However, much of the criticism is not compelling. Many critics fail to acknowledge dramatic improvements in monitoring after the first year of the program, including a significant tightening of standards. Many critics wrongly criticize what they consider over- or underpaying for CERs as undermining global reductions or "inefficient," even though the price paid for CERs has no bearing on reductions or efficiency, but only on equity.[5] Plus few critics make any attempt to compare the beneficial effects of CER trades that are legitimate with ill effects from CER trades that are not. More importantly, critics fail to consider obvious ways to correct the flaws in Kyoto that make carbon trading through the CDM mechanism problematic. Changes that render all objections to full international carbon trading moot, including objections to selling offsets for sequestration increases, are discussed in Chapter 10.

Notes

1. For an insightful and highly readable treatment of international climate negotiations see Chichilnisky and Sheeran (2009).

2. This conclusion is so counterintuitive that many people completely misunderstand the point. The result is a great deal of misplaced criticism of carbon trading. As a matter of fact, even professional environmental economists sometimes misunderstand this point.

3. While the location of the reduction has changed, the trade has not changed who pays for the reduction. The Canadian company has paid for the reduction—presumably less than it would have cost to make the reduction itself in Canada—even though the reduction took place in Mexico.

4. Many critics fail to understand that carbon trading of legitimate CERs under the CDM not only reduces the cost of compliance for MDC sources and governments—which is good, not bad, because it makes it easier to lower MDC caps even further—but also provides a substantial benefit to LDCs, as explained in Chapter 9.

5. Some climate justice activists who want to shut down the CDM cite the work of Michael Wara, at the Stanford Program on Energy and Sustainable Development and Stanford Law School, who supports an "improved" CDM (Wara 2006; Wara and Vic-

tor 2008). Wara strongly criticized the CDM executive board certification of CERs for capturing and destroying HFC-23 at refrigerant plants and N_2O at Teflon plants in China in the first year of the program. But his criticism was that MDC buyers paid much more for these CERs than it cost Chinese sellers to make the emission reductions, which Wara incorrectly described as "inefficient." In fact, the price paid for CERs has nothing to do with efficiency but only with how the efficiency gain from trade is distributed between buyers and sellers of CERs. It is ironic that climate justice activists cite work whose criticism was that too much of the efficiency gain from CER trade went to sellers in LDCs and too little was captured by MDC buyers as reason to shut down the CDM.

Chapter 9

Criticisms of Kyoto

The Kyoto treaty, which went into effect in 2005 and has now been ratified by every country except the United States, will expire in 2012. In this chapter we first review what Kyoto got right before carefully evaluating various criticisms that have been voiced.

What Kyoto Got Right

The Kyoto Protocol has been criticized from every conceivable angle. In Chapter 8 we discovered that some criticisms of carbon trading under Kyoto are misplaced while others have merit. But Kyoto got a number of key issues right, and as we look forward to a post-Kyoto treaty it is important to understand what is right about the Kyoto Protocol as well as what is wrong.

The first thing negotiators in Kyoto got right was that climate change will not be averted unless countries *mutually agree to binding emission reductions in an international treaty*. As discussed in the previous chapter, any idea that voluntary actions on the part of countries, or even small groups of countries in consort, will secure reductions sufficient to avert climate change is pure fantasy. Theory predicts that a voluntary approach will not work. The free-rider dilemma is a huge obstacle to averting climate change, and anyone who fails to understand this has no hopes of solving the problem. Moreover, the historical record between the meetings in Rio and in Kyoto five years later confirms what theory predicted. When signatories to the United Nations Framework Convention on Climate Change (UNFCCC) reconvened in Kyoto, they had no choice but to admit that lofty promises made in Rio had, by and large, proved empty, as global emissions had continued to escalate between 1992 and 1997.

Unlike the participants in Rio in 1992, those assembled in Kyoto in 1997 recognized the essential relationship between all international treaties and national sovereignty. Sovereignty leaves countries free to do as they please, which implies that if an action benefits a country enough to outweigh the costs to the country itself, treaties are not generally required to compel such behavior. Treaties are needed to elicit behavior only when the costs of an action exceed the benefits to the country itself, and the enforcement of a treaty will inevitably be felt as an infringement on national sovereignty. What makes it worthwhile for a country to sign treaties even though they infringe on its sovereignty and require behavior whose costs exceed the benefits for the country itself is that the country gets something in exchange. In general, what the country gets in exchange is a commitment from other countries to do likewise. The key point is that these commitments from other countries can dramatically change the calculus of national self-interest. In the case of climate change, it would not benefit individual countries more than it costs them to reduce their own emissions if others do not do likewise because no single country can prevent climate change. On the other hand, if a country's reduction wins similar reductions from other countries in exchange, then the benefit to each country from its own reduction *combined with everyone else's reduction* can far exceed its own reduction costs. This is why emission reductions must be mutually agreed to and binding.

The second thing Kyoto got right was that a diplomatic mechanism is necessary to overcome the incentive for every country to wait for other countries to sign a treaty before it does. In particular, Annex-1 countries had every reason not to sign the Kyoto Protocol until other Annex-1 countries had signed before them. The Kyoto Protocol finessed this "Alphonse-Gaston" problem by creating a trigger mechanism often used by international diplomats. The protocol stipulated that the treaty would not become binding until enough Annex-1 countries had ratified the treaty to account for 55 percent of emissions from all Annex-1 countries in 1990. This removed the disincentive for a country to sign for fear that it would have committed itself to mandatory reductions only to discover that other Annex-1 countries had failed to do so, choosing instead to ride for free on early signers binding commitment.

Of course, in the end not all Annex-1 countries did sign the Kyoto Protocol—the United States chose instead to free ride. And with the benefit of hindsight it is also apparent that the trigger mechanism failed to eliminate all advantages for late signers. While Japan, for example, signed quickly,

Russia delayed signing until it became the last hope of reaching the necessary 55 percent threshold after President Bush was reelected in 2004 and it was clear that the United States would continue its refusal to sign. By delaying ratification, Russia gained leverage that Japan did not enjoy as an early signer. Russia parlayed its leverage to increase its ability to profit from the fact that the dramatic decline in Russian gross domestic product (GDP)—and therefore carbon emissions—after 1990 left projected Russian emissions for 2012 well under its cap. As a condition for signing, Russia insisted that Annex-1 countries be permitted to buy more allowances in the international carbon market than had been initially agreed to in Kyoto, knowing this would increase the demand and therefore the price of allowances in a market where Russia had every reason to expect to be a big seller. But at least the trigger mechanism protected countries that were willing to commit early to mandatory reductions in exchange for a substantial portion of similar countries doing likewise from fear of a terribly nasty surprise. The trigger mechanism meant that if most other countries failed to sign, early signatories were not bound by any commitments because the treaty would not go into effect.

But the most important thing that Kyoto got right was the recognition that countries bear different responsibilities for causing climate change, countries have different capabilities to bear the costs of averting climate change, and efforts to mitigate climate change should reflect these "differential responsibilities and capabilities." Kyoto explicitly recognizes that countries where the majority of citizens have yet to enjoy the benefits of economic development should not be expected to bear the same burdens as more developed countries in order to prevent climate change. As discussed in the previous chapter, the Kyoto Protocol implemented this fundamental commitment to fairness in a very dramatic and palpable way by requiring mandatory emission reductions only from more developed, Annex-1 countries. Underdeveloped countries were classified as non-Annex-1 countries, which were not subjected to mandatory caps under Kyoto.

Failure to treat differently countries that *do* bear different responsibilities and *do* have different capabilities would make an international treaty unfair. Any treaty that effectively denies poor countries any real possibility of economic development would be inhumane and unconscionable. Unlike Rio, Kyoto did *not* honor fairness only with pretty words and unenforceable intentions. Instead, Kyoto embedded fairness into the core structure of the treaty itself. Not surprisingly, many criticisms and proposals to revise Kyoto have had the purpose of "correcting" this atypical historical "error" and putting us back on the usual track of meaningless genuflections toward international economic justice without any substance.

Too Little, Too Late

A major criticism of Kyoto is that it did too little to reduce global emissions. Many environmentalists and climate scientists have pointed out that a beginning is not a solution, and while a beginning may be acceptable progress toward solving some problems, beginning to solve a life-and-death problem is not worth much if it still leaves you dead. Even in 1997 the consensus among climate scientists was that a 5.2 percent global reduction in emissions of Annex-1 countries only by 2012 was not a strong enough beginning to avert climate change. Critics also charged not only that failure to cap emissions in less developed countries (LDCs) created the possibility that any reduction in more developed countries' (MDC) emissions would be canceled out by increases in LDC emissions, but also that the Clean Development Mechanism (CDM) would puncture holes in the cap on MDC emissions and thereby weaken the effectiveness of the treaty even more. Having begun discussion of these criticisms of carbon trading in Chapter 8, we examine charges that carbon trading makes Kyoto little more than a scam later in this chapter.

More importantly, every year since 1997 has provided new evidence about the pace and dangers of climate change and indicated that even deeper reductions than previously believed necessary are required. The science also indicates that the sooner emission reductions are made, the more effective they are at averting the crisis. So promising bigger reductions later, particularly when those making the promises know they will no longer be in office when the bigger cuts come due, is a predictable ploy we should not fall victim to. In other words, a commitment to reduce emissions by a certain amount over the next five years is far more credible than a commitment to reduce emissions by a much larger amount thirty-five years from now. Both science and politics call for *front-loading* rather than back-loading the global emission reduction schedule.

Before the climate Conference of the Parties (COP) meetings in Copenhagen in December 2009, the need to reduce global emissions more than Kyoto had called for was widely acknowledged by many government delegations as well as by almost all environmentalists. Demands for reductions of 80 percent or more by 2050 and refusal to settle for reduction schedules that are backloaded were strongly supported by environmental non-governmental organizations (NGOs), demonstrators in the streets of Copenhagen, and delegations from threatened island nations and many of the world's poorest countries. Unfortunately, popular sentiment that we need to pick up the pace in setting and enforcing reduction targets received no support in the form of concrete commitments from key government delegations.

Monitoring Problems

Perhaps no area of climate policy is more misunderstood than measuring and monitoring. As explained in Chapter 7, all environmental policies require monitoring and enforcement, and we should not expect any policy to be self-enforcing because under any policy polluters are better off if they can claim they have emitted less than they actually have. But with regard to an international climate treaty there is a huge difference between (1) monitoring country compliance with caps on national emissions during a calendar year (i.e., policing governments who are the signatories), and (2) figuring out how much credit to award a particular project for reducing emissions (i.e., policing the international carbon market). Failure to understand crucial differences between the measurement problems posed by these two completely different tasks has been the source of a great deal of confusion and many misplaced criticisms of Kyoto.

Of course, when we measure national emissions during an entire calendar year, the scale of what we measure is much, much greater than measuring how many tons a single project reduces emissions. Nonetheless, measuring national annual emissions is far easier than measuring the amount by which a particular project reduced greenhouse gas (GHG) emissions. The reason is that in the first case we do not need to create a hypothetical scenario of what would have happened had something not occurred. None of the complications introduced because we must establish a hypothetical baseline to measure "additionality" and control for "leakage" when awarding emission reduction credits to a single project raise their ugly heads when we measure annual national emissions. But all these problems immediately arise as soon as we try to measure how many fewer tons were emitted because an applicant for certified credits undertook a particular project.

Measuring national emissions: How will the Kyoto treaty managers measure national GHG emissions in 2012? Many people will be surprised to learn that the treaty staff will not attempt to measure the amount of different GHGs coming out of all the smokestacks, automobile exhaust pipes, and cows in a country. As a result, there will be very few, if any on-site inspections.[1] Instead, treaty staff will estimate national carbon emissions based on statistics already supplied by governments to the United Nations about (1) the goods and services produced by their various industries and agriculture during 2012, (2) the predominant technologies used in those productive sectors in 2012, and, most importantly, (3) the amount of fossil fuels consumed by their energy and transportation sectors in 2012. Since burning or cutting down forests also releases carbon, additional information about deforestation during 2012 may also be collected from governments, although satellite photos are more likely to be relied on. Will the resulting estimates of national emissions in 2012 be perfect? No, they will not. But just as the equally imperfect estimates of national emissions in 1990 they will be compared to were agreed on with very little squabbling when countries ratified Kyoto, the estimates for 2012 will be agreed on with very little squabbling between treaty staff and national governments. In other words, the estimates of national emissions in 2012 will allow very little opportunity for governments to challenge rulings. The estimates will be good enough to determine if governments of Annex-1 countries lived up to their treaty obligations, and even good enough to determine how much countries fell short of meeting their caps for purposes of assessing fines or penalties.

Interestingly, it would be even easier to measure the amount of carbon sequestered during 2012 in the national territory of each country—although the staff will not perform this calculation since Kyoto does not award credit for preserving existing sinks. Thanks to the system of global satellites already in place, every square inch of planet Earth can be monitored from the sky to see what is located there. Thanks to global biological mapping, we know what flora is on all that land, and thanks to global temperature and rainfall records, we know how much carbon the particular flora on all that land sequestered during the year given temperature and humidity conditions. This means that not only is measuring annual carbon emissions for a country relatively straightforward, but measuring annual *net* carbon emissions for a country (i.e., annual carbon emissions minus annual carbon sequestration) is equally straightforward.

Measuring emission reductions for projects: On the other hand, how does the Kyoto staff decide how many credits to certify for a project that applies for certified emission reduction credits (CERs)? As explained in Chapter 8, certification is done through the CDM, and it is the CDM executive board that is the final arbiter. The CDM has its own professional staff, but relies on designated national authorities and designated operational entities to evaluate project design documents. The CDM executive board is supposed to grant CERs only if (1) the project would not have taken place in any case (i.e., the project was not part of business as usual); (2) the project created a real reduction in GHG emissions that is "additional" (i.e., above and beyond what would have occurred had the project not taken place at all); and (3) the project does not create "leakage" (i.e., the project does not cause an increase in emissions elsewhere in the country that would not have occurred had the project not happened).

Determining (1) requires guessing what the applicant would have done without the incentive of being able to sell emission credits. Only if the project would not have occurred in a business-as-usual scenario is it supposed to be awarded credits. Determining (2) and (3) both require establishing a hypothetical baseline, a scenario of what would have happened had the project never occurred. Does this sound complicated? Yes, it is. Difficult? Yes, it is. Does it require difficult judgment calls? Yes, it does. Does it sound like whatever decision the executive board makes could easily be questioned and challenged? You bet!

As if all these problems were not enough, a further difficulty those who must decide how many CER credits to award particular projects must face, but those measuring *annual* net national emissions do not face, is timing and permanence. This problem can be particularly troubling when awarding credits for sequestration services that continue over a number of years and may or may not be guaranteed permanently. Projects often change emissions and sequestration for many years, and while it does not matter where changes in net carbon emissions occur, it does matter when they occur, and it matters whether or not the changes are permanent. The earlier reductions in net emission take place, the more valuable they are in averting climate change. And, obviously, a permanent reduction in net emissions is far more valuable than a reduction that is only temporary.

Now that we are clear that measuring annual national emissions is different—and easier—than measuring how much a particular project reduces emissions above and beyond what would have occurred in any case, we are ready to render a definitive judgment with regard to various criticisms of carbon trading under the Kyoto Protocol. First we review the prima facie case for carbon trading as "savior" that promotes greater efficiency and equity. Then we consider the case against carbon trading as a "scam" that undermines efforts to reduce global emissions, creates inefficiencies, and aggravates global injustice.

The Case for Carbon Trading

The efficiency case for international carbon trading: Empirical studies estimate large differences in the costs of reducing carbon emissions from sources in different countries, in which case prohibiting trading significantly inflates the overall cost of achieving global reductions.

Minimizing reduction costs should take a back seat to more important issues—namely, will the policy reduce emissions sufficiently to prevent climate change, and will the policy distribute the costs of doing so fairly? However, while efficiency may be secondary, this does not mean it does not play an important role in averting climate change. Reducing carbon emissions will increase costs for corporations—which is why corporations routinely lobby to minimize the size of mandated reductions. But reducing emissions

181

also imposes costs on society as a whole. The easiest way to understand why reducing emissions impose costs on people other than corporations is to remember that corporations always try to pass on higher costs to their customers in the form of higher prices, and whenever demand is not infinitely elastic they are able to do so, at least in part. More generally, there are significant social costs associated with reducing carbon emissions. Going without bread or milk for two days until next week's shopping trip because gas prices have gone up is a minor inconvenience. Replacing your old furnace, washing machine, or clothes drier with new, energy-efficient home appliances can cost thousands of dollars. A Toyota Prius costs considerably more than a Ford Focus because building a hybrid engine that gets fifty miles per gallon costs more right now than building a traditional engine that gets twenty-five.

Some environmentalists deny this fact and claim there are no social costs associated with moving from a fossil-fuel-based economy to an economy based on renewable energy sources. Unfortunately, ignoring transition costs does not eliminate transition costs, which are, in fact, significant. Moreover, ignoring transition costs leads people to be oblivious to the importance of devising a conversion plan to share the transition costs equitably. Of course, fossil fuel and corporate lobbies greatly exaggerate the transition costs in their attempt to frighten the public and forestall action to avert climate change. An excellent study released in October 2009 by Economics for Equity and the Environment demonstrates that the transition costs, while real, are much less than fearmongers suggest and that stabilizing GHG concentrations at 350 parts per million would be a very inexpensive insurance policy for our species and the planet (Ackerman et al. 2009b).

Of course, the real social benefits of reducing emissions will come in the form of damage avoided because climate change is averted. These real benefits are much greater than the true social costs incurred in doing so—which is why it is efficient to reduce emissions and terribly inefficient to continue to fail to do so. But in the short run, while we are still developing new technologies and ways to produce and consume without burning large quantities of fossil fuels, it is foolish to deny there are social costs associated with reducing emissions. In the short run, it will cost more to transport ourselves, more to heat and cool our homes and businesses, and more to produce everything that requires energy, including much of our food, once we put a price on carbon.

Besides avoiding wastefulness, the best reason to search for policies that minimize these social costs is that, the lower the cost, the greater reductions we can make and the sooner we can make them. This is why anyone interested in hastening and increasing abatement—which is anyone seriously concerned about climate change—should be very much in favor of making sure abatement is done efficiently. Yes, corporations lobby for cost efficiency in order to save themselves money. But just because progressives do not give priority to saving corporations money does not mean we should not support efficient abatement.

The equity case for international carbon trading: Since some climate justice activists are among the most outspoken critics of international carbon trading, it may come as a surprise that the strongest argument for international carbon trading is that it acts to reduce international economic injustice. Under Kyoto only MDCs have mandatory caps, which means that only MDCs are compelled to bear *any* of the costs of averting climate change. If MDCs were forced to make all their reductions domestically, this would cost them more than when they can buy some of their reductions from sources in LDCs for less than it would cost them to make those reductions themselves—which is why sources in MDCs who will have to make reductions lobbied for this option. But whether it costs them more or less, it is sources in MDCs who bear all the costs of averting climate change under Kyoto.

Without trading, not only would the costs to MDCs be higher, but also LDCs would have no opportunity to gain financially from trading. Of course, LDCs and MDCs alike benefit from averting climate change with or without trading, but without trading LDCs would enjoy no additional financial benefits from Kyoto. However, when sources in LDCs are allowed to sell credits to sources in MDCs, not only do LDCs benefit from averting climate change while bearing none of the costs of doing so, but LDCs also enjoy a substantial financial gain because they only sell credits when the price they get for a CER is higher than their cost to produce the reduction.

The economics is simple: Since many of the cheapest abatement opportunities are located in LDCs, there is an efficiency gain from reducing emissions there rather than in MDCs. When a source in an MDC responsible for a reduction buys a CER from a source in an LDC, the seller and buyer share the efficiency gain. The higher the price paid for the CER, the more of the efficiency gain from locating the reduction where it is cheaper is captured by the seller in the LDC. The lower the price of the CER, the more of the efficiency gain is captured by the buyer in the MDC.

But if international trade and capital liberalization aggravate global inequalities, why would international carbon trading do the opposite? This question deserves a serious answer. When there are differences in the opportunity costs of producing goods in MDCs and LDCs, there are potential efficiency gains from specialization and trade. The terms of trade divide the efficiency gain between the countries. When loans lead to larger increases in productivity in LDCs than MDCs, international lending yields an efficiency gain. The interest rate on international loans divides the efficiency gain between LDC borrowers and MDC lenders. However, the problem in the case of international trade and investment is that as long as capital is scarce globally, the interest rates and terms of trade that the laws of supply and demand generate predictably distribute the lion's share of the efficiency gains from international trade and investment to the MDCs, thereby widening the gap between the haves and have-nots. Moreover, empirical evidence about the effects of the expansion of free-market trade and international finance on global inequality over the past thirty years strongly supports what theory predicts: Expansion of free-market international trade and investment systematically aggravates global inequalities and inequities (Hahnel 2005b). But in the case of carbon trading the situation is different.

Kyoto forces MDCs to bear the *entire* cost of averting climate change by imposing caps *only* on MDCs. In this context, when carbon trading shares the efficiency gain from locating reductions where they are cheaper between sellers and buyers of CERs, the result is that part of the reduction in costs to MDCs is transferred to LDCs as a pure financial gain. Under Kyoto, LDCs get the benefit of averting climate change at no cost to them with or without carbon trading. Without carbon trading, that is all they get. But with carbon trading, LDCs get an additional financial gain from capturing part of the reduction in costs to MDCs that carbon trading creates. When LDCs and MDCs sit down to play the game of divide the efficiency gain from carbon trading between them, under Kyoto the MDCs have already put up all the chips they are playing for! Even if MDCs recapture most of their chips, any MDC chips that LDCs capture when they sell CERs simply puts them that much farther ahead than they would have been had they never had the opportunity to sit down at the carbon market gaming table and play with what is in effect "house money" provided by the MDCs.

In sum, the case for international carbon trading on efficiency grounds is that international carbon trading lowers global reduction costs. This not only reduces the human costs of averting climate change, but also makes it easier to lower MDC caps on emissions even further. The case for embracing carbon trading on equity grounds is that as long as MDCs have tighter caps than LDCs, carbon trading generates a significant flow of income from more to less developed countries that would not occur otherwise.

The Case Against Carbon Trading

What arguments do critics offer against international carbon trading? Which arguments hold no water? Which arguments make valid points because of flaws in the Kyoto Protocol that could be corrected in a post-Kyoto treaty?

We have already reviewed a number of common criticisms. Some people argue that like most international trading of one kind or another, carbon trading will aggravate global inequalities. As just explained, while this criticism is compelling on both theoretical and empirical grounds with regard to international trade and investment under free-market conditions, it is not compelling in the case of international carbon trading *provided* national caps are set equitably. This is even true if MDC buyers prove to be sharpsters who recapture the lion's share of the efficiency gain from locating reductions where they are cheaper in LDCs.

Others claim that when CERs are bought in lieu of reductions in emissions by sources in MDCs, this punctures holes in the global cap on carbon. This criticism circulates so widely in some progressive environmental circles that it is often taken to be an uncontested "fact." This criticism was analyzed at great length in Chapter 8, where we arrived at the following conclusions: (1) Carbon trading *cannot* puncture holes in the global cap on emissions as long as the source selling the CER is located in a country with a cap. (2) Even if the source selling the CER is located in a country without a cap, as long as the CER is properly evaluated it does not puncture a hole in the global cap on emissions. (3) *Only* when the CDM executive board awards illegitimate credits for projects in countries without caps are holes punctured in the cap on aggregate emissions from all Annex-1 countries and the effectiveness of the treaty weakened.

Still other critics warn that if we turn emission rights into a commodity, Wall Street will integrate CERs into its next toxic, financial cocktail, leading to yet another financial crisis. As explained in Chapter 7, if international finance is not subjected to effective regulation we will in all likelihood suffer another financial crisis. But this will occur whether or not CERs are an ingredient in the recipe for toxic assets. However, if the international financial system is tamed by prudent and competent regulations, CERs should pose no danger in this regard. However, there are other objections people have raised to carbon trading still to consider.

Not all emissions are equivalent: One argument against carbon trading reduces to the claim that not all emissions are equivalent and trading nonequivalent reductions is problematic. While this argument is valid for many pollutants, it does not apply in the case of carbon dioxide. To paraphrase Gertrude Stein, "a ton of carbon is a ton of carbon is a ton of carbon." For many pollutants, how much damage is caused and who suffers the damage depends on where the source is located. What environmental economists refer to as *hot spots* can occur whenever pollutants are not uniform—that is, when effects differ depending on the source, as is generally the case when the damage caused by an emission is greater closer to the source. But carbon dioxide is a perfect textbook case of a *uniform* pollutant: it makes no difference whether a ton of carbon is emitted by automobiles driving on the streets of

Chicago or by a power plant on the outskirts of Beijing, because the damage is the same whenever a ton of carbon reaches any part of the upper atmosphere surrounding Earth. In other words, it makes no difference where we reduce carbon emissions as far as the damage they cause is concerned, which means our only concerns should be (1) how much it costs to reduce emissions from different sources, and (2) who pays for those costs. The "trade" part of a cap-and-trade policy for carbon emissions works to allocate the reductions to wherever they cost the least. What many critics of carbon trading fail to understand is that *who pays* for reductions can be determined independently from *where* the reductions occur.

Many critics also object to trading emissions reductions for increases in sequestration (taking carbon out of the atmosphere), arguing that the two are not equivalent. But this is also not true in the case of carbon dioxide, the major GHG. Increases in the concentration of GHGs in the atmosphere cause climate change. It is the carbon cycle—where natural processes emit carbon dioxide and other natural processes sequester carbon dioxide—which human activity has pushed dangerously out of balance. And it is balance in the carbon cycle we must restore. Since taking one ton of carbon out of the atmosphere reduces concentration levels by exactly the same amount as reducing carbon emissions by one ton, the two are completely equivalent, which means that science tells us it is *net* emissions, not emissions, which matters. Since there is no difference in benefits from reducing emissions and increasing sequestration, our only concerns should be what they cost and who pays. And again, trading can lowers costs, and who pays those costs can be determined independently from where emissions or sequestration occurs. Think of it this way: If one is willing to pay a certain amount to reduce a ton of carbon emissions this year, one should also be willing to pay the same amount—neither a penny more nor less—to increase sequestration of a ton of carbon this year. There is no more reason to ban trading sequestration increases for emissions reductions than there is to ban trading of carbon emission reductions that occur in different places.[2]

Carbon trading reduces pressure on MDCs to undergo necessary changes: Many people see carbon trading as a loophole permitting the MDCs to weasel out of making necessary adjustments to their carbon-guzzling domestic economies and unsustainable lifestyles. These critics argue that we need to put maximum pressure on MDCs—where carbon emissions per capita are highest and therefore conversion to carbon neutrality is most urgent—to replace fossil fuels with renewables and develop new energy-saving habits of consumption. They argue that preventing MDCs from trading increases pressure on them to change, whereas allowing them to buy foreign credits enables them to postpone necessary domestic transformations.

It is true that we want to put maximum pressure on the advanced economies to change their unsustainable economic way of life. It is true that climate change will not be averted unless energy, transportation, agricultural, and industrial sectors in MDCs are completely transformed and consumption patterns become far more energy-efficient. It is true that the sooner these monumental tasks are tackled by MDCs, the better our chances of avoiding catastrophic climate change will be. And it is also true that Kyoto has failed to launch the advanced economies on this path. But banning carbon trading is not the right way to pressure MDCs to transform their unsustainable economies. The way to increase the pressure is to *lower their caps*, not to make it unnecessarily difficult for them to meet their caps—which is what banning trading does.

The Appendix to Part IV on climate control treaties illustrates why applying more pressure on MDCs by lowering their caps is preferable to applying more pressure by banning trading. In the appendix the marginal cost of reductions in MDCs is the same in Treaty #5 as it is in Treaty #3; in other words, the pressure on MDCs to change their habits is equal in both cases. However, because Treaty #5 allows trading through a CDM while Treaty #3 does not, Treaty #5 produces a much greater global reduction in emissions for the same amount of "pain." In other words, Treaty #5 is much more effective at preventing climate change. In the end, MDC governments will have to regulate, tax, or cap carbon emissions—as well as spend massive sums on economic conversion. The way to force them to launch an all-out "Green New Deal" is to lower their national caps dramatically in the international treaty that will follow Kyoto in 2012, while simultaneously making it as cheap as possible for them to meet lower caps by allowing full carbon trading. Moreover, since trading makes reductions easier, it increases the likelihood of winning the crucial political battles that lie ahead to lower caps even more than what can be won today.

We should not settle for less reduction than we could get for a given level of pain. Of course, those of us who are convinced that the danger of climate change is much greater than many yet realize should do our best to convince the public to tolerate the highest pain threshold we can get it to agree to. But having gotten agreement to tolerate as much pain as we can, we should then set caps as low as that pain threshold permits and get the highest emission reduction that level of pain can achieve. We do that by allowing international carbon trading. Restricting or banning trading is wasting pain by getting less reduction for the pain than we could have.

Another way to see it is this: Why should we prevent fruit growers from picking low-hanging fruit when it is available and instead force them to pass over low-hanging fruit and pick fruit from higher branches? If we want to force fruit growers to pick *both* the low-hanging *and* the high-hanging fruit, we can accomplish this goal by increasing the amount of fruit we require them to pick. But no useful purpose is served by forcing fruit growers to pass over low-hanging fruit and pick fruit from higher branches instead. If we want to force fossil-fuel-burning utilities in MDCs to undergo major, costly conversions, the way to do this is to lower the emission caps on MDC countries so they will have to not only buy the cheaper allowances but also undertake more costly conversions of their own plants.

Carbon trading will impoverish LDCs in the future: This argument takes two forms. Some critics worry that if LDC sources are allowed to sell offsets to MDCs now, when offset prices are low, then twenty years from now LDCs will have used up all their cheap ways to reduce emissions and they will be stuck with expensive ways when they are finally required to reduce their emissions by an international treaty. This argument is unpersuasive. If this conjecture about the trajectory of prices for offsets is correct, all LDC governments have to do to avoid the unfortunate fate projected for them is *not* sell offsets now if prices are low, wait for offset prices to rise, and then either sell offsets later at higher prices or use their cheap means of reducing emissions to meet their own emission reduction requirements later. This argument for banning or limiting the sale of CERs by LDCs is nothing more than paternalism, pure and simple. "We" should bar LDCs from managing their new wealth—which is what lenient national caps combined with many cheap opportunities to reduce carbon emissions amounts to—because "we" think they will foolishly screw themselves by misjudging price trajectories that someone else miraculously guesses correctly?

Others argue that the problem is not that LDC governments are stupid, but that they are at the service of domestic elites and will use income from CER sales not to benefit the poor and finance development but to further the elites' lavish lifestyles. But, if this is true, it implies—quite conveniently—that there is never any reason to reallocate wealth or income from MDCs to LDCs since any transfers would presumably be misappropriated by LDC elites. This argument suggests that winning fairer terms of trade or reparation payments for climate injustice is as pointless as securing a steady flow of revenue from MDCs to LDCs through sales of CERs.

REDD dispossesses indigenous communities: Critics have attacked a new feature of Kyoto called Reducing Emissions from Deforestation and Degradation (REDD) because they claim it dispossesses indigenous peoples and forest communities. The need to provide positive incentives to protect forests was first raised by the Coalition of Rainforest Nations in 2005 at COP 11. It gained more political traction when new estimates indicated that carbon emissions from deforestation and forest degradation account for 20 to 25 percent of global emissions, which is more than the emissions caused by the entire global transportation industry. The REDD proposal was hammered out at COP 13 in Bali in 2007, to be put to a vote at COP 15 in Copenhagen.

REDD is an attempt to correct for a perverse incentive Kyoto created to destroy existing forests in non-Annex-1 countries. Because national emissions are not capped in non-Annex-1 countries, and because there is no payment for ongoing carbon storage and sequestration services, Kyoto provides no incentive to protect forests from being burned off to create pastureland for cattle or from being cut down to be sold as timber even though deforestation releases large amounts of carbon. On the other hand, the CDM creates a positive incentive to plant trees after deforestation to sell as sequestration offsets since these projects can demonstrate additional sequestration and thereby qualify for certification. The temptation to destroy forests for commercial benefit and then replant in order to sell sequestration offsets is perverse because even if we ignore innumerable other valuable environmental services standing forests provide, such as species preservation, soil conservation, and water cleansing, the release of carbon from destroying existing forests in the present does far more to accelerate climate change than the additional sequestration from newly planted trees does to avert climate change in the future.

REDD was designed to eliminate this perverse incentive by awarding credits for preserving threatened forests. Of course, determining if a forest is threatened requires establishing a business-as-usual baseline, which, as we have seen, is not easy. And capping emissions in non-Annex-1 countries would have been a simpler way to discourage deforestation since it would have penalized carbon emissions that result from deforestation. Nonetheless, for the first time, REDD made protecting existing forests in LDCs financially valuable and thereby made control over existing forests more valuable than before. And that is the catch, according to climate justice critics: REDD gave global corporations and landed aristocracies an incentive to dispossess forest people and grab land titles even if they did not want to search for minerals or oil, burn the forest to make pastureland, or log it off for timber sales.

Historically, when oil or minerals are discovered on native lands, dispossession has often been the result. And even when native people retain possession of their lands, traditional ways of life are often destroyed by the activity necessary to reap financial rewards from new resource extraction opportunities. By design, REDD does make forests inhabited by indigenous peoples more valuable. But in this case, if forest dwellers can retain possession of their lands, they can reap financial rewards without destroying the forests and upsetting their traditional ways of life in any way. REDD rewards forest people financially for maintaining their traditional ways of life. All they have to do is avoid expulsion by global sharpsters. Perhaps climate justice activists and advocates for the rights and well-being of indigenous people should concentrate their efforts on helping forest dwellers keep their lands instead of denouncing a program willing to pay them considerable amounts for continuing to live exactly as they prefer.

Efficiency Problems

The truth is that we still do not know how much carbon trading will be permitted under the Kyoto Protocol because the day of reckoning has yet to arrive and because even after lengthy negotiations at COP meetings in Marrakesh and Bali following Kyoto, COP 15 in Copenhagen failed to reach a final resolution of all outstanding issues regarding what will and will not be counted. So how carbon trading will actually be treated under Kyoto in 2012 remains a moving target.

To the extent that trading fails to relocate reductions to where they are least costly, there is an efficiency loss. This could be due to restrictions on emissions trading that prevent efficiency-enhancing trades from taking place. Or it could be due to trading bogus credits that locate reductions where they are actually more expensive. One thing is clear at this point. There will be some loss of efficiency under Kyoto due to both problems.

Neither those who want many more projects approved through the CDM nor those who want the CDM to tighten up on its criteria for awarding credits are having it all their way. The environmental community, focusing on projects that have been approved but should not have been, wants the CDM executive board to tighten its certification process. Sources wishing to sell or buy credits, and governments supporting those sources, complain of delays, pointing out that the pipeline waiting to be evaluated by the CDM keeps getting longer and longer. There is now strong support for replacing approval on a project-by-project basis with approval for large numbers of projects that host governments would propose as a package deal. As discussed in Chapter 8, when the CDM gives credits for bogus projects or awards more credits than it should, this punctures holes in the global cap. It also disrupts an efficient pattern of allocating reductions globally. On the other hand, when fear of making mistakes leads the CDM to reject valid projects or causes the pipeline of applications to get longer and longer, this is inefficient as well. And whatever else they may accomplish, restrictions on trading between Annex-1 countries and sources located within non-Annex-1 countries raise the global cost of achieving reductions. In Chapter 10, changes to avoid these problems in a post-Kyoto treaty are proposed and discussed.

Equity Problems

Of course, some people consider the Kyoto treaty unfair simply because it would require the United States to cut emissions by 7 percent while it does not require China to cut emissions at all for the time being. But this notion of fairness implicitly presumes that all countries should share the costs of averting climate change equally. This view either ignores the facts that not all countries contributed equally to causing the problem and not all countries are equally capable of contributing to solving the problem, or else this kind of thinking denies that differential responsibilities and capabilities are relevant to how the costs of averting climate change should be distributed. But unlike the U.S. Senate and President Obama, whose behavior in Copenhagen implicitly denied that any such differences deserve to be considered, progressives—like the delegations from the 160 countries that signed the UNFCCC in Kyoto—do understand that differential responsibility and capability must be taken into account in a fair solution to the problem of climate change.

There are many progressives, and even more people from the third world, who say that the best part of the Kyoto Protocol was that it did more than pay the usual lip service to international economic justice when dealing with climate change. Because it treats MDCs—who bear the major responsibility for having overstocked the atmosphere with GHGs and who are wealthy enough to bear the costs of fixing a problem they created—differently than it treats LDCs—who did little to cause the problem and have less means available to them to help solve it—many progressives and third world residents consider Kyoto to be exemplary. However, although incorporating the principle of common but differential responsibilities and capabilities into the core structure of the treaty through the distinction between Annex-1 and non-Annex-1 countries was a powerful commitment to international climate justice, it may not have been the fairest way to implement the principle.

In Chapter 10, an alternative approach pioneered by the authors of the Greenhouse Development Rights framework will be explored, and changes based on that framework will be proposed to make a post-Kyoto treaty even more consistent with international climate justice. Suffice it to say for now that just as it would be unfair to treat the United States and China equally when per capita cumulative emissions since 1990 in the United States were seven times more than in China, and per capita GDP in the United States is six times more than in China, it is also unfair to treat China and the Democratic Republic of the Congo equally when per capita cumulative emissions since 1990 in China were fifty times more than in the Congo, and per capita GDP in China is nine times more than in the Congo. Yet this is what Kyoto does by classifying China and the Republic of the Congo both as non-Annex-1 countries.

Enforcement Problems: The Invisible Elephant

There is very little space devoted to enforcement in treaty documents, and discussion of how enforcement will be carried out at COP meetings has been most notable by its absence. The Kyoto treaty states that countries that exceed their caps will be required to make up the difference plus an additional 30 percent penalty and will also be suspended from making transfers under emissions trading programs. But as we approach the witching hour, emissions in many countries have increased to the point where there is no chance they will be able to meet their Kyoto cap by 2012, and it is increasingly apparent that nobody believes Kyoto will be enforced. In which case, if I have refused to pay my bill and have no intention of doing so, adding a penalty of 30 percent will not accomplish much.

While many other issues have been the subjects of heated debates at COP meetings since Kyoto, enforcement has all the markings of the proverbial elephant that is invisible to everyone sitting with it in the room. Yet without a credible answer to how an international climate treaty will enforce negative consequences on violators, one could argue that the treaty, and all the debate that surrounds it, is little more than a tale "full of sound and fury, signifying nothing." In the absence of a world government, all international treaties face similar problems. There are no easy answers to how to deal with recalcitrant violators. However, Kyoto is not the first international treaty to confront these admittedly difficult problems, and there are ways to increase the cost to countries that do not live up to their treaty commitments. One can make a strong case that too little attention has been devoted to how Kyoto will solve enforcement problems compared to all the attention devoted to other issues. In any case, ways to solve what is admittedly a difficult problem in a post-Kyoto treaty are discussed in Chapter 10.

Notes

1. Why the Chinese delegation in Copenhagen insisted that China would not tolerate on-site inspections and why anyone else cared one way or the other is a mystery that has led to much speculation and finger-pointing. Maybe it was a calculated ploy on China's part to sabotage negotiations. Or perhaps the United States and the United Kingdom chose to overreact to a threat they knew to be meaningless in order to blame China for the breakdown in negotiations. Both explanations may even be true. Whatever the reasons, it is a reminder that for all the careful planning, positioning, and strategizing that negotiating teams engage in, in the heat of the moment negotiators can be clueless.

2. As discussed above, while increasing sequestration by a ton is obviously equivalent to reducing emissions by a ton since both decrease atmospheric concentration by one ton, important issues of *permanence* and *timing* must be considered when trading sequestration for emissions reduction. If an emission reduction is permanent while an increase in

sequestration is only temporary, they are clearly not equivalent. Also, if the entire emission reduction occurs now while the bulk of the sequestration increase occurs later, they are not equivalent because reducing atmospheric concentration levels now reduces the likelihood of climate change more than equal reductions that occur later. However, this does not mean that trading sequestration offsets is impossible. It simply means that more care must be taken in determining what increases in sequestration are *equivalent* to a decrease in emissions. For an excellent example of how to go about comparing sequestration increases in Philippine forests with emission reductions in MDCs, see Sheeran (2006).

Chapter 10

Beyond Kyoto

In the aftermath of the train wreck in Copenhagen, it is very difficult to predict what a post-Kyoto treaty would look like or even if there will be an international treaty that succeeds Kyoto in 2012. However, this also means that thinking through key elements needed in a post-Kyoto treaty is important and timely. This chapter briefly presents the case for five concrete changes that would make a post-Kyoto cap-and-trade climate treaty more effective, efficient, and equitable. A brief discussion of whether or not these changes can garner political support and how the climate justice movement can play a positive role follows.

Let Science Set the Caps

For a number of reasons, we should insist that scientists who study the climate, not economists, are the experts best suited to advise us about how much reduction in global net emissions is necessary. (1) Climate scientists are more likely to be right about the dangers of climate change than economists, much less the business community, whose interests do not coincide with the social interest. (2) The scientific community is miraculously speaking with a single voice once we discount a handful of scientists who are clearly in the employ of fossil fuel industries, whereas other communities are a cacophony of wildly contradictory advice. (3) Most importantly, the scientific community uses the logic of insurance, which, as explained in Chapter 2, is better suited to treating climate change, where uncertainties are great and the downside risk is literally unthinkable, than the alternative logic of cost-benefit analysis favored by mainstream environmental economists. In the case of climate change, people quite reasonably want to know what reductions are required to make us safe. Weighing costs and benefits is something sensible people do only when they already feel safe. In other words, climate scientists have instinctively used the appropriate methodology, whereas economists and politicians have become bogged down in a cost-benefit framework that is inappropriate in the case of climate change.

Climate scientists have also proved the best negotiators for an aggressive response to the danger of climate change. The power of their testimony has now moved reductions of 80 percent or more by 2050 or sooner smack into the middle of the bargaining table and fixed discussion on the necessity of stabilizing atmospheric concentrations of greenhouse gases (GHG) at 350 parts per million or less. As discussed in Chapter 2, for decades mainstream economists recommended a minimalist response to climate change based on an inappropriate methodology and large-scale models driven by unrealistic and indefensible assumptions.[1] "Expert" testimony from these mainstream environmental economists bolstered resistance to dealing with climate change that was orchestrated by denialists, the fossil fuel industry, and the U.S. Chamber of Commerce. Since putting a dollar figure on the damage from cataclysmic climate change is quite difficult, if not impossible, mainstream models traditionally limited their estimate of damages to the case of moderate climate change. In effect, mainstream economic climate models simply left the central issue out of their calculations. Fortunately, climate scientists have recently succeeded in refocusing attention on what has always been the key issue—what is necessary to avoid cataclysmic climate change and keep us reasonably safe. In truth, economists have no expertise relevant to deciding how much we need to reduce carbon emissions to be safe from cataclysmic climate change, whereas climate scientists do have expertise relevant to this decision. Economists can only make useful suggestions about how to minimize the overall costs of achieving necessary reductions, and, more importantly, progressive economists can make helpful recommendations about how to distribute those costs in ways that reduce rather than further aggravate global inequities.

Caps for All

As explained in Chapter 8, trading certified emission reduction (CERs) credits that are completely bogus between Annex-1 governments or private parties within Annex-1 countries cannot undermine global reductions as long as national, annual emissions are monitored accurately and governments are held to their treaty commitments. Trading of bogus carbon credits can puncture holes in the global emissions cap only when projects in non-Annex-1 countries where national emissions are not capped sell bogus CERs to governments or sources in Annex-1 countries with caps. The obvious solution to this problem is to cap emissions in all countries—that is, eliminate the distinction between Annex-1 and non-Annex-1 countries altogether. Our motto should be "No cap, no trade."

As discussed in Chapters 8 and 9, some activists in the climate justice movement fail to understand that capping national emissions in all countries would plug all holes in the global emission cap created by trading bogus carbon credits. But others who do understand this idea still worry that capping emissions in all countries would not be fair. They argue it is not fair to cap emissions of poor countries who are least responsible for causing climate change and least able to bear the costs of curtailing climate change. Climate justice activists, as well as governments in poor countries, argue that capping emissions in poor countries effectively prevents them from developing and catching up with the developed economies.

These arguments that capping emissions in every country would be unfair are correct *if the caps are wrong*. However, none of these arguments against capping emissions everywhere holds true if caps are set equitably. Setting equally restrictive caps for all would be grossly unfair. But sensible people, and even sensible governments, understand this. As discussed in Chapter 8, for equity reasons not all Annex-1 countries were given the same caps under Kyoto. Moreover, in its plan to meet its commitments under Kyoto, the European Union (EU) assigned much lower caps to more developed countries (MDCs) such as Germany and France, and higher caps to less developed countries (LDCs), including caps that allowed emissions to increase for Portugal and Ireland. Once it is understood that *capping everyone does not mean the same cap for everyone*, it becomes apparent that we can achieve equity and, at the same time, prevent erosion of global emission reductions resulting from failure to cap emissions in all countries. Moreover, there is no reason we cannot allow very poor countries to increase emissions for some time, as long as the increase is capped.

Equitable Caps: The Greenhouse Development Rights Framework

One excellent proposal for determining equitable caps for developed and developing countries alike is the Greenhouse Development Rights Framework proposed by Paul Baer, Tom Athanasiou, and Sivan Kartha (2007). Their practical formula for assessing countries' "responsibility" and "capability" addresses an important problem about international equity. Critics have pointed out that while more people in LDCs have failed to benefit from successful economic development than in MDCs, nonetheless there are some poor people living in MDCs who also should have a right to benefit from economic development and not have to bear the costs of preventing climate change. Likewise, while there are fewer wealthy people in LDCs than there are in MDCs, there are some wealthy people in LDCs who have enjoyed development and can afford to bear part of the cost of preventing climate change. The authors of the Greenhouse Development Rights Framework propose a practical way to divide those who have already enjoyed the benefits of economic development in any country—and therefore can reasonably be expected to bear the costs of preventing climate change now that we know what kind of problems fossil-fuel-based development creates—from those who have not yet enjoyed development—and therefore should not be expected to bear the costs of preventing climate change.[2] The Greenhouse Development Rights Framework goes on to create a very practical formula to assign differential caps to all countries on a continuum that considers only a country's residents who have enjoyed economic development, combining those residents' "responsibility"— their *per capita* emissions since 1990—and those residents' "capacity"—their *per capita* gross domestic product (GDP).

By treating countries differently on a continuous basis, instead of a dichotomous basis as the Kyoto Protocol does by designating countries as either Annex-1 or non-Annex-1, a post-Kyoto international treaty would become much fairer. Not all MDCs are equally responsible and capable. More importantly, not all LDCs are equally responsible and capable. As explained in Chapter 9, China should not be treated the same way as the United States, nor should the Republic of the Congo be treated the same way as China, as it is under Kyoto. The Greenhouse Development Rights formula would give the United States tighter (lower) caps than China and would give China tighter (lower) caps than the Republic of the Congo. Of course, the more we allow developing countries to increase emissions before reaching their caps, the lower the caps on industrialized countries must be in order to meet a given level of global reductions.

Nobody is suggesting that achieving agreement on different caps for all countries will be politically easy. But achieving agreement on different caps for Annex-1 countries was not easy, yet agreement was finally reached in Kyoto. Moreover, debating the merits of different formulae for assigning caps is a far more constructive way to organize the discussion on national caps than discussing different caps on an ad hoc basis. In any case, the answer is simple, no matter how difficult negotiations may prove: Capping all countries is the only way to guarantee that we will meet our global emissions reduction goal. Capping all countries is also the only way to reap the full efficiency gain possible from carbon trading without risking undermining the overall reduction target when trading of bogus credits punctures holes in the global cap. Finally, equity can be achieved by varying the caps for different countries sufficiently using a formula such as the one already developed by the authors of the Greenhouse Development Rights Framework, which permits emissions increases for some time in the poorer countries.

Capping Net Emissions

At the international conference on climate change in Rio de Janeiro in 1992, attendees wisely recognized that it was net emissions—carbon emitted minus carbon sequestered—that mattered. However, in the intervening years between Rio and Kyoto, what was hammered out were agreements about percentage reductions in emissions to be achieved by 2012 for different industrialized countries, not reductions in net emissions. As a result, problems have arisen with sequestration offsets.

For example, *after* percentage reductions were set in Kyoto, the United States argued that it deserved credit for sequestration from U.S. standing forests and from agricultural practices that sequester carbon in soils. In some estimations, this would have cut the amount the United States was required to reduce its carbon emissions by almost half of what had been agreed to in difficult international negotiations over required emission reductions for different industrialized countries. Canada and some other MDC countries presented similar petitions. If these petitions for sequestration credit had been granted, the reduction in global emissions envisioned at Kyoto would have been seriously eroded. Of course, if the shortfall in global emissions reductions had been matched by an equal increase in global sequestration, there would have been no problem, since it is net emissions that matter. But critics pointed out correctly that much of the credit being asked for was not for an *increase* in sequestration; instead, credits were being demanded for a great deal of sequestration that was taking place anyway. The problem was that percentage reductions were negotiated for emissions, not net emissions, and then petitions for sequestration credit in lieu of emission reductions came in after the fact.

Capping net emissions in the national territory of a country—rather than capping only emissions—would also solve an important problem arising from projects in non-Annex-1 countries selling offsets for sequestration increases. As already explained, under Kyoto's Clean Development Mechanism (CDM), a project can receive CERs if it increases carbon sequestration. So creating a tree plantation can qualify for CERs because it is easy to demonstrate that new trees planted are sequestering carbon that would not have been sequestered had the trees not been planted. But the CDM executive board does not grant CERs for carbon stored and sequestered by existing forests that are conserved because it is difficult to know whether or not the forest would have been preserved in any case. As discussed in Chapter 9, this created a perverse incentive to replace existing forests with tree plantations in non-Annex-1 countries, which led to the Reducing Emissions from Deforestation and Degradation REDD proposal.[3] At this point it is not clear if REDD will ever be approved. If REDD is not approved, there is no financial compensation for conserving existing forests under Kyoto and the perverse incentive to destroy existing forests and replace them with tree plantations will persist. But if REDD is finally approved, the executive board of the CDM will face the challenging task of establishing a hypothetical baseline in order to make sure that conservation is "additional" and creates no "leakage." After all, it was because these measurement problems were deemed intractable that forest conservation was excluded from receiving credit under the CDM in the first place.

It is extremely important to solve this problem. As explained in Chapter 9, carbon emissions from deforestation and degradation exceed total emissions from the transportation sector worldwide, according to recent estimates. Even if we do not take other environmental benefits from forest conservation into account, destroying existing forests is very counterproductive simply from the perspective of net carbon emissions. If the original forest is preserved intact, it continues to store large quantities of carbon and also sequester more carbon each year. On the other hand, if the existing forest is logged off and young trees are planted in its place, net emissions will be higher and occur sooner. The young trees may grow faster and therefore sequester more carbon than the original forest, but any increase in annual sequestration pales in comparison to the release of carbon that immediately accompanies deforestation. From a net carbon emission perspective, it is better to conserve existing forests than destroy forests, even when deforestation is followed by replanting.[4]

But what if *net* emissions were capped in the country in question? In this case, since the treaty would hold the government responsible for national net emissions, the government would have an incentive to discourage activities that increase net emissions and encourage activities that decrease net emissions within its borders. The international treaty need not dictate to governments how they go about doing this. Since conservation almost always yields fewer net emissions than deforestation followed by replanting, national governments would be foolish not to enact domestic policies that make sure that conservation is also financially more attractive. Capping national net emissions provides the proper incentive for governments to find ways to discourage deforestation, eliminates the perverse incentive to destroy and replant that currently exists under Kyoto in countries without caps who can sell sequestration offsets, and does not burden the CDM with the headache of judging additionality and leakage with regard to conservation projects. The only thing the treaty must measure is annual, national, net emissions, which, as explained in Chapter 9, is straightforward and relatively noncontroversial. Again, the solution is simple: Cap national net emissions rather than emissions.

Besides capping national emissions in every country rather than only emissions in Annex-1 countries, besides capping national emissions according to differential responsibility and capability using something like the Greenhouse Development Rights formula, which gives poor countries caps above their current emissions to allow them to develop, and besides capping national net emissions rather than emissions, what else needs to be done to address valid criticisms of the Kyoto Protocol?

A New Sheriff for the Carbon Market

As long as emissions from non-Annex-1 countries are not capped, there is no choice but to give an international agency the authority to review applications for CERs from sources in those countries. Applicants have every incentive to cheat and pretend they are reducing emissions even if they are not—that is, even if reductions are not "additional" or produce "leakage." More importantly, there is no incentive for non-Annex-1 country governments to blow the whistle on bogus proposals for CERs by home country applicants. Even if a proposal is bogus, there are no negative ramifications for anyone else in the home country since non-Annex-1 country emissions are not capped. So why should a non-Annex-1 government agency disapprove bogus applications that will give a home country applicant a profit, even if the government agency does not collect part of the bogus profit in bribes? For this reason, Kyoto had no choice but to create an international professional bureaucracy to play the role of sheriff for the international carbon market.

However, as hardworking, honest, and professionally competent as the CDM executive board and its staff may be, the CDM is an international bureaucracy subject to the pressures all international bureaucracies respond to. In the end, its officers have nothing at stake but their salaries and reputations. Meanwhile, they are subject to predictable political pressures from different sides. On the one hand, international environmental organizations concerned with preserving the integrity of global reductions apply political pressure on the CDM to tighten standards and deny certification to questionable projects. On the other hand, those who wish to sell or buy CERs, governments that lobby for business interests operating in their territory, and those who favor the income flows from MDCs to LDCs that CER sales generate all apply political pressure on the CDM to approve more projects and increase the volume of CER trading.

As discussed in Chapter 9, the result has been suboptimal in two ways. While many projects approved have been legitimate, a troubling number of bogus projects have also been approved, undermining planned global emissions reductions and generating inefficiencies and inequities. Meanwhile, those worried about the negative effects of bogus projects have succeeded in limiting application of the CDM mechanism by continuing to press Annex-1 countries to meet their reduction quotas "predominantly" from internal reductions and by excluding certain categories of projects deemed too difficult to monitor. These limits on trading have led to a failure to minimize the global cost of achieving reductions and have also limited the transfer of income from MCDs to LDCs.

If an international bureaucracy were the only sheriff we could find to monitor the legitimacy of international carbon trades, we would have no recourse but to accept whatever outcome results from this predictable tug-of-war or abandon carbon trading among private parties and forgo the considerable cost reductions and desirable income transfers legitimate trading provides. But fortunately there is a better sheriff available *once net emissions are capped in all countries*. Once such caps were established, planned global reductions would be secured even if bogus CERs were traded—including bogus CERs for sequestration offsets. Furthermore, the governments of all countries would have a powerful incentive to prevent private parties within their borders from selling bogus CERs in the international carbon market. It is in the interest of country governments *whose national net emissions are capped* to keep private parties operating within their territories from selling more CERs in the international carbon market than the amount by which a project actually reduces emissions or increases sequestration above and beyond what would have occurred had the project not been undertaken. As already explained, if country governments whose net emissions are capped failed to prevent bogus sales, either those governments or their citizens would suffer the adverse consequences of having to cover the shortfall by reducing net emissions or buying more CERs than they would have had to otherwise.

Under an international treaty that enforces caps on net emissions in all countries, national governments and the citizens they represent are the ones who lose when residents are certified to sell more CERs than they should. No doubt national governments will appreciate all the assistance they can get from the professional staff of an agency of the international climate treaty with expertise in establishing baselines to measure additionality and detect leakage. But it is national governments that should be put in charge of final approval for projects within their own borders seeking to sell CERs in international carbon markets.

Very little would be required to make this change. At present, designated national authorities (DNAs) in non-Annex-1 countries must approve project design documents (PDDs) before they are submitted to the CDM executive board for evaluation and final certification. The problem is that in countries without caps there is no incentive for DNAs to disapprove projects even if they are illegitimate, and DNAs routinely rubber-stamp proposals. However, once net emissions are capped in all countries, governments would be foolish to allow their DNAs to rubber-stamp bogus projects. Once net emissions are capped in all countries, after PDDs are evaluated by the MDC executive board and awarded CERs on a provisional basis, DNAs should *then* be allowed to approve or nix the deal.

It is very important to protect the integrity of a climate treaty from difficult problems that arise in monitoring the integrity of carbon trading. Problems inherent in measuring and monitoring the integrity of sales of carbon credits are much greater than in measuring annual national net carbon emissions. Measuring annual national net emissions involves none of the dilemmas associated with establishing a hypothetical baseline necessary to measure additionality and detect leakage or judging the permanence or timing of emission reductions or sequestration increases. Since all these problems intrude when making judgments about equivalences for individual trades, it is advantageous to protect the integrity of the climate treaty from problems associated with monitoring carbon trading between private parties. For all these reasons, we should cap annual national net emissions for all countries, make monitoring and enforcing national caps the top priority of the international treaty organization, and shift responsibility for certifying emission reduction credits for individual projects to the governments where projects are located.

Having protected the global interest and prevented damage to the global cap by any bogus carbon trading that does occur, what remains is to be sure that those who have the most to lose from illegitimate carbon credits are in charge of accreditation. Once a country's annual net emissions are capped, its own government should have final approval over proposals by any of its residents who wish to sell credits in the international carbon market because those who seek to sell bogus credits are seeking to exploit their fellow citizens.

In sum, to fix Kyoto we need to take the following five steps: (1) Embrace the advice of climate scientists and lower the global cap on emissions sufficiently to stabilize atmospheric concentrations of GHGs at 350 parts per million and keep the average increase in global temperature below 2 degrees Celsius. (2) Cap emissions in all countries. Once we do these two things, we will be assured that the treaty is *effective*—that is, it really will reduce the risk of cataclysmic climate change to an acceptable level—and that, even if bogus carbon credits are traded, they will not puncture holes in the global emission cap. (3) Set national caps using a formula along the lines of the Greenhouse Development Rights Framework, which accounts for differential responsibility and capability on a continuous basis and awards LDCs much higher caps than MDCs, including caps for LDCs that allow increases in emissions sufficient for them to develop. Once we have done this, we will have distributed the costs of averting climate change fairly and not denied anyone, living anywhere, the right to benefit from economic development; furthermore, carbon trading will generate a massive annual flow of income from richer to poorer countries without resort to acrimonious and unprofitable debates over climate reparation payments. (4) Cap national net emissions rather than emissions. This will eliminate existing perverse incentives and provide effective incentives for conservation and sequestration without burdening the international treaty organization with difficult measurement problems, as REDD would do. Finally, (5) appoint national governments as the new sheriff to oversee accreditation for carbon trading between private parties. While this does not make the job of judging additionality and leakage any less difficult, it puts the decision in the hands of a sheriff with a great deal to lose if sellers receive more credits for a project than the amount by which the project actually decreases net emissions, above and beyond what would have taken place otherwise.

Why Not an International Carbon Tax?

The train wreck in Copenhagen raised the question whether it might not be better to scrap the Kyoto framework altogether and try to get countries to agree on an international carbon tax instead. Even though many criticisms of Kyoto are unfounded, other criticisms are valid, and nobody denies there are problems with Kyoto. In early negotiations there was support, particularly from Europe, for an international carbon tax. Moreover, the cap-and-trade framework hammered out in Kyoto was championed principally by Al Gore and the delegation from the United States, which remains the only country not to sign the agreement. Finally, as we saw in Chapter 7, progressive economists traditionally favor taxes over cap-and-trade programs for a number of good reasons. So why should progressives not abandon the Kyoto cap-and-trade framework as a failed experiment and push for an international carbon tax in its place? There are three compelling reasons why this would be a fatal mistake.

First, the international community has invested twelve years negotiating a cap-and-trade format, and given the urgency of the problem as compared to the speed of international diplomacy we should not want to start all over again. While some people propose now switching from cap-and-trade to an international carbon tax in good faith, those who have long opposed doing anything significant to avert climate change are now dangling a carbon tax in front of our noses as a cynical ploy to delay negotiations further. Those who want a serious and timely response to climate change should be very careful not to witlessly aid and abet those maneuvering for further delays.

Second, as explained above, the scientific community has positioned us to win global caps that are, even if not a "solution," a decent deal in present circumstances. Caps that stabilize GHG concentrations in the atmosphere at 350 parts per million and keep the average global temperature from rising by more than 2 degrees Celsius would be a tremendous step forward to prevent climate change before it is too late. This is quite a change from a few years ago and is largely due to the powerful testimony coming from climate scientists. On the other hand, nobody believes we have any chance of winning political support for an international carbon tax high enough to reduce emissions by nearly this much. In other words, strictly from an emission reduction perspective we are poised to get a much better deal than we could ever hope to get with an international carbon tax.

Nor is this surprising. When tax levels are debated it is economists who are the experts. How high should a tax be? Ask an economist. On the other hand, when we ask how low does a cap on emissions need to be to keep us safe, people sensibly ask climate scientists. Those who want an aggressive response to climate change should want the political debate to play out the second way, with climate scientists telling us what caps make us safe—not the first way, with economists telling us how high to set a carbon tax based on their estimates of how costly the tax will be to the economy. It is important to remember that mainstream environmental economists have not testified in favor of an aggressive response to climate change and are unlikely to recommend a tax that is high enough. If we change the subject from caps to taxes, we witlessly take the microphone out of the hands of climate scientists and hand it back to economists.

But neither of these is the most important reason that progressives should prefer a cap-and-trade treaty to an international carbon tax. The most compelling reason is that there is no practical way to make an international carbon tax nearly as fair as we can make a cap-and-trade policy. One issue is how effective the treaty will be at averting climate change. That concerns how much and how fast global emissions are reduced, and as explained above, cap-and-trade is a better bet to get the job done than an international tax. The second important issue is how the costs of achieving those reductions will be distributed among countries, some of which bear much greater responsibility for current GHG concentrations in the atmosphere than others, and some of which have much greater capacity to bear the costs of solving international problems than others. A uniform global carbon tax places a more or less equal burden on all countries, principally in the form of higher energy costs in the short and medium run. *If* the international treaty organization collected this tax from every country, then *in theory* the treaty organization could redistribute the tax revenue in a way that was fair to poorer countries—for example, compensate China more for imposing as high a carbon tax as the United States, and compensate the Republic of the Congo even more. But it is highly improbable that countries would let the United Nations collect an international carbon tax. It is far more likely that any international carbon tax treaty would instead require participating governments to impose a uniform carbon tax and then collect the tax from its own citizens. Having done so, does anyone imagine that the U.S. Senate would agree to send tens, if not hundreds of billions of dollars per year collected from U.S. citizens to the government of China?

So the overwhelming problem with an international carbon tax is that the tax revenues would not be distributed back to countries as "reparation payments" in a way that fairly compensates poor countries. On the other hand, under a cap-and-trade treaty, redistribution is done by giving wealthier countries tighter (lower) caps than poorer countries and then allowing sources in richer countries to "buy" cap space from projects in poorer countries through carbon trading. To secure international economic justice under an international carbon tax system, MDC governments would have to collect tax revenues from their own citizens in order to make reparation payments to LDC governments. Under the cap-and-trade treaty proposed above, sources emitting GHG in MDCs would make even larger payments to projects located in LDCs in order to lower their own compliance costs and boost their own bottom lines. At present, achieving agreement to do the latter seems far more likely than the former.

It is increasingly apparent that lumping countries into two groups—Annex-1 MDCs, all given more or less the same mandatory cap, and non-Annex-1 LDCs, all given no caps—is not the best way to set caps for both efficiency and equity reasons. But, as explained, it would be easy to fix this problem in the tradition of the Kyoto Protocol. Assigning caps for all countries according to the Greenhouse Development Rights Framework formula would perfect the Kyoto system of distributing the costs of averting climate change according to "differential responsibilities and capabilities" by assigning very different caps to different countries on a continuum based on the per capita cumulative emissions since 1990 and the per capita GDP only of citizens who have already benefited from economic development. By capping emissions in all countries, we prevent any trading of bogus credits in international carbon markets from puncturing holes in the cap on global emissions; and by treating countries differently on a continuous instead of a dichotomous basis the treaty would also be more fair.

In sum, there is still a chance of winning a decent deal for poor countries through an improved cap-and-trade post-Kyoto treaty, whereas there is little chance of moving the climate justice agenda forward if we go back to the idea of an international carbon tax. With caps higher than current emissions for LDCs, and caps way below current emissions for MDCs, carbon trading could generate the biggest transfer of resources from rich countries to poor countries that the world has ever seen.

Can It Sell in Brussels, Beijing, and Buffalo?

Can the kind of modifications proposed gather enough political support to be incorporated into a post-Kyoto treaty? Even if these changes would make an international treaty more effective, efficient, and fair—which they would—they are of limited interest if they are politically impossible.

Particularly in light of the setback in Copenhagen and the failure of the United States Senate to pass any climate legislation whatsoever, it is easy to be skeptical about the prospects for an effective and fair climate treaty. Nor does the present alignment of political power particularly favor progressive forces, although that could change quickly if ruling elites continue to fail to respond effectively to the current economic crisis; the very process of winning an effective, fair international climate treaty could catalyze other progressive changes as well. But perhaps the best way to pose the question is this: Do these demands give us our best chance of winning something worthwhile?

The EU: The EU has a better track record of being willing to support an effective and fair climate treaty than either the United States or China, so let us begin in Brussels. Since the EU is the strongest supporter of Kyoto, the five-point program outlined above should play well in Brussels because it affirms support for the essential features of Kyoto—the necessity of binding caps on national emissions agreed to jointly and enforced by an international treaty, and sharing the costs of averting climate change according to differential responsibilities and capabilities. Placing caps on national emissions in all countries should also please Brussels since it gives the EU more global emission reductions in exchange for its own reductions. Since the program allows for full carbon trading, it also allows the EU to lower the cost of meeting its commitments while ensuring that bogus trading by others cannot puncture holes in the global cap. If the EU's historical resistance to full carbon trading was based on fears about holes, this program should assuage those fears. However, this program would require the EU to agree to a lower cap for itself. As everywhere, there are different political forces at work in the EU.

The Great Recession has caused some governments to become less willing to undertake more burdens. On the other hand, the recession has temporarily lowered emissions, and European delegations in Copenhagen were the only ones who arrived ready to commit to more aggressive reductions if other countries proved willing to do likewise. This program essentially reinforces the must-do, progressive impulse that is stronger in Europe than elsewhere.

China: How might China react? China has argued forcefully that its under-developed status should exempt it from any mandatory cap. Moreover, unlike some smaller and weaker LDCs that can be subjected to outside pressure, China has made it perfectly clear that it will not be bullied into submission on this or any other subject. So it might appear there is no chance of selling this program in Beijing since it replaces China's non-Annex-1 exemption from any mandatory cap with a mandatory cap, no matter how lenient. Moreover, the science is very clear on this: Because China is so large, unless China does reduce emissions at some point there is no way to prevent climate change, period. So does this mean "game over"?

The question we need to ask is how China might be induced to do something it is not willing to do at this point—accept a mandatory cap. The program outlined above offers some important inducements. While China would not get nearly the free ride the Republic of the Congo would get under the Greenhouse Development Rights Framework, it would certainly be treated fairly given its low per capita cumulative emissions and low per capita GDP relative to the United States, Europe, and Japan. For some years Chinese caps would be set above its current emissions under the Greenhouse Development Rights formula, so the caps would not impinge on its economic growth for now. Moreover, the five-point proposal would also permit China to sell more credits since MDC purchases would no longer be limited, as is the case under Kyoto. If China's main concern is economic competitiveness vis-à-vis the United States, the EU, and Japan, this program would guarantee China a permanent competitive advantage compared to any country whose GDP per capita remained higher than China's. China might also risk the anger of poorer countries and lose leadership status among LDCs if it blocks a treaty that would provide countries that are considerably poorer than China with more preferential treatment. Finally, if China continues to reject any manda-tory cap, no matter how favorable, and insists instead on cutting emissions voluntarily, it will discover that the price for this kind of sovereignty is quite high. Voluntary reductions buy no quid pro quo reductions on the part of others in exchange, and as the most populous country in the world China benefits more when others reduce their emissions than any other country.

The United States: Of course the U.S. Senate—even when the Democratic Party had a sixty-seat majority—would not have ratified the treaty outlined above. The recommended changes do address the most common reason senators voiced for rejecting Kyoto, namely that emissions were not capped in China. Moreover, the proposed changes increase the scope for carbon trading, which the United States has long demanded. But those were never reasons—they were merely excuses—for not ratifying Kyoto.

The reason the U.S. Senate will not ratify a treaty like the one outlined above is simple. The antiquated U.S. Constitution not only gives a senator from Wyoming who represents only 544,270 constituents the same vote as a senator from California who represents 36,961,664 constituents, but also requires the U.S. Senate to ratify any treaty by a two-thirds majority vote. This means that if thirty-four senators, many of whom represent remarkably few people and are easy targets for industry to bully or buy, oppose a treaty, it cannot be ratified. In almost all other countries, international treaties can be ratified by a simple majority vote of their democratically elected parliament or legislature. But because there are thirty-four U.S. senators who are largely immune from the popular will, who hold a stranglehold on the treaty ratification process in the United States, and who prefer for the United States to ride for free on whatever sacrifices the rest of the world makes to avert climate change, the world's richest country and largest emitter of GHGs will not join the civilized world to solve arguably the greatest problem humanity has ever faced. Does this mean "game over"?

The United States has long been a bigger obstacle to an effective and fair international climate treaty than any other country. The performance of the Obama administration in Copenhagen demonstrated that this continues to be the case even though a different political party controls the White House and both Houses of Congress. In the case of the United States there are two questions worth asking: (1) Do the proposed changes provide the best opportunity for eventually winning U.S. support for an international climate treaty that is effective and fair? If not, (2) do the proposed changes best equip the rest of the world to proceed without U.S. ratification for the time being and to increase the pressure on the United States to join the civilized world in the long run?

We could easily make a strong case that the proposed changes are the best deal the United States *should* hope to get. While the United States has a mandatory cap, so does every other country. While the U.S. cap is tight, it is no tighter than that of any other country with the same responsibility and capability. In other words, this treaty would not ask the United States to pull greater than its fair share. It also guarantees that its sacrifices would not go in vain because they would be accompanied by reductions elsewhere in the world sufficient to achieve the result of averting cataclysmic climate change, certainly a result that everyone in the United States would benefit from. The treaty would also provide the unlimited access to international carbon markets that the United States government has long asked for as a means of minimizing the costs of living up to its responsibilities.

Most importantly, the proposed modifications permit the rest of the world to proceed as they should without U.S. ratification for the time being. It keeps U.S. intransigence from derailing the only process that has any chance of preventing climate change equitably. It also gives the rest of the world the best opportunity to put more and more pressure on the United States to come around.

Just as it was possible to implement Kyoto without U.S. participation, it is also possible to implement the kind of treaty outlined above beginning in 2012 without U.S. participation. When the United States refuses to ratify and participate in a post-Kyoto treaty, the rest of the world can argue even more powerfully and irrefutably that this is a clear case of free riding by the country most responsible for causing the problem it refuses to help solve and most capable of shouldering burdens necessary to solve it. At that point the only kinds of pressure the world can ever bring to bear on the world's greatest military power and largest economy can be considered: travel restrictions for U.S. citizens; expelling the United States from the Olympic Games and the World Cup; recalling foreign ambassadors to Washington; expelling U.S. ambassadors abroad; United Nations resolutions condemning U.S. behavior. The World Trade Organization has already signaled its willingness to authorize retaliatory tariffs against countries that unfairly award themselves competitive advantages by refusal to curb carbon emissions. Besides levying fines, these are the same kinds of measures an international climate treaty must resort to when a signatory nation fails to live up to its treaty obligations. While none of these measures will sway a U.S. government that persists in remaining obdurate, they do impose real costs that a rational calculation by U.S. policymakers should weigh in the balance.

A Useful Role for Environmental Justice Activists

Exemplary mass actions: Only climate change denialists, special interests tied to the fossil fuel industries, or people who have been hypnotized by demagogues or are paying no attention fail to understand that both domestic and international political responses to the danger of climate change have been woefully inadequate to this point. Climate change is an urgent problem and delay is deadly. Anyone who cares about averting climate change should be thankful that the criminally negligent performance of official government delegations and a number of heads of state in Copenhagen in December 2009 did not go without a massive and powerful protest. There is a crucial role for climate justice activists and the *street heat* they bring. Protests in the galleries of national congresses and parliaments where elected representatives serve special interests and refuse to approve effective, fair domestic policies; protests at international meetings where government delegations free ride and obstruct, where too little is accomplished, and where justice is sacrificed, are all productive and desperately needed. The larger the demonstrations and the greater the anger over the failure of authorities to do what is required, the better. "Keep the Oil in the Soil and the Coal in the Hole" campaigns, which mobilize citizens to engage in mass protests and civil disobedience at mine sites, at wellheads, and, better yet, at company headquarters and CEOs' residences, can also be an important and positive catalyst. When governing elites are playing Nero's fiddle while our world burns, outrage is the only sane response.

However, dogged determination, heroic protest, and civil disobedience can be only one part of an effective strategy to reduce carbon emissions sufficiently to avert climate change. Unless an effective cap-and-trade international treaty is approved and enforced, unless governments are forced to implement effective domestic policies, demonstrators engaging in civil disobedience will be rounded up and arrested by armed police and military personnel to no avail. So just as it is counterproductive for mainstream environmental nongovernmental organizations and progressive politicians to denounce the tactics of demonstrators who are playing an important, positive role in averting climate change equitably, it is also counterproductive for radicals who put their lives on the line to accuse those working tirelessly for a more effective and fair international treaty and better domestic policies of misleading the public and selling "pretend solutions." We will need much more of both kinds of efforts to succeed, and the sooner climate change radicals and reformers recognize this, the more successful we all will be.

Expose bogus carbon trading: As explained above, we will not avert climate change without ratifying and enforcing an international climate treaty that caps national emissions in all countries and allows for carbon trading. Therefore ill-informed attacks on all forms of carbon trading, in all circumstances, are extremely counterproductive. Trashing carbon trading only weakens efforts to avert climate change fairly and undermines the credibility of the climate justice movement.

However, as explained earlier, there will be powerful incentives for individual parties to sell bogus carbon credits, allowances, and offsets. Buyers cannot be relied on to prevent this because buyers have no reason to care if an allowance is bogus or not as long as it is accredited; and judging how much credit a project legitimately deserves is often quite difficult. While an international treaty that successfully enforces caps on net national emissions will prevent bogus trading from puncturing holes in the global cap and thereby undermining global reductions in net emissions, bogus trading is nonetheless terribly unfair. When a source in one country gets away with selling a bogus credit to a source in another country, it cheats everyone else in the country where the sale originated. A cap on national emissions in the country of origin prevents the bogus sale from puncturing a hole in the global cap, but it does so by forcing others in the country where the sale originated to plug up the hole the bogus sale created. In other words, sale of an illegitimate carbon credit unfairly forces someone else in the country to bear the cost of reducing its emissions, increasing its own sequestration, or purchasing a credit in the international carbon market when it should not have had to.

Sales of bogus credits by sources located in poor countries are particularly unfair because those who are unfairly forced to bear the cost of plugging the hole are residents of poor countries who, in general, can least afford to do so. This is an area where international climate justice activists who prioritize protecting the interests of poor residents in poor countries can be of great help. Monitoring accreditation for fraud and exposing sales of bogus credits can be very useful. But to be useful those performing this valuable service must not be confused about what is at stake. As long as the sale is from a country whose national emissions are capped, it cannot puncture a hole in global reductions. So that should not be the basis for the criticism. Instead, a bogus carbon credit is an act of environmental injustice inflicted by the sellers on their fellow citizens. Just as prosecutors who want to win convictions must accuse defendants of the crime they committed rather than some other crime, climate justice activists need to accuse the sellers of bogus carbon credits of the crime they actually commit. The crime is exploitation of one's fellow citizens. The crime is not undermining global emission reductions when the country of origin for the sale has its national emissions capped.

Question the economic system: In Part II we reviewed important theories from both mainstream and heterodox schools of economics and discovered a number of ways in which the private enterprise market system puts the environment at risk. Like Pogo, we have found the enemy, and he is us! Not "us" the people. Nor is the enemy population growth or advanced technologies per se. But "us" meaning the defining institutions of "our" economic system bear primary responsibility for putting more and more strain on the natural environment, strain that has now reached crisis proportions in the form of climate change. Who will raise these important issues and resist the temptation to sugarcoat painful truths about our present economic system?

Who will point out that markets *predictably* overproduce goods whose production or consumption generates negative external effects and consequently leads us to pollute too much? Who will point out that markets *predictably* undersupply public goods since all can free ride on what others provide, so markets consequently provide insufficient incentives to protect the environment? Who will point out that it would be irrational for private owners *not* to extract natural resources—including coal, oil, and natural gas—faster than is socially desirable whenever rates of profit are higher than a socially responsible rate of time discount? Who will explain how markets for labor and consumer goods create perverse incentives that lure people to take too much of their productivity gains as individual consumption and too little as more environmentally friendly collective consumption and leisure time? Who will criticize the culture of consumerism that business interests promote because it profits them, and the perverse environmentally destructive effects of market biases on preference development? And who will point out that markets fail to generate information necessary to know how high corrective environmental taxes and subsidies should be, while spawning powerful political lobbies with interests in underestimating the size of necessary correctives?

Climate justice activists and spokespersons are among the most reliable voices pointing out how and why giant corporations and market forces are the most powerful enemies of the natural environment today. Climate justice activists are among the best at explaining how those fighting to protect the environment must invariably swim against the current in our private enterprise market system, which often rewards environmentally destructive behavior and punishes environmentally responsible behavior. Last, but not least, climate justice activists are willing to explore possibilities of system change in order to replace perverse incentives with incentives for economic decision-makers to respect and protect the environment instead.

Prospects for the human and other species may ultimately hinge on whether our current economic system is replaced by a qualitatively different economic system, a system unencumbered by a dysfunctional growth imperative and with no elites to prey on their fellow humans and the natural environment. Climate justice activists have played an increasingly important role in exploring the kinds of changes discussed briefly in the conclusion.

Notes

1. In addition to the studies criticizing key assumptions responsible for misleading conclusions in mainstream economic models cited in note 9 in Chapter 2, interested readers should also consult Stanton, Ackerman, and Kartha (2009), Laitner et al. (2003), Hall and Behl (2006), Kahouli-Brahmi (2008), and Edenhofer et al. (2006).

2. Unfortunately, there is no way to compel national governments to use the leeway afforded them by higher caps to benefit poor citizens rather than wealthy elites without interfering in the internal affairs of sovereign states. But at least a treaty whose caps were

determined according to the Greenhouse Development Rights formula could not be accused of denying any people the right to enjoy the benefits of economic development no matter where they lived.

3. It is likely that the CDM executive board would approve CERs for a project proposal to clear-cut an existing forest and replace it with a tree plantation. However, if the project proposal were to create a tree plantation on land that had already been clear-cut, it might well be approved. A change in ownership might prove necessary to secure approval, but that is hardly an insurmountable hurdle in today's business world.

4. Besides serving as carbon sinks, standing forests also provide other important environmental services. As habitats for endangered species they are crucial in efforts to protect biodiversity. They are also water purifiers and soil protectors. Any policy that fails to provide effective incentives for forest conservation is seriously flawed. Any policy that creates perverse incentives to destroy forests is criminally incompetent.

Appendix to Part IV

Exercise on Climate Control Treaties

This exercise is designed to illustrate some of the political and economic issues that play key roles in discussions about how to design an international treaty to avert climate change.

Imagine three countries sitting down to negotiate a global climate change agreement: the United States, Russia, and India. Consider the United States and Russia as more developed countries (MDCs), termed Annex-1 countries in the Kyoto Protocol, and India as a less developed country (LDC), or a non-Annex-1 country. Below are equations for both the marginal costs (MCs) and total costs (TCs) of reducing greenhouse gas (GHG) emissions for all three countries. As a country reduces emissions by more and more, the MC of reducing emissions rises. This is because presumably a country will use the least costly options for reducing emissions first and gradually move on to using higher-cost methods as more emissions reductions are required. It is also typically the case that the MC of emissions reduction is lower in developing countries. This is because LDCs have engaged in relatively little emissions reduction, or abatement, so many low-cost opportunities for reducing emissions still exist there.

The MC and TC of emissions reduction (abatement) for the three countries are expressed in billions of dollars, where X is the number of tons of GHG emissions reduced by each country:

United States	$MC_{us} = 5X_{US}$	$TC_{us} = 2.5X_{US}^2$
Russia	$MC_R = 2X_R$	$TC_R = X_R^2$
India	$MC_I = X_I$	$TC_I = X_I^2/2$

Initially There Is no International Treaty

While each country has potentially unlimited "rights" to emit carbon into the upper atmosphere, the United States chooses only to "exercise" its "right" to emit 400 tons, Russia chooses only to exercise its right to emit 250 tons, and India chooses only to exercise its right to emit 200 tons. As a result, global emissions are 850 tons. The international community has identified a 10 percent reduction in global carbon emissions as necessary to minimize the risks of dangerous climate change.

Treaty #1: The treaty requires each country to reduce its emissions by 10 percent.

1. How much emissions reduction would each country have to do?

United States:	$(.10)400 = 40 = X_{US}$
Russia:	$(.10)250 = 25 = X_R$
India:	$(.10)200 = 20 = X_I$
Global:	$(40 + 25 + 20) = 85 = X_G = (.10)850$

2. What would be the cost of the last ton of emissions reduced in each country?

United States:	$MC_{US} = 5X_{US} = 5(40) = \$200$
Russia:	$MC_R = 2X_R = 2(25) = \$50$
India:	$MC_I = X_I = 1(20) = \$20$

3. What would be the total cost for each country?

United States:	$TC_{US} = 2.5X_{US}^2 = 2.5(40)^2 = \$4,000$
Russia:	$TC_R = X_R^2 = (25)^2 = \$625$
India:	$TC_I = X_I^2/2 = (20)^2/2 = \$200$

4. What would be the total cost of emissions reduction for the world?

$TC_G = \$4,000 + \$625 + \$200 = \$4,825$

5. Comment on any inefficiencies and inequities in this treaty.

Efficiency: After each country has reduced its emissions by 10 percent, the MC of reduction is different in the three countries. We therefore know we failed to minimize the global costs of reduction, which means the pattern of reductions this treaty yields is *in*efficient. To illustrate: The last ton reduced in the United States (the 40th ton reduced) costs $200, while the last ton reduced in Russia (the 25th ton reduced) costs only $25. Had we reduced 39 tons in the United States (instead of 40) and 26 tons in Russia (instead of 25), we would have achieved the same level of global reductions, 850, but we could have saved $200 – $25 = $175—that is, TC_G would have been $4,650 instead of $4,825.

Equity: For simplicity assume that the benefits of achieving a global reduction of 85 tons are the same for all three countries. While the United States is paying more than Russia, which is paying more than India, to achieve this global reduction, we might argue that it is still unfair for India to bear this much of the cost because India did much less to create the problem in the first place, since Indian per capita cumulative emissions are much lower than per capita cumulative emissions of the United States and Russia, and because India is less able to bear the cost of preventing climate change, since per capita gross domestic product (GDP) is much lower there. We could also argue that the treaty now explicitly limits each country's "right" to release carbon into the upper atmosphere, but distributes the remaining rights very unfairly. The treaty implicitly awards the United States rights to emit (400 – 40) = 360 tons, but awards Russia only rights to emit (250 – 25) = 225 tons, and India only rights to emit (200 – 20) = 180 tons. We could argue this is unfair for three reasons: (1) Since per capita cumulative emissions are highest in the United States and lowest in India, India should be awarded the most rights to emit more carbon dioxide in the future and the United States should be awarded the fewest rights to emit more—whereas this treaty does just the opposite. (2) Since emission rights are a new form of wealth and per capita wealth is lowest in India and highest in the United States, India should receive the most emission rights and the United States the fewest—whereas this treaty does just the opposite. (3) It is more difficult to achieve economic development when consumption of fossil fuel is limited. Since India is least developed and the United States is most developed, India should receive the most emission rights and the United States the fewest—whereas this treaty does just the opposite.

Treaty 2: The treaty calls for a 10 percent reduction in global emissions, but exempts India from making any reductions and permits no trading of emission rights.

1. How much emissions reduction would each country have to do?

To make the two treaties equivalent, global reductions must be the same: X_G must again be 85, but now $X_I = 0$. Assume we require the United States and Russia to make the same percentage reduction, p, in their emissions. In this case we have:

$$X_{US} + X_R = 85; \ 400p + 250p = 85.$$

Solving the second equation for p: $650p = 85$; $p = 85/650 = .13077$; that is, the United States and Russia must each reduce by 13.077 percent.

United States: (.13077)400 = 52.308 = X_{US}
Russia: (.13077)250 = 32.692 = X_R
India: $0 = X_I$
Global: 52.308 + 32.692 + 0 = 85 = X_G

2. What would be the cost of the last ton of emissions reduced in each country?

United States: $MC_{US} = 5X_{US} = 5(52.308) = \$261.54$
Russia: $MC_R = 2X_R = 2(32.692) = \$65.38$
India: [Note: $MC_I = X_I = 1(1) = \$1$ if India reduced emissions by 1 ton]

3. What would be the total cost for each country?

United States: $TC_{US} = 2.5X_{US}^2 = 2.5(52.308)^2 = \$6,840.32$
Russia: $TC_R = X_R^2 = (32.692)^2 = \$1,068.77$
India: $TC_I = X_I^2/2 = (0)^2/2 = \$0.00$

4. What would be the total cost of emissions reduction for the world?

$$TC_G = \$6,840.32 + \$1,068.77 + \$0 = \$7,909.09$$

5. Comment on the effects of excluding India from mandatory reductions on efficiency and equity.

218

Efficiency: Treaty #2 is even less efficient than Treaty #1 since $7,909.09 > $4,825. This is why people sometimes argue that achieving equity can come at the expense of efficiency. The cost of treating India fairly—not requiring it to reduce emissions at all—has raised the global cost of reducing emissions by 85 tons by $7,909.09 – $4,825 = $3,084.09. The reason is that none of the reduction is taking place in India, where the costs of reduction are lowest. Note that the first unit reduced in India would have cost only $1! We are also distributing reductions inefficiently between the United States and Russia since the MCs are different in these two countries. We could lower TC_G by having more of the reductions in Russia, where the last unit of abatement cost only $65.38, and fewer of the reductions in the United States, where the last unit of abatement cost $261.54. But since Treaty #2 does not permit carbon trading between the United States and Russia, the inefficient pattern of abatement in those two countries will not be eliminated.

Equity: Clearly Treaty #2 treats India more fairly than Treaty #1. The implicit distribution of emissions rights—that is, new wealth—is now, for the United States, $400 – 52.308 = 347.692$ (which is less than 360), and for Russia, $250 – 32.692 = 217.308$ (which is less than 225). While India is given potentially limitless emission rights, under Treaty #2 India will only "exercise" its rights to emit 200 tons. That is all India chose to exercise before there was any treaty, and since this treaty does not allow India to sell any of its new wealth, India will continue to emit 200 tons, as before.

Treaty #3: The treaty calls for a 10 percent reduction in global emissions, exempts India from making any reductions, reduces U.S. and Russian emission rights by the same percentage—13.077—but permits unlimited trading of emission rights between Annex-1 countries (that is, between the United States and Russia).

1. How much would each country have to reduce its emissions?

Once again $X_{US} + X_R = 85$ and $X_I = 0$. But now instead of $400p + 250p = 85$, meaning that the United States and Russia will each reduce its emissions by the same percentage, p, the pattern of emissions reductions will be determined by the condition: $MC_{US} = MC_R$. This is because the United States and Russia will keep trading emission rights until there are no longer any mutually beneficial deals to be struck, which will be the case only when MC_{US} becomes equal to MC_R. So $5X_{US} = MC_{US} = MC_R = 2X_R$, or $X_{US} = (2/5)X_R$. Substituting for X_{US} in the first equation above, $(2/5)X_R + X_R = 85$, and $X_R = (5/7)85 = 60.714$, and therefore $X_{US} = 24.286$.

219

United States: $24.286 = X_{US}$
Russia: $60.714 = X_R$
India: $0 = X_I$
Global: $24.286 + 60.286 + 0 = 85 = X_G$

2. What would be the cost of the last ton of emissions reduced in each country?

United States: $MC_{US} = 5X_{US} = 5(24.286) = \$121.43$
Russia: $MC_R = 2X_R = 2(60.714) = \$121.43$
India: [Note: $MC_I = X_I = 1(1) = \$1$ if India reduced emissions by 1 ton]

3. What would be the total cost of the reductions carried out in each country?

United States: $TC_{US} = 2.5X_{US}^2 = 2.5(24.286)^2 = \$1,474.52$
Russia: $TC_R = X_R^2 = (60.714)^2 = \$3,686.19$
India: $TC_I = X_I^2/2 = (0)^2/2 = \$0.00$

However, the total cost to the United States is not just the cost of reducing its own emissions by 24.286. That reduction is not sufficient to achieve a 13.077 percent reduction from 400, which is all the United States has the "right" to emit. Consequently, the United States will have to buy emission rights from Russia. Like Treaty #2, Treaty #3 gives the United States the right to emit (1 − .13077)400 = 347.692 tons. The United States will also reduce 24.286 tons, as calculated above. Therefore, the United States will need to purchase [400 − 347.692 − 24.286] = 28.022 emission rights from Russia. The price of each emission right will be $121.43 because Russia would accept no less (since that is what it will cost Russia to reduce its last ton) and the United States will pay no more (since the United States could reduce another ton itself for that amount). So $121.43(28.022) = $3,402.71, and the total cost to the United States—that is, the cost of reducing emissions internally by 24.286 tons, *plus* the cost of buying 28.022 emission rights from Russia—is $1,474.52 + $3,402.71 = $4,877.23.

The total cost to Russia of reducing emissions by 60.714—which exceeds a 13.077 percent reduction from 250 by 28.022 tons—is reduced by the amount Russia gains from selling 28.022 emission rights to the United States. At a price of $121.43 each, Russia reduces its total costs by $121.43(28.022) = $3,402.71 when it sells 28.022 emission rights to the United States. So the total cost to Russia—that is, the cost of reducing emissions internally by 60.714 tons, *minus* the revenue received from selling 28.022 emission rights to the United States—is $3,686.19 − $3,402.71 = $283.48.

4. What would be the total cost of emissions reduction for the world?

$$TC_G = \$4,877.23 + \$283.48 + \$0 = \$5,160.71$$
$$(\text{also } TC_G = \$1,474.52 + \$3,686.19 + \$0 = \$5,160.71)$$

5. Comment on the effects of emission trading between Annex-1 countries on efficiency and equity.

Efficiency: Treaty #3 is more efficient than Treaty #2 because it allows reductions to be reallocated from the United States to Russia until the marginal reduction costs are equal in the two countries. TC_G are lowered by $7,909.09 – $5,160.71 = $2,748.38. However, Treaty #3 is still not as efficient as it might be. The 85th ton reduced costs $121.43 (whether it is reduced in the United States or in Russia). If instead the 85th ton were reduced in India, it would cost only $1!

Equity: The distribution of emission rights under Treaty #3 is the same as under Treaty #2, so the equity implications of the wealth distribution are the same. The efficiency gain ($7,909.09 – $5,160.71 = $2,748.38) from reallocating reductions from the United States to Russia until the marginal reduction costs are equal in the two countries achieved by Treaty #3 is divided between the United States ($6,840.32 – $4,877.23 = $1,963.09) and Russia ($1,068.77 – $283.48 = $785.29). There is no change for India. Under both Treaty #2 and Treaty #3, India benefits from prevention of climate change at no cost.

Treaty #4: The treaty calls for a 10 percent reduction in global emissions, exempts India from making any reductions, reduces U.S. and Russian emission rights by the same percentage—13.077—but permits unlimited trading of emissions rights between all countries, including India; that is, full use of a Clean Development Mechanism (CDM).

1. How much emissions reduction would each country have to do? (Note: Treaty #4 does not require India to reduce emissions; however, since India can now sell emission reduction credits to the United States and Russia, India will benefit by reducing emissions, as illustrated below.)

We now have two conditions: $X_{US} + X_R + X_I = 85$, and $MC_{US} = MC_R = MC_I$. Since $MC_{US} = 5X_{US}$, $MC_R = 2X_R$, and $MC_I = X_I$, from the second condition we get

$$5X_{US} = 2X_R = X_I, \text{ or } X_R = (5/2)X_{US} \text{ and } X_I = 5X_{US}.$$

Substituting into the first equation, $X_{US} + (5/2)X_{US} + 5X_{US} = 85$, giving $X_{US} = 10$.

United States: $10 = X_{US}$
Russia: $25 = X_R$
India: $50 = X_I$
Global: $10 + 25 + 50 = 85 = X_G$

2. What would be the cost of the last ton of emissions reduced in each country?

United States: $MC_{US} = 5X_{US} = 5(10) = \$50$
Russia: $MC_R = 2X_R = 2(25) = \$50$
India: $MC_I = X_I = 1(50) = \$50$

3. What would be the total cost for each country?

Total costs for each country associated with the reductions it carries out itself are as follows:

United States: $TC_{US} = 2.5X_{US}^2 = 2.5(10)^2 = \$250$
Russia: $TC_R = X_R^2 = (25)^2 = \$625$
India: $TC_I = X_I^2/2 = (50)^2/2 = \$1,250$

However, the United States and Russia will have to buy emission rights from India as follows:

The United States will buy: $400 - (1 - .13007)400 - 10 = 42.308$
Russia will buy: $250 - (1 - .13007)250 - 25 = 7.692$
India will sell: $42.308 + 7.692 = 50$

Emission rights will sell for $50 each because the MC of reductions is now $50 in all three countries, so no country will pay more than $50 for a credit or sell a credit for less than $50. Therefore, it will cost the United States an additional $50(42.308) = $2,115.40, it will cost Russia an additional $50(7.692) = $384.60, and India will gain $50(50) = $2,500 from selling emission rights through the CDM, and therefore the total costs for the three countries are:

United States: $TC_{US} = \$250 + \$2,115.40 = \$2,365.40$
Russia: $TC_R = \$625 + \$384.60 = \$1,009.60$
India: $TC_I = \$1,250 - \$2,500.00 = -\$1,250.00$

4. What would be the total cost of emission reductions for the world?

$TC_G = \$2,365.40 + \$1,009.60 - \$1,250 = \$2,125$ (also $TC_G = \$250 + \$625 + \$1,250 = \$2,125$)

5. Comment on the effects of a CDM on efficiency and equity.

Efficiency: Treaty #4 has minimized the global cost of reducing global emissions by 85 tons: TC_G Treaty #4: $2,125 < TC_G Treaty #1: $4,825 < TC_G Treaty #3: $5,160.71 < TC_G Treaty #2: $7,909.09. We also know this because the marginal costs of reduction are the same in all three countries, so there is no way to reallocate emission reductions and lower global costs. Comparing the total cost of reducing emissions by 85 tons under Treaty #4 and Treaty #3, the efficiency gain produced by the CDM is $5,160.71 – $2,125 = $3,035.71. It is distributed as follows: U.S. total costs have fallen by $4,877.23 – $2,365.40 = $2,511.83. Russian total costs have risen by $1,009.60 – $283.48 = $726.12. (This is because the CDM allowed India to replace Russia as the seller in the lucrative market for emission rights.) And India now enjoys a profit of $1,250.

Equity: Treaty #4 awards the same emission rights—that is, new wealth— as Treaty #2 and #3: the United States (347.692), Russia (217.308), and India (potentially limitless). However, the CDM in Treaty #4 allows India to make more profitable use of its emission rights by selling some of them to the United States and Russia. Under Treaty #2 and #3, India could not sell any of its new wealth to the United States and Russia. The CDM allows India to sell emission rights, which it has every incentive to do as long as reducing emissions costs less than the price India receives. In the market for emission rights, supply (50 emission rights supplied by India) will equal demand for emission rights (42.308 from the United States and 7.692 from Russia) when the price of an emission right is $50. So under this treaty, the reduction of 50 of the 85 tons reduced globally will take place in India, which will cut back on its emissions from 200 to 150 tons. However, even though the reductions are taking place in India (where they are cheaper), the costs of achieving those reductions are being paid for by the United States and Russia.

The United States and Russia are paying more than it costs India to reduce 50 tons. The total cost of reducing the 50 tons in India is $50^2/2 = $1,250. The United States and Russia pay India $50(50) = $2,500. But this does not mean the United States and Russia are overpaying India by $1,250. We could just as easily argue the United States and Russia are underpaying India because it would have cost the United States and Russia much more than $2,500 to reduce those 50 tons themselves. By comparing the total costs under Treaty #3 and Treaty #4, we can calculate how much more it would have cost the United States and Russia: From Treaty #3 we know the total cost to the United States and Russia combined of reducing all 85 tons themselves is $5,160.71. From Treaty #4 the total cost to the United States and Russia combined (when they can purchase 50 of the 85 tons from India) is $2,365.40 + $1,009.60 = $3,375. Therefore the United States and Russia have saved $5,160.71 – $3,375

= \$1,785.71 by purchasing 50 emission rights from India. Rather than speak of over- or underpaying, it is more accurate to say that the United States and Russia are sharing with India the efficiency gain from relocating 50 tons of reduction from the United States and Russia to India. In this case, the United States and Russia are getting \$1,785.71 of the efficiency gain, and India is getting \$1,250 of the efficiency gain. If the division of the efficiency gain were allocated through some political process or even through direct negotiation, it could be divided differently. However, this is how the efficiency gain will be allocated if we leave it to be settled by the laws of supply and demand in a free market for emission rights. The efficiency gain from this market transaction, like the efficiency gains from all market transactions, is divided between sellers and buyers according to the relative price elasticities of supply and demand. Whoever has the lower price elasticity will always capture more of the efficiency gain.

Warning: There is an important implicit assumption in the above analysis and an explicit warning is in order. We have assumed that India will actually reduce its emissions by 50 tons when it sells 50 emission rights to the United States and Russia. Of course this is what the executive board of the CDM in the Kyoto Protocol is supposed to ensure when it certifies emission rights for sale, namely that there was actually that number of tons reduced additional to what would have occurred in any case. But Treaty #4 gives India unlimited emission rights. When India could not sell emission rights, it only found it in its interest to "exercise" its right to emit 200 tons. But since India can now sell emission rights at \$50 apiece, why would India not want to "exercise" its right to emit more than 200 tons—in which case global emissions would no longer decline by 85 tons? As long as India has unlimited emission rights, there will be what economists call a perverse incentive for India to try to sell bogus emission rights. Selling a real reduction that cost only \$15, say, for \$50 is a good deal. But if you can sell a "pretend" reduction that cost nothing for \$50, that is an even better deal! We began to evaluate this problem in Chapter 8 but devote more attention to it in Chapters 9 and 10.

However, even if the CDM avoids cheating—that is, selling rights to emit that do not correspond to real reductions—it is sometimes criticized for other reasons we review in Chapter 9. Some people criticize it precisely because it does what it is designed to do—lower the cost of emissions reductions for MDCs. These critics argue that by lowering the cost of carbon emissions in the United States and Russia—in our exercise from \$121.43 to \$50 a ton—the CDM has reduced incentives for MDCs to search as hard as they would have otherwise for new renewable energy and energy conservation technologies. As discussed in Chapter 9, supporters of the CDM respond by saying, "If you want to keep the marginal cost of emissions high in the

MDCs, it is better to do so by reducing emission caps on MDCs by more than 13.077 percent rather than by making it more costly for them to reduce emissions by limiting their use of the CDM." To see how this might work, we consider Treaty #5.

Treaty #5: The treaty calls for reducing global emissions by whatever percentage is necessary to keep the price of carbon emissions as high as $121.43 in the United States and Russia while allowing unlimited emission trading between all countries.

    1. How much emissions reduction would each country have to do?

$$MC_{US} = 5X_{US} = 121.43, \text{ which gives } X_{US} = 24.29$$
$$MC_R = 2X_R = 121.43, \text{ which gives } X_R = 60.72$$
$$MC_I = X_I = 121.43, \text{ which gives } X_I = 121.43$$

$X_G = 24.29 + 60.72 + 121.43 = 206.44$, which is much greater than 85 and therefore moves us much further in the direction of reducing global emissions. While an 85-ton reduction was a 10 percent reduction from pretreaty emission levels, $206.44/850 = .24287$ is a 24.287 percent reduction. While unlimited trading guarantees that we will achieve this much larger reduction at the lowest possible global cost, nonetheless the global cost will be considerably higher because the overall reduction is considerably higher.

    2. What would be the cost of the last ton of emissions reduced in each country?

By design the MC of emission reductions in each country is $121.43 in order to keep the pressure on the United States and Russia to search for renewable and energy efficiency as high as it was under Treaty #3.

    3. What would be the total cost for each country?

Total costs for each country associated with internal reductions are as follows:

United States: $TC_{US} = 2.5X_{US}^2 = 2.5(24.29)^2 = \$1,475.01$
Russia: $TC_R = X_R^2 = (60.72)^2 = \$3,686.92$
India: $TC_I = X_I^2/2 = (121.43)^2/2 = \$7,372.62$

However, the United States and Russia will have to buy emission rights from India. If we continue to exempt India from any mandatory reductions and reduce emission rights in the United States and Russia by the same percentage, we can calculate the percentage reduction, p that will be necessary as follows:

$400p + 250p = 206.44$, which gives $p = .3176$. In other words, the United States and Russia will both have to reduce emissions by 31.76 percent in order to achieve a global reduction of 24.287 percent since we are not limiting India's emission rights at all.

The United States will buy: $400 - (1 - .3176)400 - 24.29 = 102.75$
Russia will buy: $250 - (1 - .3176)250 - 60.72 = 18.68$
India will sell: $102.75 + 18.68 = 121.43$

Emission rights will sell for $121.43 each. Therefore it will cost the United States an additional $121.43(102.75) = \$12,476.93$, it will cost Russia an additional $121.43(18.68) = \$2,268.31$, and India will gain $121.43(121.43) = \$14,745.24$ from selling emission rights through the CDM:

United States: $TC_{US} = \$1,475.01 + \$12,476.93 = \$13,951.94$
Russia: $TC_R = \$3,686.92 + \$2,268.31 = \$5,955.23$
India: $TC_I = \$7,372.62 - \$14,745.24 = -\$7,372.62$

4. What would be the total cost for the world?

$TC_G = \$1,475.01 + \$3,686.92 + \$7,372.62 = \$12,534.55$.
(also $\$13,951.94 + \$5,955.23 - \$7,372.62 = \$12,534.55$)

5. Comment on the effects of creating a high price on emissions in Annex-1 countries to stimulate research and innovation in energy conservation and renewables.

Efficiency: Treaty #5 is efficient in the sense that it minimizes the global cost of achieving a 24.287 percent reduction in global emissions. But a larger efficiency question is what percentage global reduction is efficient in the first place! This depends, of course, on how great the benefits of avoiding climate change are compared to the costs associated with doing so. In theory, we should keep reducing emissions up to the point where the global benefit of the last ton reduced is equal to the cost of reducing it. Depending on how large the benefits of reducing emissions may be, that may mean that only a 10 percent reduction in emissions is warranted (i.e., efficient) or it may mean that a 24.287 percent reduction is warranted (i.e., efficient).

However, all attempts to estimate and quantify the benefits of avoiding climate change have proved very unsatisfactory—and without such an estimate, a cost-benefit analysis (CBA) is impossible. So instead of deploying a CBA approach to answering the question of what percentage reduction in global emissions is efficient, more and more analysts are approaching this part of the policy debate as an insurance issue, as explained in Chapter 2. We ask scientists to tell us what percentage reductions are necessary to reduce the risk of possibly cataclysmic climate change to a level we find acceptable. If they tell us we need a 10 percent reduction, then we design a policy to achieve that target. If they tell us we need a 24.287 percent reduction, we make that our target. Right now, most climate scientists believe that the percentage global reduction that is considered politically realistic is significantly below the level science says is necessary to reduce risk to an acceptable level. In this case, something more along the lines of a 24.287 percent reduction would be more efficient than a 10 percent reduction.

Equity: Because Treaty #5 leads to a larger global reduction and still gives India potentially unlimited emission rights, there are fewer emission rights to be awarded to the United States and Russia. The United States is awarded $(1 - .3176)400 = 272.96$, which is less than the 347.692 the United States received under Treaty #4. Russia is awarded $(1 - .3176)250 = 170.60$, which is also less than the 217.308 Russia received under Treaty #4. Notice that while the total cost of Treaty #5 to the United States and Russia is much higher, tightening global reductions from 10 percent to 24.287 percent benefits India by allowing India to sell more emission rights ($121.43 > 50$) at a much higher price ($\$121.43 > \$50$)! This means that non-Annex-1 countries stand to gain a considerable amount financially if the global reduction target is reduced under a Kyoto-type treaty, in addition to all the benefits they will enjoy by reducing the amount of climate change they must live with.

Conclusion

A Winning Political Strategy

The first step in formulating any political strategy is to distinguish between friends and enemies. Unfortunately, many organizations fighting to better protect the environment have done a poor job in this regard, although some have discovered their error and recently changed course. To turn environmental destruction into environmental restoration, it is not sufficient to design effective policies. A political coalition determined enough and powerful enough to implement these policies must be built.

Pollution taxes, cap-and-trade policies, regulations prohibiting destructive products and technologies, and substituting public or community stewardship for free access to important common pool resources can substantially change incentives and outcomes even while production for profit and the market system persist. However, these steps to prevent environmental destruction require challenging freedoms that corporations have long taken for granted and implementing policies that curb the rule of market forces. Once this is recognized, it should be apparent that trying to make the environmental coalition attractive to large corporations and adopting a pro-market ideology are ultimately self-defeating. While pro-market rhetoric may open access to some ears and while concessions like giving away pollution permits free of charge to corporate polluters may reduce their opposition temporarily, this approach will never produce a political coalition that can adequately protect the environment. Instead, it further empowers the organizations and forces driving environmental destruction in the first place.

The coalition to protect the environment must be built from those who are most harmed by environmental destruction and those with the most to gain from doing the work we now know is necessary to convert our energy sector from fossil fuels to renewables and reconfigure our entire economic infrastructure. Future generations are clearly harmed by environmental destruction and benefit from environmental protection, but they cannot be organized into a political force to fight for environmental protection today. And while those who have the time and energy to fight for future generations out of solidarity are a critical part of a successful environmental coalition, they have not provided enough troops to turn the tide of battle. Fortunately, there are two other constituencies that have a great deal to gain from environmental protection— those who live in poor communities and those who need jobs over the next two decades. Together, these groups comprise the overwhelming majority of ordinary Americans.

Because they are less powerful than richer communities, poor communities are generally less successful in the political game of "not in my back yard" (NIMBY). For this reason poor communities usually suffer most from environmental destruction and have the most to gain from its prevention.[1] As long as the environmental movement remains an upper-middle-class movement, it will continue to lack support from a constituency that objectively has every reason to support protecting the environment, provided policies are designed to also protect it from bearing an unfair portion of the costs of doing so.

As of April 2010 there were 15 million Americans under- or unemployed, and the economy needs to create 100,000 new jobs each month to provide for new entrants into the labor force. Right now, unless we retrofit old houses, businesses, and government buildings, unless we build new buildings that are much, much more energy-efficient, unless we build and install huge numbers of wind turbines and solar panels, unless we replace industrial agriculture with environmentally sustainable agriculture, and unless we replace our current roads and cars with rail lines, bike paths, high-speed trains, trolley cars, and bicycles—all ASAP—we will not avoid cataclysmic climate change by mid-century. Moreover, it is becoming increasingly apparent to any who care to see that in the neoliberal global economy "jobless recoveries" in the advanced economies have become the norm. The only way to put the unemployed back to work and generate strong job growth in the U.S. economy for the next generation will be to put people to work retrofitting the entire economy to become carbon-neutral.

We are in the midst of two crises that cry out for one solution—the grandmother of all economic conversion programs. We need a Green New Deal on the scale of the conversion program that took us from a depressed peacetime economy to a fully employed wartime economy at the onset of

World War II.[2] Hopefully more labor leaders will realize that the best and perhaps only chance to put America back to work again is through a Green New Deal. And hopefully more environmental leaders will realize that not all production is *un*economic and environmentally destructive. Right now the kind of economic do-over necessary to correct a mammoth historic mistake that has saddled us with an energy sector, economic infrastructure, and technologies that are rapidly leading us down a path to environmental disaster will require decades of full employment to fix.

The key is remembering that poor and working people have other needs besides environmental protection and restoration. They need affordable housing and transportation. They need to be able to pay for food and utility bills. If the environmental movement makes demands that threaten other vital interests of ordinary people, it will never build a sufficiently powerful coalition to protect and restore the environment. And unless the environmental movement supports progressive movements fighting to meet people's other needs, it can hardly expect people working in those movements to rally to its cause and contribute enough political muscle to move the environmental agenda forward.

There will be significant costs as well as benefits associated with moving from unsustainable to sustainable patterns of work and consumption. Protecting ordinary people from being the ones who have to bear these costs is not only the right thing to do, it is the smart thing to do to build a successful environmental coalition. If coal miners and automobile workers are compensated while being retrained for new green jobs, they will be less likely to oppose putting a price on carbon. If affordable housing in old city neighborhoods is available because it is restored and subsidized, young families who need decent housing will not oppose zoning measures preventing suburban sprawl from gobbling up green space surrounding metropolitan areas. If farmers are given transfer development rights in exchange for development rights on their own land, they will be less likely to oppose the downzoning of farmland that smart growth requires because they will not be asked to take a financial loss. If public transportation is convenient and cheap, people who cannot afford to live near their work will be less likely to demand wider highways as the solution to gridlock. If regressive FICA taxes are reduced, people will be less likely to oppose new green taxes needed to correct perverse, environmentally destructive incentives. Environmental protection is efficient not because there are no costs, but because the benefits outweigh the costs. This means that all who *would* be harmed can be fully compensated. It is just as important for the environmental movement to come up with policies that *do* fully compensate different categories of ordinary people who might otherwise be harmed as it is to come up with policies that are effective at stopping environmental de-

231

struction. Otherwise there will never be a coalition strong enough to impose policies that actually stop environmental abuse.

Is Reform Enough?

More and more environmentalists are beginning to suspect that while policy reforms and a political coalition powerful enough to win them are urgently needed, protecting the environment may ultimately require more dramatic changes in the economy than the kinds of policies discussed in Parts III and IV.

Why swim upstream? Every policy to reduce pollution or increase environmental protection discussed in Parts III and IV is merely a stopgap attempt to correct for some destructive dynamic that is an intrinsic part of the way we go about our daily economic business. It is perfectly sensible for those who fight for environmental protection and sustainable development to ask why they should settle for an economic system that requires them to always swim upstream against the current, settle for partial victories, and risk being quickly swept downstream whenever their organizing efforts falter.

Of course, environmentalists must fight for prudent regulation to prevent the Mineral Management Department of the U.S. Department of the Interior from approving leases for deep-sea oil wells like Deepwater Horizon when corporations unconvincingly claim that they have developed fail-safe drilling technologies and stand ready to contain damage in case what they argue is impossible should ever happen. But why should environmentalists continue to tolerate an economic system where giant corporations like BP can capture the regulatory framework erected to prevent them from engaging in socially detrimental activities and can exert so much political influence that in the midst of one of the greatest environmental catastrophes of all time the leadership of both political parties insisted on keeping provisions to *expand* deep-sea drilling in legislation under consideration? According to BP's latest estimates, all the oil it could ever have drained from the Deepwater Horizon field would have barely sufficed to slake U.S. consumption for five days. How great must the ideological and financial power of the oil industry be to make a majority of our elected politicians think—even as the leak continued to spew unknown amounts of oil into the Gulf of Mexico six weeks after the explosion—that it makes sense not only to keep hundreds of other wells no different from Deepwater Horizon operating in the Gulf of Mexico, but to pass new legislation to make it easier for oil companies to obtain licensing to drill even more wells just like Deepwater Horizon? Just because totalitarian communism and central planning were not a better answer does not mean there is no better way to coordinate our economic activities than to leave giant multinational corporations driven by market forces in charge of what and how we produce.

Limits of consciousness-raising and green consumerism: The modern environmental movement has raised popular awareness of the importance of protecting the environment to a degree few would have predicted possible forty years ago. In addition to indigenous communities who always better understood how their fates were linked with the fate of the natural environment, there are now billions of people worldwide who value environmental protection, and millions who self-consciously strive to be socially responsible "green consumers." But it is increasingly apparent that consciousness-raising and green consumerism are not enough to prevent environmental deterioration. As long as individual consumers and businesses are penalized financially for socially responsible behavior, and handsome profits are to be made by any who are willing to be less socially responsible than others, the environment will continue to deteriorate despite higher levels of environmental awareness and admirable personal sacrifices. If consciousness-raising and reforms continue to come up short, what kind of "big think" changes might be necessary to get the job done?

Institutional Solutions Versus Technical Solutions

When environmentalists discuss big changes, they usually gravitate toward dramatic new technologies for producing and living. Many environmentalist writers challenge pessimistic conventional wisdom about the promise of solar, wind, and geothermal energy technologies. Organic and permaculture farming do not go wanting for enthusiastic advocates. Creative ideas about how to build passive houses and carbon-neutral buildings abound. And debates over the pros and cons of hydrogen-powered cars, the feasibility of "clean coal," and of course the risks and costs of nuclear energy continue unabated. But while environmentalists have not been shy about offering "big think" technical solutions to environmental problems, with some notable exceptions they have been less prone to talk about changes in our basic economic institutions. The environmental movement has traditionally drawn out our engineering impulse more strongly than our social science impulse.

Challenging mainstream thinking about technologies is important. But it bears asking why engineers working in the mainstream of their profession fail to provide the analyses so many environmentalists feel are needed. Are the professional engineers and agronomists who work for corporations and universities really less intelligent than environmental activists who may sometimes have engineering degrees but are often only amateurs? If not, then presumably there are institutional reasons we fail to get the kind of analysis environmentalists think we need from so many of our professionals. Stories abound of corporate, government, and university discrimination against engineering

233

and scientific research agendas that are environmentally friendly, while funds are lavished on research agendas that will expand corporate profits. But it is important to recognize that this systematic bias reflects an underlying problem in important economic, political, and educational institutions responsible for research. In any case, if we are going to solve our environmental problems, it is as important to challenge mainstream thinking about economic institutions as it is to challenge conventional engineering wisdom. What kind of system changes could eliminate perverse incentives that punish individual actors when they do the socially responsible thing, and instead reward behavior that protects and restores the environment?

When Small Is Beautiful

When environmentalists do think about institutional responses to environmental problems, they often praise the virtues of downsizing our economy and recommend some form of *community-based economics* (CBE).

Supporters of CBE offer a vision of largely self-reliant, local economies governed by the kind of direct democracy once used in New England town meetings.[3] Advocates of CBE seek to avoid the negative repercussions of both markets and bureaucratic planning by eliminating the "problem" these allocative mechanisms address—coordinating a division of labor among geographically dispersed groups. By decentralizing large, national economies into small, autonomous economic communities, CBE advocates also hope to promote face-to-face democratic decision-making, eliminate the need to transport large volumes of goods over long distances, and create incentives for local communities to take the environmental effects of their activities into account. Promoters of CBE argue that while participatory democracy does not work in large groups where people do not know each other and cannot meet face-to-face, it can work in small communities where it is possible for people to know each other personally. They argue that a great deal of long-distance transportation of goods is both unnecessary and *un*economic when environmental costs are taken into account. And supporters of CBE also reason that once the consequences of choices fall "in my back yard," the IMBY principle will induce local communities to better protect their environment.

Not surprisingly, CBE comes in many different flavors, some more radical and some less so. Murray Bookchin, founder of the school of social ecology, is the best-known proponent of post-capitalist, libertarian municipalism (Bookchin 1986; Bookchin and Biehl 1998). Howard Hawkins (1993), a long-time activist and 2006 Green Party candidate for the U.S. Senate in New York, has also written along similar lines. David Korten and Paul Hawken have argued in books that have reached wide audiences that an ecological

234

society can best be achieved through democratic pluralism (Hawken 1993; Korten 1999). Gar Alperovitz (1973, 2005) and Michael Shuman (2000) have both written widely about the advantages and feasibility of what Shuman calls self-reliant communities and Alperovitz calls a decentralized, pluralist commonwealth. E.F. Schumacher's (1973) classic defense of localism spawned a whole school of Buddhist economics. Kirkpatrick Sale (1996, 2002) is a well-known proponent of bioregionalism. Herman Daly argues for a less radical version of regional self-reliance (Daly and Farley 2003), while Roy Morrison (1995) has written persuasively about a more radical vision he calls ecological democracy. These are only some of the different versions of CBE that appear in a wide-ranging and growing literature.

CBE is a healthy reaction against an excessively global division of labor that has become exceedingly *un*economic as multinational corporations stretch environmentally destructive supply chains in order to appropriate a larger share of the global economic pie more often than to take advantage of true comparative advantages. CBE is a healthy reaction against the loss of control by local communities over their economic destinies, and a healthy vote of confidence in people's abilities to manage their own economic affairs. And supporters of CBE are certainly correct that if those who decide how much pollution is warranted were the same as those who suffered the consequences of pollution, we would be far more careful about our wastes. However, while CBE offers an important positive alternative to neoliberal global capitalism, it leaves many questions unanswered, and small is not always beautiful.

And When It Is Not

In a community-based economy, the IMBY principle works only for local pollutants—that is, for pollutants that adversely affect only the inhabitants of the local community where they are generated. It does not work when one community fouls not only its own nest with pollution but the nests of other communities as well. What happens when sulfur dioxide from a utility plant located in a county in Ohio comes down as acid rain on hundreds of counties in Pennsylvania, New York, and Connecticut, or when run-off carrying manure from a chicken farm on a tributary of the Capon River in West Virginia contributes to dead zones in the middle of the Chesapeake Bay? In a community-based economy, there would be insufficient incentive for the community where the utility plant or the chicken farm is located to curb its polluting activities, because only part of the negative consequences would occur IMBY, while a significant part of the negative effects would take place NIMBY, but in someone else's backyard instead. To simply observe that local communities would have an incentive to negotiate with each other regarding curbing emissions of nonlocal pollutants, and point out that they are free to do so is no more helpful than observing that nation states today have an incentive to negotiate with each other on curbing carbon emissions to prevent climate change, and pointing out that they are free to do so.

More generally, when push comes to shove, no version of CBE proposes that communities be entirely self-sufficient. However, advocates of CBE fail to explain both how to decide how much integration is desirable, and how to manage whatever division of labor between communities is agreed on. Joel Kovel provides an eloquent critique of extreme localism:

> A pure community, or even "bioregional" economy is a fantasy. Strict localism belongs to the aboriginal stages of society: it cannot be reproduced today, and even if it could, it would be an ecological nightmare at present population levels. Imagine the heat losses from a multitude of dispersed sites, the squandering of scarce resources, the needless reproduction of effort. . . . There needs to be, in any economy, an interdependence whose walls are not confinable to any township or bioregion. (Kovel 2003, 156)

In other words, it turns out that autonomous communities are really only semiautonomous for a number of good reasons: (1) Not every local community can produce everything its members will want to consume. (2) Even if complete self-sufficiency were possible, whenever there are significant differences in opportunity costs of producing goods in different communities, it is inefficient to forgo a division of labor. (3) Whenever there are true *economies of scale* that surpass the customer base of a local community, it is inefficient to forgo a division of labor between communities. (4) If communities were completely self-sufficient, serious inequities would arise whenever some communities were better endowed with natural, produced, or human capital than others.

But when CBE enthusiasts are forced to acknowledge that communities will be only *semi*autonomous, they fail to explain how the "semi" part should be handled. Instead of concrete proposals or procedures, we invariably find either unconvincing assertions that in this case markets will somehow generate fair and efficient outcomes, or what amounts to hand-waving accompanied by declarations of faith that when the time comes democratic communities can sit down together and work things out between themselves satisfactorily. But it is not enough simply to say that relations between communities "must be nondependent, nonmonetary, and noninjurious" (Sale 1996, 483). In the likely event that communities rediscover the advantages of some division of labor, it is important to have well-thought-out procedures for how communities that are only semiautonomous should go about agreeing upon and managing the division of labor among them.[4]

Wanted: An Environmental Benefit-Revealing Mechanism

As discussed in Chapter 5, a critical failing of market economies is that they provide no quantitative information about how much damage pollution causes so we know how high to set corrective Pigovian taxes.[5] This vacuum gives rise to the necessity of trying to generate quantitative estimates of the benefits of environmental protection through stopgap measures that, as we discovered in Chapter 2, inspire less confidence the more we know about them. The best that can be said about contingent valuation surveys, travel cost studies, and hedonic regression is that they are better than nothing. But just because markets do not induce people to reveal how much they are damaged when the environment is permitted to deteriorate does not mean we cannot design a different economic system that generates accurate estimates of pollution damage as part of its normal procedures, taking these damages into account when deciding what and how to produce. The *participatory planning procedure* in an economic model known as a *participatory economy* (Albert and Hahnel 1991, 1992) is designed to induce participants to reveal truthfully how much worse off they truly believe they would be if the environment were degraded in different ways, and then charge any who damage the environment as a by-product of producing socially valuable goods and services for the amount of damage caused.[6]

In the participatory planning procedure used to allocate scarce productive resources and distribute consumption goods in a participatory economy, communities of all who are affected by a particular pollutant are given the right to restrict its emission. In the language used to discuss the Coase theorem in Chapter 6, the "victims" are awarded the "property right" not to be polluted. While an affected community may choose to ban emissions entirely, it can also permit as high a level of emissions as it chooses, for which the community will be compensated according to a quantitative estimate of the damages it incurs based on the final estimate of the damage per unit of pollutant that emerges from the planning procedure.

In each iteration of the planning procedure, an iteration facilitation board (IFB) quotes a current estimate of the damage caused by releasing a unit of each pollutant. Both the enterprises proposing to emit the pollutant and the community of affected parties respond to this "signal." Enterprises propose how much they want to emit, knowing they will be charged for those emissions an amount equal to the current estimate of the damages per unit times the number of units they propose to emit. This means damage from emissions becomes part of production costs, implementing the "polluter pays" principle. The community of affected parties proposes how many units of the pollutant it is willing to allow to be released, taking into account that it will

237

be compensated by an amount equal to the current estimate of the damages per unit times the number of units allowed to be released. In other words, the affected community has a right not to be polluted if it so chooses. On the other hand, if it chooses to permit a certain amount of pollution to occur, it is compensated for the damage it chooses to endure. This is important since often the benefits of permitting low levels of emission far outweigh the damages from low emission levels.

Why does the procedure yield an accurate estimate of the damage caused by pollutants, and lead to an efficient level of pollution? In most cases it is reasonable to assume that as emission levels increase, the costs to victims of *additional* pollution rise and the benefits to producers of permitting *additional* pollution fall. In this case the efficient level of pollution is the level at which the cost of the last unit emitted is equal to the benefit from the last unit emitted. What will happen if the IFB quotes an estimate of damages that is less than the estimate at which the last unit of emissions causes damages equal to benefits? In this case the affected community will not find it in its interest to permit as much pollution as polluters would like; that is, there will be excess demand for permission to pollute, and the IFB will increase its estimate of the damage caused by the pollutant in the next round of planning. If the IFB quotes an estimate of damages that is higher than the estimate at which the last unit of emissions causes damage equal to benefits, the affected community will offer to permit more pollution than polluters will ask permission to emit; that is, there will be an excess supply of permission to pollute, and the IFB will decrease its estimate of the damage caused by the pollutant in the next round.

There is no incentive for pollution victims to pretend they are damaged either more or less than they really are or for polluters to pretend they benefit more or less than they really do from being allowed to pollute, because each would fare worse by responding untruthfully than by responding truthfully to the signals sent by the IFB. Consequently, when the IFB adjusts its estimate of the damages for all pollutants until the sum total of requests to pollute are equal to the permission to pollute, we end up with as accurate an estimate of the true damages caused by different pollutants as can be hoped for, and also the efficient level of pollution.[7]

Under traditional assumptions the above procedure will (1) reduce pollution to "efficient" levels, (2) satisfy the "polluter pays" principle, (3) compensate the actual victims of pollution for the damage they suffer, and (4) induce polluters and victims to truthfully reveal the benefits and costs of pollution. In other words, the procedure is what economists call "incentive compatible." Uncorrected markets accomplish none of these four goals. And while in theory markets *could* reduce pollution to efficient levels *if* corrective Pigovian taxes were set equal to the magnitude of the negative external effect, because markets are not incentive compatible for polluters and pollution victims, markets provide no reliable way to estimate the magnitudes of corrective taxes for pollutants.

However, there is an important problem: In an inegalitarian economy the damage-revealing mechanism outlined above would unfairly allocate pollution to poorer communities. If there were rich and poor communities, poor communities would be more inclined to bolster their income by offering to tolerate more pollution than rich communities would agree to tolerate even if poor communities had as strong a preference for a clean environment as did rich communities. Consequently, this procedure should only be used in the context of an economy that is far more egalitarian than any today.[8] Only if communities have comparable incomes would it be advisable to allow them to express whatever differences of opinion they have about the dangers of different pollutants, and whatever differences in preference they may have for income versus environmental amenities, as the above procedure allows them to do. In *The Political Economy of the Environment* (2002), James Boyce elaborates on a number of ways a more egalitarian distribution of wealth and income would benefit the environment. One more advantage of egalitarianism should be added to his excellent list: An egalitarian economy creates an opportunity to implement an environmental-benefit-revealing mechanism that is sorely needed if we are to manage our relations with the natural environment sensibly, whereas inegalitarian economies make this impossible because they would turn any such mechanism into a transmission vehicle for generating environmental injustice.

It's Planning, Stupid!

Because environmental problems have become so pressing, it would be inappropriate not to travel back to the present in closing. Unfortunately, even if we got all the prices right—even if we miraculously imposed Pigovian taxes and subsidies that fully corrected for all the different externalities that abound in market economies, and in particular put a price on carbon emissions equal to the damage they cause—it would be naive to assume that the capitalist financial system could be relied on to steer sufficient investment resources into energy conservation and renewable energy to protect us from cataclysmic climate change. Asset bubbles are too attractive to capitalist finance, and thinking long-run is not Wall Street's forte. While competent regulation of the financial sector is desperately needed, all this would accomplish would be to prevent more financial crises. It would not mean that our savings would be marshaled quickly and forcefully enough to make the investments necessary to tackle the unprecedented makeover our fossil-fuel-guzzling economies require.

We need a dramatic increase in the portion of national incomes devoted to investment rather than consumption. We need an even more dramatic reordering of investment priorities. And we need all this sooner than ASAP. This is not something that a private financial sector is equipped to carry out even if it is regulated and relatively safe from speculative excesses. Nor is it something that small, semiautonomous, community-based economies are suited to accomplish even though building examples of sustainable, egalitarian communities is helpful to show the way forward. We need investment planning. We need investment planning on a national scale. We need the kind of investment planning that the federal government carried out from 1939 to 1943 when the U.S. economy was converted from a peacetime economy operating at two-thirds speed to a wartime economy running on all cylinders. And we need this kind of investment planning now.

Sadly, the Obama administration squandered its first opportunity to do what will eventually be required. In the first months of the new administration, the U.S. financial system was paralyzed and had ceased to function. Not only had credit for Main Street dried up, but also the major players on Wall Street had so fouled their own nests with assets of unknowable toxicity that they would not even risk lending to each other! Popular anger and disgust with Wall Street was at an all-time high. The need to pump loans to businesses and state and local governments to prevent further layoffs was apparent to most ordinary people even if not to their leaders in Washington. In short, the early months of 2009 were the best opportunity since 1929 not only to impose strong regulatory reform on a clueless and discredited financial industry, but also to require banks that were literally in hock to the federal government to lend in accord with social priorities set by the government.

While there was much debate in the winter of 2009 over how many *billions* of dollars in the fiscal stimulus would go for "green jobs," the opportunity to direct *trillions* of dollars into "green investment" was allowed to slip, unnoticed, through our hands. The federal government could have easily required banks to reprioritize investments in exchange for the bailouts they needed to stay alive. Quid pro quo is not unbeknownst to politicians, except apparently in the case of bank bailouts. Better still, the federal government could have nationalized major banks either without compensation or by purchasing a majority of their shares at the low prices they were selling for at the time, which would have cost taxpayers far less than the generous bailouts without conditions that the Obama administration bestowed upon the banks instead.

Of course, placing major financial institutions in the hands of the federal government is no guarantee that the government will use them wisely to implement a massive green investment conversion program. And there is little reason to believe that Obama's chief economic advisers, Laurence Summers and Timothy Geithner, who were too clueless to understand how to respond to the financial crisis of 2008–2009, or too beholden to Wall Street, would have proved wise enough to know how to respond to the larger economic and ecological crises that can only be solved through a massive green investment conversion program. On the other hand, knowing what the right investment priorities are will not be sufficient if the government has inadequate means for getting them implemented.

Economic conversion during World War II was not primarily directed through the financial system. The War Department simply informed General Motors that the government would be purchasing large numbers of tanks to replace the fall in household demand for automobiles caused by gasoline rationing and forced savings through war bonds, after which General Motors had no problems obtaining loans for what were very profitable conversion investments. While the climate crisis will eventually become a national emergency, since the Energy Department is not likely to be awarded a budget as large as the War Department received during World War II, for the foreseeable future the government would have to use the financial system to carry out the Green Investment New Deal that will be necessary.

This means that a big part of a successful response to climate change will take the form of investment planning administered through a publicly controlled financial sector. Unfortunately, at the moment the financial sector controls the government rather than the other way around. And outside the Pentagon there is little experience with investment planning in the United States. As a matter of fact, "planning" is such a dirty word in the United States that in the past we have had to use a euphemism like "industrial policy" to even talk about it. Embracing and perfecting the practice of investment planning through the financial system will not be easy in the United States, but it will be necessary if we are to respond successfully to the ecological crisis we now face.

Notes

1. For an excellent study of struggles against environmental destruction waged by poor communities, see Martinez-Alier (2002), especially chapters 5, 6, 7, and 8.

2. Unfortunately the most visible and powerful spokesperson for a Green New Deal, Van Jones, was dismissed in the early days of the new administration by President Obama when Jones was singled out for attack by the right-wing media. The best parts of Jones's book, *The Green Collar Economy* (2008), are his insights about the difference between winning and losing political strategies for both the environmental and the labor movements.

3. For an excellent survey and defense of CBE on ecological grounds, see Curtis (2003).

4. I have suggested to supporters of CBE that the *participatory planning procedure* that is part of an economic model known as *participatory economics* can provide a concrete solution to their problem. Instead of making an arbitrary choice about how much integration there will be among communities that can only be *semi*autonomous, this procedure is designed to reveal how much economic integration versus decentralization is warranted by differences in opportunity costs, while giving communities and workers a great deal of decision-making autonomy regardless of whatever degree of integration is chosen. See Hahnel (2007b).

5. An environmental-benefit-revealing mechanism is the same as a pollution-damage-revealing mechanism. A quantitative estimate of the damage more pollution causes is the same as a quantitative estimate of the benefit derived from reducing pollution and protecting the environment.

6. For a fuller explanation of how the planning procedure incorporates a pollution-damage-revealing mechanism, see Hahnel (2005a, 195–207).

7. One might well ask why problems that arise in Coasian negotiations are less likely to arise in this procedure. The short answer is that when "polluters" and "victims" negotiate with each other directly, it is clear how they could use "private information" to their advantage. In this case, however, they are both participating in a procedure where they respond to a "signal" from the IFB, not knowing if this will be the final planning round or not. If they try to game the system by responding untruthfully in an attempt to influence the signal in the next round, they run the risk of having not done the best they could for themselves if the signal in this round equates permission and requests for emissions, and therefore the current round is the last round. See Hahnel (2011) for a comprehensive treatment of how the planning procedure either avoids or minimizes perverse incentives that plague Coasian negotiations.

8. The model of a participatory economy is an egalitarian economy where income differences between different communities would be very small, which is why this pollution-damage-revealing procedure does not run the risk of creating environmental injustice in that context.

References

Ackerman, Frank. 2009. *Can We Afford the Future?* London: ZED.

———. 2010. "Cost-Benefit Analysis of Climate Change: Where It Goes Wrong." In *Economic Thought and U.S. Climate Change Policy*, ed. D.M. Driesen, 61–82. Cambridge, MA: MIT Press.

Ackerman, Frank, Stephen DeCanio, Richard Howarth, and Kristen Sheeran. 2009a. "The Limitations of Integrated Assessment Models of Climate Change." *Climatic Change* 95: 297–315.

Ackerman, Frank, Elizabeth Stanton, Stephen DeCanio, Eban Goodstein, Richard Howarth, Richard Norgaard, Catherine Norman, and Kristen Sheeran. 2009b. *The Economics of 350: The Benefits and Costs of Climate Stabilization*. Economics for Equity and the Environment. www.e3network.org/papers/Economics_of_350.pdf.

Ackerman, Frank, Elizabeth Stanton, and Ramon Bueno. 2010a. "Fat Tails, Exponents, Extreme Uncertainty: Simulating Catastrophe in DICE." *Ecological Economics* 69, 8: 1657–1665.

———. 2010b. "CRED: A New Model of Climate and Development." Stockholm Environment Institute, Working Paper WP-US-10-03. April 28.

Albert, Michael, and Robin Hahnel. 1991. *The Political Economy of Participatory Economics*. Princeton, NJ: Princeton University Press.

———. 1992. "Participatory Planning." *Science & Society* 56, 1: 39–59.

Alperovitz, Gar. 1973. "Notes Toward a Pluralist Commonwealth." In *Strategy and Program*, ed. Staughton. Lynd and Gar Alperovitz, 49–109. Boston: Beacon Press.

———. 2005. *America Beyond Capitalism*. Hoboken, NJ: Wiley.

Anderson, Terry, and Donald Leal. 2001. *Free Market Environmentalism*. Rev. ed. New York: Palgrave Macmillan.

Asafu-Adjaye, John. 2000. *Environmental Economics for Non-Economists*. Singapore: World Scientific.

Baer, Paul, Thomas Athanasiou, and Sivan Kartha. 2007. *The Right to Development in a Climate Constrained World: The Greenhouse Development Rights Framework*. Berlin: Heinrich Boll Foundation, Christian Aid, EcoEquity, and the Stockholm Environmental Institute. (An updated, second edition is available as a PDF file at www. ecoequity.org.)

Bookchin, Murray. 1986. *Post Scarcity Anarchism*. Montreal: Black Rose. (First edition 1970.)

Bookchin, Murray, and Janet Biehl. 1998. *The Politics of Social Ecology*. Montreal: Black Rose.

Boulding, Kenneth. 1966. "The Economics of the Coming Spaceship Earth." In *Environmental Quality in a Growing Economy*, ed. Henry Jarrett, 3–14. Baltimore: Johns Hopkins University Press.

Boyce, James. 2002. *The Political Economy of the Environment*. Cheltenham, UK: Edward Elgar.

Boyce, James, and Mariano Torras. 2002. "Rethinking the Environmental Kuznets Curve." In *The Political Economy of the Environment*, ed. James Boyce, 47–66. Cheltenham, UK: Edward Elgar.

Burkett, Paul. 2006. *Marxism and Ecological Economics: Toward a Red and Green Political Economy*. London: Palgrave Macmillan.

Camerer, Colin. 2003. *Behavioral Game Theory: Experiments in Strategic Interaction*. Princeton, NJ: Princeton University Press.

Canning, Catherine. 1996. "The Laundry Detergent Market." *Household and Personal Products Industry*, April.

Chichilnisky, Graciela, and Kristen Sheeran. 2009. *Saving Kyoto*. London: New Holland.

Coase, Ronald. 1960. "The Problem of Social Cost." *Journal of Law and Economics* 3: 1–44.

Commission on Racial Justice. 1987. *Toxic Wastes and Race in the United States: A National Report on the Racial and Socio-Economic Characteristics of Communities With Hazardous Waste Sites*. New York: United Church of Christ.

Costanza, Robert, John Cumberland, Herman Daly, Robert Goodland, and Richard Norgaard. 1997. *An Introduction to Ecological Economics*. Boca Raton, FL: St. Lucie Press.

Curtis, Fred. 2003. "Eco-localism and Sustainability." *Ecological Economics* 46: 83–102.

Daly, Herman. 1995. "Summary of the Economic Growth Debate: What Some Economists Have Learned but Many Have Not." In *A Survey of Ecological Economics*, ed. Rajaraman Krishnan, Jonathan Harris, and Neva Goodwin, 125–128. Washington, DC: Island Press.

Daly, Herman, and John Cobb Jr. 1989. *For the Common Good: Redirecting the Economy toward Community, the Environment, and a Sustainable Future*. Boston: Beacon Press.

Daly, Herman, and Joshua Farley. 2003. *Ecological Economics: Principles and Applications*. Washington, DC: Island Press.

DeCanio, Stephen. 2003. *Economic Models of Climate Change: A Critique*. London: Palgrave-Macmillan.

Domar, Evsey. 1946. "Capital Expansion, Rate of Growth and Employment." *Econometrica* 14, 2: 137–147.

Duesenberry, James. 1949. *Income, Saving and the Theory of Consumer Behaviors*. Cambridge MA: Harvard University Press.

Edenhofer, Ottmar, Kai Lessmann, Claudia Kemfert, Michael Grubb, and Jonathan Köhler. 2006. "Induced Technological Change: Exploring Its Implications for the Economics of Atmospheric Stabilization: Synthesis Report from the Innovation Modeling Comparison Project." *Energy Journal*, special issue 1: Endogenous Technological Change and the Economics of Atmospheric Stabilization, 207–222.

REFERENCES

Farrell, Joseph. 1987. "Information and the Coase Theorem." *Journal of Economic Perspectives* 1, 2: 113–129.

Foster, John Bellamy. 1994. *The Vulnerable Planet: A Short Economic History of the Environment*. New York: Cornerstone Books.

———. 2000. *Marx's Ecology: Materialism and Nature*. New York: Monthly Review.

———. 2002. *Ecology Against Capitalism*. New York: Monthly Review.

———. 2009. *The Ecological Revolution: Making Peace With the Planet*. New York: Monthly Review.

Foster, John Bellamy, and Fred Magdoff. 2010. "What Every Environmentalist Needs to Know About Capitalism." *Monthly Review* 61, 10: 1–30.

Goodstein, Eban. 1995. *Economics and the Environment*. Englewood, NJ: Prentice Hall.

———. 1999. *The Trade-Off Myth: Fact & Fiction About Jobs and the Environment*. Washington, DC: Island Press.

Greenwood, Daphne, and Richard Holt. 2010. "Growth, Development, and Quality of Life." In *Economic Pluralism*, ed. Robert Garnett, Erik Olsen, and Martha Starr, 160–175. New York: Routledge.

Grossman, Gene, and Alan Krueger. 1995. "Economic Growth and the Environment." *Quarterly Journal of Economics* 60: 353–377.

Hahnel, Robin. 1999. *Panic Rules! Everything You Need to Know About the Global Economy*. Boston: South End Press.

———. 2001. "Endogenous Preferences: The Institutionalist Connection." In *Crossing the Mainstream: Ethical and Methodological Issues in Economics*, ed. Amitava Dutt and Kenneth Jameson, 315–331. Notre Dame: University of Notre Dame Press.

———. 2002. *The ABCs of Political Economy: A Modern Approach*. London: Pluto Press.

———. 2005a. *Economic Justice and Democracy: From Competition to Cooperation*. New York: Routledge.

———. 2005b. "What Mainstream Economists Won't Tell You About Neoliberal Globalization." *Socialist Studies* 1, 1: 5–29.

———. 2007a. "The Case Against Markets." *Journal of Economic Issues* 41, 4: 1139–1159.

———. 2007b. "Eco-localism: A Constructive Critique." *Capitalism Nature Socialism* 18, 2: 62–78.

———. 2009a. "Climate Risks: Lessons From the Financial Crisis." Policy Brief 5. Economics for Equity and the Environment. www.e3network.org/briefs/Hahnel_Climate_Financial_Risks.pdf.

———. 2009b. "From Competition and Greed to Equitable Cooperation: What Do Pluralist Economists Have to Offer?" In *Economic Pluralism*, ed. Robert Garnett, Erik Olsen, and Martha Starr, 145–159. New York: Routledge.

———. 2009c. "Why the Market Subverts Democracy." *American Behavioral Scientist* 52, 7: 1006–1022.

———. 2011. "Wanted: A Pollution Damage Revealing Mechanism." Under review at *Eastern Economic Journal*.

Hahnel, Robin, and Michael Albert. 1990. *Quiet Revolution in Welfare Economics*. Princeton, NJ: Princeton University Press.

Hall, Darwin, and Richard Behl. 2006. "Integrating Economic Analysis and the Science of Climate Stability." *Ecological Economics* 57: 442–465.

Hardin, Garrett. 1968. "The Tragedy of the Commons." *Science*, December 13, 1243–1248.

Harris, Jonathan M. 2002. *Environmental and Natural Resource Economics: A Contemporary Approach*. Boston: Houghton Mifflin.

REFERENCES

Harrod, Roy. 1939. "An Essay in Dynamic Theory." *Economic Journal* 49: 14–33.

Hawken, Paul. 1993. *The Ecology of Commerce*. New York: HarperCollins.

Hawkins, Howard. 1993. "Community Control, Workers' Control, and the Cooperative Commonwealth." *Society and Nature* 1, 3: 55–85.

Heilbroner, Robert. 1989. "Tune-Up for the Market." *New York Times Magazine*, September 24.

Hicks, John. 1939. *Value and Capital*. Oxford, UK: Clarendon Press.

Hunt, E.K., and Ralph d'Arge. 1973. "On Lemmings and Other Acquisitive Animals: Propositions on Consumption." *Journal of Economic Issues* 7, 2: 337–353.

Ishiguro, Shingo. 2003. "Comparing Allocations under Asymmetric Information: Coase Theorem Revisited." *Economic Letters* 80: 67–71.

Jones, Van. 2008. *The Green Collar Economy: How One Solution Can Fix Our Two Biggest Problems*. New York: HarperCollins.

Kahouli-Brahmi, Sondes. 2008. "Technological Learning in Energy-Environment-Economy Modeling: A Survey." *Energy Policy* 36, 1: 138–162.

Kneese, Allen, and Ronald Ridker. 1972. Predicament of Mankind. *Washington Post*, March 2: B1.

Korten, David. 1999. *The Post-Corporate World: Life After Capitalism*. Bloomfield, CT: Kumarian Press.

Kovel, Joel. 2003. *Enemy of Nature: The End of Capitalism or the End of the World*. London: ZED.

Kreps, David. 1990. *A Course in Microeconomic Theory*. Princeton, NJ: Princeton University Press.

Kuznets, Simon. 1955. "Economic Growth and Income Inequality." *American Economic Review* 1: 1–28.

Laitner, John, Stephen DeCanio, Jonathan Koomey, and Alan Sanstad. 2003. "Room for Improvement: Increasing the Value of Energy Modeling for Policy Analysis." *Utilities Policy* 11: 87–94.

Martinez-Alier, Joan. 2002. *The Environmentalism of the Poor*. Cheltenham, UK: Edward Elgar.

Marx, Karl. 1967. *Capital*, vol. 1. New York: International Publishers. (First edition 1867.)

Maume, David Jr., and Marcia Bellas. 2001. "The Overworked American or the Time Bind? Assessing Competing Explanations for Time Spent in Paid Labor." *American Behavioral Scientist* 44, 7: 1137–1156.

Meadows, Donela, Dennis Meadows, Jorgen Randers, and William Behrens III. 1972. *Limits to Growth: A Report for the Club of Rome's Project on the Predicament of Mankind*. New York: Universe Books.

Morrison, Roy. 1995. *Ecological Democracy*. Boston: South End Press.

Nordhaus, Richard, and James Tobin. 1972. "Is Growth Obsolete?" *Economic Growth*. National Bureau of Economic Research General Series #96E. New York: Columbia University Press.

Ochs, Jack, and Alvin Roth. 1989. "An Experimental Study of Sequential Bargaining." *American Economic Review* 79: 355–384.

O'Connor, James. 1998. *Natural Causes: Essays in Ecological Marxism*. New York: Guilford.

Olson, Mancur. 1965. *The Logic of Collective Action: Public Goods and the Theory of Groups*. Cambridge, MA: Harvard University Press.

Osborne, Martin. 2004. *An Introduction to Game Theory*. Oxford, UK: Oxford University Press.

Osborne, Martin, and Ariel Rubinstein. 1994. *A Course in Game Theory*. Boston: MIT Press.

REFERENCES

Ostrom, Elinor. 1990. *Governing the Commons: The Evolution of Institutions for Collective Action.* Cambridge, UK: Cambridge University Press.

Pigou, Arthur C. 2009. *Wealth and Welfare.* Ithaca NY: Cornell University Library. (First edition 1912.)

Pindyck, Robert, and Daniel Rubinfeld. 2001. *Microeconomics.* Englewood, NJ: Prentice Hall.

Rawls, John. 1971. *A Theory of Justice.* Cambridge MA: Harvard University Press.

Roemer, John. 1981. *Analytical Foundations of Marxian Economic Theory.* Cambridge, UK: Cambridge University Press.

Rosser, Barkley, Jr. 1999. "On the Complexities of Complex Economic Dynamics." *Journal of Economic Perspectives* 13, 4: 169–192.

———. 2005. "Complexities of Dynamic Forestry Management Policies." In *Economics, Natural Resources, and Sustainability: Economics of Sustainable Forest Management,* ed. Shashi Kant and R. Albert Berry, 191–200. Dordrecht: Springer.

Roth, Alvin. 1997. "Bargaining Experiments." In *Handbook of Experimental Economics,* ed. John Kagel and Alvin Roth, 253–348. Princeton, NJ: Princeton University Press.

Rubinstein, Ariel. 1982. "Perfect Equilibrium in a Bargaining Model." *Econometrica* 50: 97–109.

——— 1985. "A Bargaining Model with Incomplete Information About Time Preferences." *Econometrica* 53: 1151–1172.

Sale, Kirkpatrick. 1996. "Principles of Bioregionalism." In *The Case Against the Global Economy,* ed. Jerry Mander and Edward Goldsmith, 471–484. San Francisco: Sierra Club Books.

———. 2002. *Dwellers in the Land: The Bioregional Vision.* Athens: University of Georgia Press.

Schor, Juliet. 1992. *The Overworked American: The Unexpected Decline of Leisure.* New York: Basic Books.

———. 1998. *The Overspent American: Upscaling, Downshifting, and the New Consumer.* New York: Basic Books.

Schumacher, E.F. 1973. *Small Is Beautiful.* New York: Harper and Row.

Schwartzman, David. 2008. "The Limits to Entropy: Continuing Misuse of Thermodynamics in Environmental and Marxist Theory." *Science & Society* 72, 1: 43–62.

Selden, Thomas, and Song Daqing. 1994. "Environmental Quality and Development: Is There a Kuznets Curve for Air Pollution Emissions?" *Journal of Environmental Economics and Management* 27: 147–162.

Shafik, Nemat. 1994. "Economic Development and Environmental Quality: An Econometric Analysis." *Oxford Economic Papers* 46: 757–773.

Sheeran, Kristen. 2006. "Forest Conservation in the Philippines: A Cost Effective Approach to Mitigating Climate Change?" *Ecological Economics* 58, 2: 338–349.

Shuman, Michael. 2000. *Going Local: Creating Self-Reliant Communities in a Global Age.* New York: Routledge.

Smith, Adam. 1999. *An Inquiry Into the Nature and Causes of the Wealth of Nations.* London: Penguin. (First edition 1776.)

Solow, Robert. 1956. "A Contribution to the Theory of Economic Growth." *Quarterly Journal of Economics* 70, 1: 65–94.

———. 1957. "Technical Change and the Aggregate Production Function." *Review of Economics and Statistics* 39, 3: 312–320.

———. 1972. *Newsweek.* March 13, 1972: 103.

Stahl, Ingolf. 1972. *Bargaining Theory.* Stockholm: Economic Research Institute at the Stockholm School of Economics.

Stanton, Elizabeth, Frank Ackerman, and Sivan Kartha. 2009. "Inside the Integrated Assessment Models: Four Issues in Climate Economics." *Climate and Development* 1, 2: 166–184.

Tietenberg, Thomas. 2003. *Environmental and Natural Resource Economics*. 6th ed. Boston: Addison Wesley.

Veblen, Thorstein. 2008. *The Theory of the Leisure Class*. Oxford: Oxford University Press. (First edition 1899.)

Wara, Michael. 2006. "The Performance and Potential of the Clean Development Mechanism." PESD Working Paper #56. http://pesd.stanford.edu.

Wara, Michael, and David Victor. 2008. "A Realistic Policy on International Carbon Offsets." PESD Working Paper #74. http://pesd.stanford.edu.

World Commission on Environment and Development. 1987. *Our Common Future*. Oxford, UK: Oxford University Press.

Zoltas, Xenophon. 1981. *Economic Growth and Declining Social Welfare*. New York: New York University Press.

Index

About the Author

Robin Hahnel is professor emeritus at American University in Washington, DC, and visiting professor in the department of economics at Portland State University in Portland, Oregon, where he now resides. He has also taught at the University of Maryland, the Catholic Universities in Panama and Peru, and Lewis and Clark College. He is the author of *Economic Justice and Democracy* (2005), *The ABCs of Political Economy* (2002), *Panic Rules!* (1999), and *The Political Economy of Participatory Economics* (with Michael Albert, 1991).